AF541798

SPECTACULAR POLITICS

SPECTACULAR POLITICS

Performative Nation-building and Religion in Modern India

CLEMENS SIX

Translated from the German by

REKHA KAMATH RAJAN

MANOHAR
2010

First published 2010

ISBN 978-81-7304-886-9

Published by
Ajay Kumar Jain *for*
Manohar Publishers & Distributors
4753/23 Ansari Road, Daryaganj
New Delhi 110 002

Typest by
Umesh Chand Nailwal
Delhi 110 092

Printed at
Salasar Imaging Systems
Delhi 110 035

To My Parents

Contents

Preface

Most parts of this book were written during an important and not less intense historical period of Indian politics, which ended with the surprising victory of the Congress party and its allies in the general elections in 2004. Since 1998, India was ruled by a fragile, but still functioning coalition of several parties under the leadership of an extreme right-wing political party, the Bharatiya Janata Party (BJP), which had successfully presented itself as a national alternative to the Congress. The general impression, under which I was at that time–together with many other observers of Indian affairs–was that India had just stepped over to a new era of post-colonial history, marked by a decisive and as such ultimate break with its own Congress-dominated past. Since Congress' renewed gain of power at the centre in 2004 and the confirmation of its clectoral hegemony five years later, this impression has somewhat faded to the background, but still exists. The repeated electoral defeats of the BJP cannot reverse the long-term transformations of India's political system, the Indian State itself as well as Indian society as a whole. The topic discussed here is no doubt strongly influenced by the impression of ruling Hindu nationalism, but is even more relevant now, as the forces of globalization and fragmentation continue to tighten their hold of India and will also in future strongly influence its political and social developments. When the BJP was ruling this country, considering the distinct strategies it had used to gain power, I found it important to reflect once again on political communication, on the ways in which political concepts, ideologies and world-views get transformed into mobilizing programmes, manufacture consent as well as consensus and finally bring power to their protagonists. What I found particularly questionable was the relationship between content and form of politics, as it was conceptualized so far in political and historical theory. Ultimately I arrived at the conclusion that both, content and form, equally determine the consequences and impact of politics in society. Thus, performance is itself politics, rather than simply its expression.

The chapter on terrorism and its strategies in South Asia was written before the terrorist attacks in Mumbai on 27 November 2008. These attacks differ in so far from the historical examples discussed here, as they were not limited to a single or a series of violent acts limited to a very short period of time such as bomb blasts or other attacks based on explosives. The Mumbai attacks of 2008 involved the police and military forces in a fierce battle, lasting several days. As distinct as these attacks may seem from a strategic point of view, they do confirm the general features of terrorism in South Asia as described in the concerned chapter included in this book. Thus, the historical remarks made here on the historical phenomenon of terrorism seem also suitable for an understanding of the Mumbai events and hopefully help to illustrate the dangerous dilemmas especially for State action.

Although I am a historian by training, and thus determined by my academic discipline to concentrate primarily on empirical, i.e. archival research, my major interest in writing on this topic was theoretical. Thus, the major focus here is on theoretical considerations related to nationalism as a historical force and the nation as a (collective and individual) mental category. Long before I started the work on this topic but even now as it is finished, I do assume that the ultimate key to make sense of the past and enhance our understanding of historical change is not so much the collection of historical sources in order to reconstruct what might have been, but the effort of theory-building based on empirical, i.e. archival evidence. In my understanding, theory-building should be the ultimate goal of historiography as a discipline since theory alone can possibly answer the question, why historical transformations have occurred and how.

The present book is the outcome of interactions with many silent witnesses in archives and libraries in India, but also with people who either engage theoretically with the history of this country and/or who have experienced a part of this history personally. A special word of thanks goes out to Peter Feldbauer to whom I owe so much, and to Dietmar Rothermund whose advice and help were invaluable and illuminating. In India I was fortunate to have the help of Swapna Banerjee-Guha in Mumbai, from whose analyses and political commitment I learnt a great deal. I was also given the opportunity to discuss some hypotheses and approaches with Partha Chatterjee in Kolkata and with Partha S. Ghosh and Sanjay Kumar in Delhi. I am grateful to late Abani Lahiri for sharing his experiences of the independence struggle and his views on Gandhi with me. I would also like to thank various institutions like the Nehru Memorial Museum & Library, New Delhi, the National Archives of India, New Delhi, the Centre for the Study of Developing Societies, Delhi, the J.N. Library of the University of Mumbai, the library of the Tata Institute for Social Sciences, Mumbai and the libraries of the Asiatic Society in Mumbai and Kolkata. A special word of thanks is also due to the staff of the Centre for Education and Documentation in Mumbai. I owe many interesting discoveries to their patience and friendly cooperation.

CLEMENS SIX

INTRODUCTION

History, Performance and Religion

This book addresses a seemingly simple question: How does one explain the historical processes through which abstract ideas such as, for example, the idea of a nation becomes a motivation for mass mobilization, political re-organization and even violence at a large scale? Formulated in this way, the question presupposes that such ideas of collective identity do not simply refer to a somewhat pre-existing phenomenon, but rather themselves need to be understood as historical products which are at one point of time defined, repeatedly contested and propagated and which finally develop a historical dynamic through which societies even of the size of India are transformed in a profound way. My starting point for reflecting on this question was the reading of an essay Georg Lukács had published for the first time in March 1919 under the impression of the Russian Revolution two years earlier. In this essay, titled 'What is Orthodox Marxism?', Lukács seeks to explain Marxist 'orthodoxy' that, in contrast to the critique of being an 'uncritical acceptance of the results of Marx's investigations', would be a distinct combination of theory and practice based on facts.[1] Lukács' starting point is a quote of Karl Marx's early critique of Hegel which reads as follows: 'Theory becomes a material force when it grips the masses.' And Lukács comments: 'Even more to the point is the need to discover those features and definitions both of the theory and the ways of gripping the masses which convert the theory, the dialectical method, into the vehicle of revolution.'[2] In what follows, neither the dialectical method nor theory as a vehicle of revolution is an issue. However, what is the central focus of this book is the question of both 'the theory and the ways of gripping the masses', namely the idea of a national collective identity, thus the theory of nationalism, as well as some distinct political strategies for 'gripping the masses', helping to transform these abstract and theoretical ideas into powerful modes of mobilization. Let me begin with some remarks on the strategies (or academically expressed, methodologies) of my own discipline, which is History, in order to explain what the contribution of the following chapters could be.

Historians, especially social historians, are generally engaged not only in reconstructing but also explaining historical action. Although historical research has, in the meantime, also produced branches within the discipline which focus on the history of mentalities and ideas, a large part of historiography remains focused on actions and attempts to retrace and explain them. In other words, historians ask why individuals or groups of people acted in the way they did and, with the help of more or less suitable theoretical models, they attempt to explain the underlying motives and motivations for human action both on the individual as well as on the collective plane.

The attempt in this book will be to find a somewhat different approach to historical actions. In contrast to, or rather, in addition to the above-mentioned perspectives in historical research, historical actions themselves, their shape as public acts will constitute the focal point here. The idea is not only to ask which historical events were directly or indirectly caused by these actions, but to clarify the role played by the concrete forms of these actions in historical processes and to see how this can be used to interpret their mode of operation. I am concerned here with a mode of operation which is different from established explanations and causalities put forward by historical research. In short, historical action which one would tend, at first glance, to interpret as symbolic and, therefore, more or less irrelevant for the explanation of historical processes, will be considered here as constitutive for the course of history by assuming that its mode of operation is on a specific and decisive plane of historical reality. Such symbolic, or spectacular, and in this sense, demonstrative political actions will be analysed in this book as constitutive principles of historical reality. It will be assumed that both as actions as well as through the mode (linguistically and concretely) of their performance in the public sphere they contain and unfold the potential for decisively influencing the course of history. How is this to be understood?

The potential of historical actions to change reality is, to begin with, easily applicable to those, chiefly, political actions which have demonstrably changed the course of history in a decisive manner. When the Head of a State uses his legitimate powers to declare war on another country there is no need for a sophisticated explanation to discover that this action gives rise to consequences that significantly alter the course of history. It is somewhat different with forms of political action which seemingly do not have, or haven't had, any direct and perceivable effects, but which become effective on another level and should, therefore, be considered important for the course of historical events. I am referring here to those symbolically-laden actions or enactments whose mode of operation consists mainly in the propagation of political contents and views and which are not, as in the case of a declaration of war, in the sphere of direct politics. Instead, this kind of actions challenge the existing political framework as a whole, i.e. redefines the central categories of the political discourse, alters the political atmosphere, creates 'public moods and sentiments' and thereby produces 'political authority'.[3] I thus proceed on the assumption that political actions have different qualities and occur at various levels. Therefore, the historical analysis must also be carried out at various levels so as to grasp all these dimensions.

In order to illustrate this concept of politics, the eminent political scientist Thomas Meyer[4] has suggested a threefold model which was not devised with reference to the history of modern India but which, in my opinion, has a global relevance. In this model the political discourse consists firstly in a 'strategy to lay down the institutional framework'. This describes those political actions with which 'the political or social conditions of decision-making and participation are re-structured'. This first level of political discourse, therefore, refers to those events that produce the structural framework for the normal course of political business. With reference to modern India this strategy for establishing an institutional framework to create the environment and the structural preconditions for post-colonial politics would mean the transition from the colonial state to a republic by establishing national democratic institutions while also incorporating the legacy of colonial administration. The point is that this strategy seeks to reorganize conditions of participatory politics in the state and therefore describes very fundamental changes.

On a second level, politics, according to Meyer, is characterized by a 'programmatic-operative strategy' that unfolds within the given institutional framework and attempts to influence political events through practical policy measures. This refers to individual measures like tax policies, economic policies or social policies which define the actual content of state action and lead to those political results which directly concern the citizens of the state. The historical significance of this dimension of politics also does not need to be justified.

The third and final level is the 'strategy of cultural argumentation' which describes political action that 'seeks to influence political decisions and actions of the citizens through compromise and persuasion'. This form of political action can be launched from all social sites, i.e. both by the state as well as by the opposition to this state. Political action of this kind does not require an institutional or operative dimension but it can still result in historically relevant changes since it is concerned with attitudes, orientations and convictions, i.e. with the political culture itself. This third dimension of political discourse is not simply an addition to the 'really decisive' operative and institutional dimensions, but it is an important field of political contests in which different actors struggle for hegemony and control. The significance of this third dimension of cultural argumentation is twofold.[5] First, the convictions and views arising out of this become the yardstick with which the citizens judge the legitimacy of operative and institutional events or structures of politics. Anyone who is successful in changing the culturally argumentative dimension of politics can also influence the other two political dimensions and thus 'make' history. Second, the dimension of cultural argumentation in politics defines the role of the citizens and thus formulates those maxims and orientations according to which the citizens define their own political authority. This dimension is, therefore, decisive if a historian wishes to analyse the self-perception and self-definition of the 'historical subjects' of political processes and should help us to define and understand the competition for power and resources more broadly than before.[6]

The central concept that is used here in the interpretation of politics as a spectacle is that of performance. The concept itself is generally traced back to John L. Austin who described those speech acts as 'illocutionary speech' in the sense of performative utterances which not only say something but also do something.[7] In such cases a linguistic utterance, like the exchange of wedding vows or a promise made, goes beyond the context of speech and thereby changes reality. Austin's speech-act theory and the question of the relationship between words and the world[8] will be taken here as a point of departure for a theoretical project that is not limited to the relationship between language and reality but also examines the relationship between actions and reality. On the basis of the example of Indian nationalism, or rather, the different forms of Indian nationalism in the twentieth century, the concept of the performative will be extended to the field of social and political actions. Performance, or the concept of performative nation-building, is thus no longer just a category of the philosophy of language but a theoretical concept of historical research which makes it possible to analyse political processes in terms of the three dimensions sketched out above. In the examples taken from India's history in the twentieth century, performative nation-building is not considered in isolation but is linked to political and social developments in order to explain the reciprocal effects of these different processes and thus, also, the specific modes of operation of performative politics. As will be demonstrated in the subsequent chapters, here performance not only means the construction of a political spectacle for the purpose of attracting maximum public attention, even more important, performance also means the communication and, if successful, assertion of certain versions of the self, i.e. the 'I' and the 'We'. Reflecting Austin's characterization of performance as 'illocutionary speech', performance is the means to constitute political and societal reality insofar as it determines the historical perception of the self and of reality.

From this understanding of political performance or performative nation-building, the link with religion follows almost automatically. Religion is *per se* an interpretation of reality which expresses itself in rituals and is also performed through rituals. In this case the ritual is not only a form of visualization or a symbolic expression of this interpretation of reality, but religion itself emerges as a reality in the ritual. Similar to performative politics, the religious ritual constitutes a reality. With reference to performative nation-building, forms of politicized religion are, therefore, interesting and vivid. In this context I do not assume that political actors simply take the ritual language of religion into the political discourse but that both, the religious as well as the political, are altered and ultimately come into existence in the course of the spectacular construction of public campaigns and events. Neither the so-called religious elements nor the political discourse are the same after their communication in performative politics. Both are profoundly defined and re-defined through their performance for a political purpose and the seemingly clear distinction between religion and a somewhat 'secular' politics becomes less and less distinguishable and thus less and less convincing. To illustrate this point, I may refer to Judith Butler who offers an interesting characterization, rather than definition, of religion, linking this concept with diverse fields of societal development such as gender relations or the politics of war. According to Butler, 'religion is not simply a set of beliefs or a set of dogmatic views, but a matrix for subject formation whose final form is not determined in advance, a discursive matrix for the articulation and disputation of values, and a field of contestation'.[9] For the discussion of performative politics and religion especially three aspects can be derived from this description. First, religion is a matrix for subject formation which shall be understood here in a double sense, i.e. subject formation in relation to the individual, the self, as well as in relation to the a collective subject, a 'We'. Second, religion has to do with the definition and propagation of values. In other words, it influences the 'cultural grounding'[10] of a society. And last, religion is a field of contestation and disputation and as such necessarily linked with political processes through which power relations and resources are negotiated. Understood in this way, religion and political strategies such as the politics of performance show several significant interrelations that can and should be analysed more in detail. Thus, although the history of modern India also provides several examples for non-religious performative politics, I find these forms of religiously defined politics most interesting and possibly historically also most significant.

A study of the historical relevance of performative actions and political rituals is not a new discovery, although the perspective has changed. John Zavos published one of the latest and especially creative contributions to the focus on performance. His short essay illustrates some benefits we can gain from this perspective on history. In his interpretation, this focus allows us to

> demonstrate a continuity not just between pre- and post-Independence political action, but also between political action that we might otherwise perceive as 'secular' and 'religious' (and therefore of a different type). Performance becomes a means of understanding politics that cuts across this problematic dichotomy. But as well as continuity, there has been change; particularly (...) the increasingly intense focus on religious and caste identities in national- and state-level politics.[11]

Thus, the benefit of a 'performative' understanding of political history is twofold: on a concrete empirical level it helps us first of all to ask and then possibly understand why we observe certain continuities in political communication from the colonial to the post-colonial era in which the former is characterized by an authoritarian, at best 'protodemocratic'[12] political system and the latter by a functioning democracy. Both periods of Indian history provide numerous examples for performative politics, although with interesting developments and alterations, even ruptures at a later stage. As my own case studies of the following chapters demonstrate, the category of performance is an appropriate tool to explain these continuities as well as changes. On a theoretical level, performative politics demonstrates the limits, if not inadequacy of clear-cut academic categories such as 'the secular' or 'the religious' because empirically the difference between the two is difficult to sustain. Especially by looking at concrete examples of performative politics such as the Khilafat movement, the Shuddhi movement or more recent cases of Hindu-nationalist mobilizations it becomes clear that these categories have to be used rather carefully to explain the character of political discourses. My approach to performative politics assumes, that both, politics as well as the so-called 'religion', are themselves to an important extent defined and constituted in the course of performative strategies and communications. The historical cases of performative politics I have chosen from India's modern history shall illustrate how the 'political' and the 'religious' are framed and defined in interdependence to each other, so that these processes of 'relating', 'diffusion' and 'interpenetration' are themselves put into the centre of our historical understanding and analysis. Through performance in politics the historical 'actors' (in the twofold sense) carry out a work of defining the 'political' and the 'religious' and thereby alter the vocabulary of politics as such. The overall framework of this definition work is the concept of the nation. I assume that it is through the focus on this particular form of (modern) collective identity that we can understand best the characteristics and strategic sense of performance in politics. The category of the nation itself hides the secrets to understand better, why and why at a particular point of time politicians (and in some cases also religious authorities) refer to the strategic repertoire of performative politics to determine the political discourse as a whole according to their agenda. At a rather superficial level, one commonality of colonial as well as post-colonial forms of performative politics is that they were all implemented with reference to an 'Indian nation', no matter how this nation was defined in detail. Obviously, the concrete understandings, i.e. the versions of this 'Indian nation' varied significantly. The history of India in the twentieth and twenty-first century could also be understood as a power struggle over the definition of this nation and its modes of exclusion and inclusion. Nevertheless, it is significant that even in Gandhi's case 'the nation' was the overall reference of performative politics and therefore also constitutes the most important reference for its theoretical understanding.

In order to analyse why—and this is no specificity of Indian history but could also be applied to any (modern) European history—nationalism is an appropriate, even necessary frame for performative politics, I start with Pierre Bourdieu's remarks on categories of commonality and collective identity. The interesting aspect of the theoretical work of the French philosopher and sociologist Bourdieu in this context is, that he developed these remarks in reference to his observations and experiences of the Algerian colonial society, where he analysed the functioning of social networks and the ruptures as well as transformations of modernity. In some of his writings Bourdieu assumes that categories of the 'We' which go beyond the family and kinship ties exceed, per definition, personal experience. The consequence is that these categories, in order to be socially, economically and politically relevant, have to be produced and re-produced through different modes than personal experience. Performative strategies, i.e. the political communication and alteration of the perception of political reality through spectacles, mass mobilizations and media events fulfil this need within a framework of nationalist politics, be it anti-colonial or post-colonial. If one assumes that the idea of the nation develops a discursive dominance in India, similar to most parts of the colonized world, during the second half of the nineteenth century, performance as politics is a logical consequence of the changing structures of political discourses since that time. Three aspects follow from this assumption.

First, in this understanding, performative nation-building, i.e. the explicit application of performative strategies within the nationalist discourse, is the result of the changing character of politics as such. Nationalism is a political ideology based on the inclusion of more and more sections of the 'national' population, i.e. the 'citizens' into the political discourse. In order for nationalism to remain credible and relevant, the modes of political communication have to be adapted to these changing requirements of the political discourse. Especially in the colonial context the question was immediate for the indigenous elite, how the claim for national self-determination and autonomy can be legitimized and sustained on the basis of a justified representation of 'the nation', a justified entitlement to 'speak for' in opposition to a colonial power claiming to know what's best for the 'subjects'. Performative politics is the strategic consequence of these alternative modes of self-perception on the side of the colonized as a 'nation' which develops from an elitist approach to a category of mass mobilization and participation during the first half of the twentieth century. Secondly, the active political communication with and participative inclusion of an increasing number of people was also a deliberate strategy of anti-colonial elites, initiated in India at a large scale by Mahatma Gandhi after the First World War in order to challenge the very basis of politics. One important continuity between the colonial and the post-colonial context was that the Independence movement as a mass movement laid the foundations not only for a politicization of a growing number of segments of Indian society. The last phases of this process are still ongoing in the form of an increasing regionalization and fragmentation of Indian politics since the 1980s which was and is also a process of increasing politicization of regions, lower castes, Adivasis, women and other 'fragments of the nation' (Partha Chatterjee). Additionally, the pre-Independence mass mobilizations can also be interpreted as a form of democracy or rather preliminary form of participatory politics, later constitutionally transformed in a functioning democracy. In any case, my understanding of performative politics emphasizes this interdependence with the ideology of nationalism. Thus, performance in politics should be analysed within a nationalist political framework. Thirdly, the historical character and functioning of performative politics is closely related to the structure of the public, i.e. primarily the question what the public or public space is. As this book covers a historical period of almost hundred years, the meaning of 'public' is an important structural precondition of politics and political communication has changed significantly during that time. The Khilafat movement was confronted with a restrictive colonial regime, seeking to control oppositional discourses as effectively as possible, especially since the end of First World War had recently increased the precariousness of the political situation in India. On the other hand, the Indian National Congress had limited organizational foundations. Both aspects determined important limitations of the access to the public. Performative politics at that point of time was an intelligible strategy to reduce this limitations and broaden the access to the public for the anti-colonial movement. During the second half of the 1980s and the first half of the 1990s, the mass mobilization campaigns of the Hindu right must be interpreted in the context of a vanishing media monopoly of the Indian State TV channel, Doordarshan. Media liberalization was an important factor in the functioning of these later forms of performative nation-building, insofar as initially the BJP successfully sidelined the Congress-controlled TV media and later used especially the private TV channels to communicate its political agenda. Another aspect in relation to the definition of the 'public' is the question who has the power to access and define it? The public is at no point of time simply given but an area of power-related contestations and competition. The question of who has access to the public and who has the power to define, i.e. broaden and limit the 'public' is an important dimension of the struggle for political power. Performative politics as a political strategy is a reaction to certain features of public space and in many cases seeks to alter these existing features by creating alternative channels of communication, not yet controlled by the powerholders. The colonial as well as post-colonial case studies in this book try to refer to these important questions of the public and public space in the case of recent Hindu nationalism, maybe, more explicit than in the case of the Khilafat or the Shuddhi movement.

Another study published a few more years ago on performative politics in western India must at least briefly be mentioned here. Using a similar theoretical approach Raminder Kaur has analysed the 'Ganapati Utsava' in Maharashtra and has interpreted it as an arena of struggle for political definitions especially on the part of Hindutva forces.[13] The analysis throws up interesting insights and conclusions about the particularities and dimensions of political confrontations and about the attempt to redefine politics and public culture in India. In contrast to Kaur and Sudipta Kaviraj, to whom Kaur refers, I don't proceed from the assumption that performative politics is necessarily limited to colonial or post-colonial societies. Although this book discusses the history of modern India, the examples mentioned are significant for global history. I agree with Kaur that performative strategies for propagating political content or for changing political culture has greater historical and current relevance in those societies where low literacy rates, for example, compel the elite to fall back on this form of political discourse. This means that the attractiveness and also the modes of operation of performative politics depends on the context and has to be linked in the analysis with the social and political specificities of, in this case, India. In the case studies that are discussed here it is, therefore, not merely a question of illustrating strategies of cultural argumentation in the history of modern India but of linking these with structural and social changes that have taken place in the country. Advancement of knowledge in historical research is only possible when these connections are established. This does not mean, however, that performative politics itself is a characteristic of colonial or post-colonial societies. On the contrary, we see that these forms of political strategy were present in Europe throughout the twentieth century and have gained significance in the most recent past. This development is linked with the changed conditions for political discourses in an era of accelerated globalization that thrusts the symbolic forms of political discourse into the foreground. The numerous reasons for these developments range from an increasing disempowerment of national political processes in favour of transnational players to a flattening of public discourses on the whole. Already some years ago, Colin Crouch suggested the term 'post-democracy' in order to analyse the transformation of Western political systems into increasingly authoritarian societies where the centres of real economic as well as political power lie beyond the reach of electoral accountability degrading democratic processes into political spectacles without almost any real political significance.[14] On the one hand, therefore, performative politics depends on the context and reacts to the structural conditions of politics of, for example, a colonial state or a colonized society. On the other hand, however, it is a global phenomenon which is lately becoming increasingly more important. In none of these contexts, however, has politics been limited to non-performative strategies–in Thomas Meyer's words: to operative and institutional strategies–but it has always been concerned with suitable and successful strategies of propagation and 'saleability'.[15] From this point of view, therefore, it appears to be a legitimate and interesting exercise to use theoretical approaches for understanding (performative) politics both in India and in Europe and to combine them in order to open up new perspectives on the history of modern India. A preliminary conclusion in relation to the character of performative politics can therefore be that it is distinguished by a critical political ambivalence. On the one hand, performance and spectacle in politics foster the politicization and participation of more and more 'citizens' in political processes. Especially in the colonial period, this is an important aspect not to be underestimated in its consequences for the way politics was defined and concretely implemented. On the other hand, performative politics signifies a depletion not only of the political discourse but also of decision-making processes as such since in these forms of political communication the shape of the political discourse increasingly defines its content.

The first chapter of this book deals with some preliminary remarks on nationalism in modern India in order to examine the association of political discourses with religion, especially in colonial India. It is important to emphasize that at the beginning of nineteenth-century religion and spirituality weren't mere details in nascent nationalism but were the real terrains for the formation of nation-building. The second chapter develops this argument further and discusses the theoretical concept of performative nation-building. As has already been pointed out, existing European and Indian theoretical approaches will be used to arrive at a model which is suited for the analysis of the case studies from the history of modern India that follow. The major theoretical inspiration is taken here from Bourdieu, who has not only developed a fruitful theory of various forms of social and individual capital, important for the understanding of nationalism as a socially hegemonic discourse, but also analysed the societal functioning of (political) rituals and repetitive action to set collective identities. The first case study in chapter 3 looks at Gandhi's Khilafat movement and his deification in the context of this movement. The connection with the organizational and structural potential of the Indian National Congress is also established here, i.e. Gandhi's strategy of mobilization through cultural argumentation is linked with the operative and institutional strategies of the Congress. Using the example of the Shuddhi movement, chapter 4 illustrates the transformation of the religious and the traditional in the framework of performative nation-building and concludes the block of case studies on colonial India. For post-colonial India chapters 5 and 6 draw on different aspects and discuss historical forms of performative politics both as politics of the state as well as (democratic) oppositional politics. Here again, the focus is not only on forms of symbolic politics but also on structural changes of statehood, of the public sphere and the social stratification of the Indian society which are reflected in the political processes. Chapter 7 is devoted to the current theme of religious terrorism in South Asia. It not only goes into the organizational and ideological enmeshment of different forms of violence legitimated by religion but also seeks to apply the theory of performative politics to terrorism as a political strategy in order to discuss the action-oriented logic of this form of violence. As mentioned in the Preface, the chapter was written long before the tragic events in Mumbai in November 2008. One of the politically and historically significant aspects of these terrorist attacks was the timespan of the attack and the subsequent violent confrontation between the terrorists and the Indian security forces lasting for several days. Seemingly, the time span itself was one of the intentions of those who planned and conducted these acts. However, retrospectively these terrorist acts confirm the approach developed in chapter 7, namely that the (performative) shape of such actions is one of their most crucial if not the most important characteristic to get their 'message' across. Chapter 8, the last chapter, sums up the theoretical conclusions from the case studies of colonial and post-colonial India by interpreting the politics of the spectacle as a synthesis of discourse and performance. In connection with established Indian approaches it also suggests a new model for the interpretation of nationalism.

NOTES

1. Lukács, 1972, p. 1.
2. Ibid., p. 2.
3. Hansen, 2004, p. 20.
4. Meyer, 1994, p. 56.
5. Ibid., p. 57.
6. Zavos/Wyatt/Hewitt, 2004, p. 3.
7. Austin, 1962.
8. Cf. for this Searle, 1969, Part 1.
9. Butler, 2009, p. 122.
10. Ibid., p. 106.
11. Zavos, 2007, p. 138.
12. Kohli, 2004, p. 260.
13. Kaur, 2003.
14. Crouch, 2004.
15. Nandy, 2000, p. 83.

CHAPTER 1

Politics, Nationalism and Religion in Modern India

AN IDEA OF INDIA: NATIONALISM IN THE COLONIAL STATE

When Mohandas Karamchand Gandhi was once asked what he thought of a Western, a European civilization, the Mahatma simply said, 'I think it would be a good idea'.[1] With this pointed response Gandhi referred to what was, in his opinion, a discrepancy between an 'idea of Europe', which he didn't elaborate on, and the political situation of those times. From an Indian perspective this situation was characterized by the colonial domination of a large section of humanity by a minority of, almost exclusively, European powers. From their modern centres of global development these powers had degraded the periphery in the south to the status of the 'not-yet-civilized' and thus to an earlier stage of real modernity and progress. Gandhi's political experience of the discriminatory, disenfranchising and impoverishing practices of colonial rule, which he shared with the then more than 300 million inhabitants of British India, is a stark contrast to an 'idea of Europe' defined mainly by Judaeo-Christian attributes and a political content derived from the Enlightenment. Gandhi's extensive writings on this theme show that, in his opinion, the ideal of Christian altruism and the enlightened concept of universal equality had been nullified by colonial politics and had thus also been denied to India through the violent suppression of oppositional politics. For Gandhi, therefore, the subject of Europe was essentially limited to an ideal dimension so long as this practice of colonial subjugation and disenfranchisement was legitimized by Europe's political self-conception. However, this idea of Europe formed itself a backdrop to Gandhi's politics as a normative ideal and it also functioned as a framework of his anti-colonial mobilization: from these Europeans who swore by the idea of Europe, Gandhi demanded consistency with and political actions corresponding to this idea. The history of the Independence struggle in the first half of the twentieth century can also be interpreted as a continuous heightening of the awareness of this discrepancy both in London as well as in the colony—a discrepancy which could no longer be maintained and justified in the face of the growing awareness in India of its own political and economic rights. The outcome of this process of diminishing acceptance of a political praxis that went against individual and collective, i.e. national, self-determination is well known and, as a historical paradigm, it became a model for other colonies also under the hegemony of European rulers.

With emancipation from colonial rule the 'peoples without a history' (Hegel) not only gained self-rule (*swaraj*) but also their own history. This, however, did not occur only by demanding a correspondence between politics and the idea of Europe. Europe's confrontation with itself which was systematically precipitated by the European-trained and, therefore, European-thinking leaders of the Independence struggle and which was translated into an anti-colonial programme was only one aspect of another, oppositional, idea of an independent India. It constituted what can be regarded as a negative backdrop for the rejection of colonial repression, it only formulated what had to be rejected in the interests of one's own rights and it turned the idea of Europe, in the context of colonial subjugation, against itself.

Along with this negatively formulated demarcation against colonial rule there was a need for a positive concept for what would follow, for a concrete self-image, more or less politically viable, as an ideal backbone for an independent India. The gaining of Independence and the concomitant rejection of European assistance on the path to modernity was based on the argument of national self-determination which, in turn, presupposed a concept of the character and the boundaries of this nation. This concept was not simply a given fact at any point of time during the colonial epoch; rather, it was fought out and defined in different ways in a lively debate about nation, collective identity, culture and history. Many different versions of an idea of 'India' were formulated in the course of these decades and they became the object of fundamental ideological controversies in which the struggle for the 'power to formulate'[2] and for political hegemony was carried out with regard to the national self-image.

Differences arose mainly in the framework of two questions. The first concerned deliberations about the elements of tradition that could constitute a collective Indian identity and the second concerned the relationship between Hindus and Muslims.[3] In the initial period of the discourse on an Indian nation there was a sense of cooperation with the colonial power as also a consciousness of the possible civilizational benefits of British rule. In 1828, Raja Rammohun Roy had taken a decisive organizational step towards national emancipation by establishing the Brahmo Samaj. In a letter written in the same year he expressed his confidence about the possibilities of a positive partnership with Britain:

> Supposing that one hundred years hence the Native character becomes elevated from constant intercourse with Europeans and the acquirement of general and political knowledge as well as of modern arts and sciences, is it possible that they will not have the spirit as well as the inclination to resist effectually any unjust and oppressive measures serving to degrade the scale of society? . . . Were India to share one fourth of the knowledge and energy of that country [i.e. Great Britain, C.S.], she would prove from her remote situation, her riches and her vast population, either useful and profitable as a willing province, an ally of the British Empire, or troublesome and annoying as a determined enemy.[4]

Despite Roy's approval of Britain and its 'benevolent rule', the letter also contains a sharp criticism of colonial practices and Roy questions laws enacted by the government 'without consulting or seeming to understand the feelings of its Indian subjects and without considering that this people have had for more than half a century the advantage of being ruled by and associated with an enlightened nation, advocates of liberty and promoters of knowledge'. These first attempts at sketching an idea of India were hesitant ones, marked by a tenor of civilizational subservience which was, however, abolished by the time the Indian National Congress was formed in 1885. The political-nationalist discourse in India employed the strategy of dividing reality into a spiritual and a material domain. This strategy preceded and ideologically justified the later phase of political action against colonial rule.[5] What is interesting and significant about this mode of thought for the course of the anti-colonial struggle is the fact that it created the first conceptual sphere of sovereignty within a colonized society long before the Independence movement could achieve its first political victories against the British. According to this understanding of colonial reality, which gained ground in the nineteenth century, the world is divided into a material, or external, domain and a spiritual, or inner, one. As far as the material sphere was concerned, which included the economy, modern technology and science, there was no doubt that the dominance and superiority of the British and the Europeans would have to be acknowledged. India would have to catch up with them in these areas through observation and imitation. The dominance of the West in this domain was explained on the basis of a quasi-natural attribution of material orientation to Western culture and tradition. In contrast to this India's superiority lay in the field of spirituality and here, at least, any interference from European domination could be rejected. This created a sphere of complete autonomy based essentially on India's history and traditions which also constituted the decisive positive difference to the colonial masters. India was thus, as a representative of the East, master in the fields of culture and religion for which it could apparently produce a much richer and a more varied heritage. This concept of the self, the Indian, is explicitly formulated for the first time by Swami Vivekananda who not only derived India's developing consciousness of itself from this, but who also used it to articulate a missionary zeal in the name of spirituality:

Let foreigners come and flood the land with their armies, never mind. Up, India, and conquer the world with your spirituality! . . . Materialism and all its miseries can never be conquered by materialism. Armies when they attempt to conquer armies only multiply and make brutes of humanity. Spirituality must conquer the West. Slowly they are finding out that what they want is spirituality to preserve them as nations.[6]

The consequence of this dual division of reality was the insistence on sole competence for formulating a national identity which was understood almost exclusively as a national culture with a marked religious imprint. This seriously curtailed the political and social jurisdiction of the colonial state and, as an interim stage, it became a precondition for self-rule. In this stage of the discourse on autonomy nationalism developed its singular strength, which initially led to a gradual autonomy in the spheres of culture and religion. In the further chain of events, however, these spheres became the main criteria for the existence of an Indian nation and thus initiated the culturally motivated rejection of foreign rule.

The reason why culture and religion were so closely linked with reflections on an Indian nation is to be seen, on the one hand, in connection with India's specific historical experience as a colony and with its rich cultural and religious landscape. On the other hand, the reason for this strong link with religion and culture can be found in the very nature of nationalism itself. Nationalism is the 'form of political thought which is based on the assumption that social ties are dependent on cultural conformity'.[7] In contrast to traditional societies where differing forms of culture are used to mark intra-societal differences nationalism propagates a common national culture which integrates all citizens into a single unit. However, the exact assessment of culture in the framework of the nationalist discourse was never the same in contemporary Indian history. Just as the idea of the nation itself was thought about and formulated in different ways, the role of culture, and especially of religion, was interpreted differently.

In the first two decades of the twentieth century the radical-national wing of the Indian National Congress under the leadership of B.G. Tilak, for example, saw the essence of the Indian nation, following the above-mentioned dual division of reality, in its cultural, i.e. Hindu character. For these nationalists this character had been a constant element in the country's history and it was this which had to be restored to its original grandeur and glory through a committed and uncompromising anti-colonialism.[8] For Bipin Chandra Pal, Tilak's comrade-in-arms from Bengal, the nation 'India' signified the following:

> If we are asked to define what nationality is, we would say that it is the individuality of a people. . . . We cannot explain the how, much less can we explain the why, of these peculiarities; all that we can say of them is that they are there, in the very constitution of these different people.[9]

Pal identified two main aspects in the specific characteristics that define the individuality of the Indian nation and, thus, set it off against other nations. These two aspects would have to be borne in mind in politics and in the formation of 'national life': a common structure of thought and a comprehensive and unified social organization. Although he doesn't elaborate on this, Pal assumes that these characteristics are quasi-natural and he calls for a political praxis which builds on this to establish India's sovereignty:

> Loyalty to our national ideals and institutions means really our only chance of living as a distinct and individual nation. It constitutes our only title to grow as an individual nation among the nations of the modern world. It is a supremely practical problem to us. Its value is positive and not negative.[10]

The national-liberals around G.K. Gokhale or Dadabhai Naoroji, on the other hand, established an ideological tradition in India's political history that was continued by Motilal and Jawaharlal Nehru.

This tradition was far more oriented towards liberal English ideas of national self-determination. Rather than viewing an Indian nation as a kind of natural constituent of history, they saw it as a 'nation in the making' which would have to develop as a multi-cultural and especially as a multi-religious society through a process of political emancipation and a rise in awareness.[11] Jawaharlal Nehru, who later became the first prime minister of independent India, carried on this liberal position with the inclusion of socialist aspects. He emphasized the importance of the future for the Constitution of an Indian nation. For Nehru, India as a unified nation didn't arise only out of the logic of the past, although his writings also contain some signs of this which are formulated in a clearly overreaching and almost lyrical manner.[12] Instead, what was decisive for the right to exist as an independent state and as a nation was, according to Nehru, the prospect of a prosperous future, for which national integration was an important prerequisite. Particularly for the initial period after Independence Nehru considered economic and social necessities as well as cooperation at the national level as the main binding force of the nation,[13] even though he didn't fully dispute the relevance of culture and religion as fundaments of a collective commonality:

> I think that at almost any time in recorded history an Indian would have felt more or less at home in any part of India, and would have felt as a stranger and alien in any other country. He would certainly have felt less of a stranger in countries which had adopted his culture or religion. Those who professed a religion of non-Indian origin or, coming to India, settled down there, became distinctively Indian in the course of a few generations, such as Christians, Jews, Parsees, Moslems. Indian converts to some of these religions never ceased to be Indian on account of a change of their faith.[14]

However, for Nehru, the factors of culture and religion had the dangerous potential of being misused and instrumentalized for–in his view–anti-national and group-based interests. Nehru's opposition to every form of political mobilization along religious lines wasn't based only on its potential danger for economic and social development at the national level. He also criticized this political strategy in principle as reactionary and pre-modern and one which would only help extend British rule in India.[15] In numerous speeches and public appearances Nehru repeatedly pointed out the irrelevance of communal politics which was being formed along the dividing lines of religion in Indian society. This kind of politics, he felt, didn't allow one to see the real themes of India's present and future, namely political independence and economic development.[16] In keeping with this Nehru summed up his own programme with regard to culture and religion in the following manner:

> The real factor to my mind is the economic factor. If we lay stress on this and divert public attention to it we shall find automatically that religious differences recede into the background and a common bond unites different groups. The economic bond is stronger than even the national one.[17]

Thus, Nehru, like many other later heads of government of post-colonial states, was concerned

> initially with establishing a regime whose purpose is to mobilize all national forces for overcoming under-development. Its rational legitimacy is based solely on this substantive purpose. The nation as the legitimizing factor of political rule internally and externally and the nation-state as the institutional framework, as an organizational form for development politics, appear at present to be the only historically possible means to solve the problems of colonial and semi-colonial countries with regard to their emancipation.[18]

This concept of nation was culturally relatively neutral and, therefore, open to the ethnic and religious diversity in the countries concerned. The fathers of independence regarded this as the most important condition for the long-term success of the project of statehood.

By emphasizing the priority of the economic factors of national development Nehru came into conflict with M.K. Gandhi in whose political biography religion and culture play a pivotal role. Nehru rejected Gandhi's explicit reference to religion in his political campaigns, whereas for Gandhi the relationship between politics and religion wasn't merely dependent on the exigencies of the situation or justified by a greater success in political mobilization, but this relationship was substantial and, indeed, necessary. When asked by a journalist in 1940 whether he still maintained what he had said in his biography that politics and religion cannot be separated and whether a commonality could be evolved in a country like India with its religious diversity, Gandhi replied:

> Yes, I still hold the view that I cannot conceive politics as divorced from religion. Indeed religion should pervade every one of our actions. Here religion does not mean sectarianism. It means a belief in ordered moral government of the universe. It is not less real but it is unseen. This religion transcends Hinduism, Islam, Christianity, etc. it does not supersede them. It harmonises them and gives them reality.[19]

For Gandhi, the permeation of political life and action with a humanistic religion of non-violence had a primarily integrative function for a nation like India. It transcended the narrow and, in end effect, divisive boundaries of the different religious communities to postulate a general and comprehensive view of a more human-oriented development. Gandhi viewed the two-nation theory, which envisaged Pakistan divided from India as a separate nation for Muslims, as a 'falsehood' since the dividing principle of religious affiliation was in contradiction to Gandhi's idea of an independent India integrated in terms of religion and culture. The nation of 'India' was, for Gandhi, a pool of heterogeneous cultural landscapes whose independent existence could only be justified if there was a consistent realization of a morally-high, human-oriented development moving towards individual and collective maturity and autonomy.

THE SPECIFICITIES OF INDIAN NATIONALISM

If a nation is defined as an 'appointed community of people' which acknowledges and achieves 'a common historical territory, common myths and memories, a public culture, a singular economy as well as the same rights and duties for all its members',[20] then this definition is not limited to a European state, but it describes a global project that can be implemented in different, locally specific, ways. Nationalism as an ideological movement, which is committed to the creation and maintenance of autonomy in terms of the right to a people's, i.e. nation's, sovereignty, always uses available cultural means that are taken from its own rich pool of cultural signifiers. The question remains controversial as to whether national consciousness is a historical phenomenon or whether it arose, or was constructed, under modern conditions.

The debate about a possible Indian nation was conducted mainly along the lines of the basic differences between the primordialist and the modernist conception.[21] Among the political actors of South Asia from different ideological camps there was, however, always a strong tendency to assume a long history of an Indian nation in order to establish one of the most important conditions for a national consciousness, viz., historical legitimacy. Regardless of the question whether an Indian nation is entirely a modern product of the anti-colonial discourse in the name of political autonomy, or whether it has historical roots, India's self-image as a historically established nation was an integral aspect of all modern political trends. This form of recourse to an 'ideal' past, to an old 'national' heritage is, by no means, only a characteristic of religious nationalism which naturally traces the nation to millennia-old traditions. It is also found in the more secular models of an Indian nation as, for example, in Nehru's writings.[22] This fact prompted Rothermund[23] to suggest the concept of 'solidarity-traditionalism' with regard to the subject of nationalism in India. This concept refers to a discursive strategy that allows political leaders, especially in (former) colonies, to establish a collective and politically effective solidarity as the emotional basis of a national consciousness:

> This solidarity has to be based on cultural and religious traditions if there is no specific tradition of a common territorial state or if this state is a colonial one imposed by foreign rulers. Solidarity-traditionalism is, therefore, a frequent feature of the nationalism of subject nations or such nations whose territorial integrity is problematic either because of external challenges or a lack of internal cohesion.[24]

In its varied articulations Indian nationalism thus exhibited specific characteristics which determine the relationship between religion and politics even today.

The first specificity of the Indian context with regard to the construction of national solidarity is its colonial past which was not only the overarching framework for the rise of nationalism but which also constituted its essential point of reference. Let us first look at colonialism as the political framework for the rise of the nationalist discourse.

Eric Hobsbawm[25] assumes that even in Western nation states the existence of a modern political system preceded the formation of the idea of nation. He, therefore, emphasizes the primary importance of economic and social transformation processes for the rise of nation states. Other authors of the modernist school, on the other hand, analyse the multifarious processes in the creation of nation states as the simultaneity of economic and social changes at the threshold of modernity.[26] According to this view, therefore, the social changes that led to the rise of modern states and the rise of nationalism as an effective ideology supporting the state were mutually dependent and also causally connected. This European simultaneity explains nationalism as a direct conceptual reaction to the requirements produced by social changes to find another legitimating factor for political power, or to challenge this power. For the Indian context–and in this sense colonialism plays a decisive role–we can only assume that state-formation occurred first which produced nationalisms only much later. For one, this resulted from the character of the state itself which, as a colonial state, was the product of a foreign conquest and, therefore, represented the exact opposite of India's national self-image. Later, however, it was this very character of the colonial state which became the actual provocation for nationalist thinking. For the other, this anteriority was caused by a dislocation in the phases of material development in South Asia. At the time when the colonial state was set-up according to European administrative criteria, it did not match the economic status of the subcontinent. By the time colonial rule was fully established a modern system of government had been imposed on India's basically agrarian, pre-modern economic and social structure. The social basis of this modern system matured only in the 1920s to create the conditions for a broad nationalist commitment. The first reason for India's exceptional position in the global history of the rise of nationalism arises out of the problematic situation created by anteriority. A territory marked by colonial conquest had not been constituted through other criteria as the territorial principle which could support a culturally defined and internally cohesive nation whose self-conception could achieve the highest possible measure of cultural integration. It is true that the British, to a certain extent, created a national market which, like in Europe, was one of the main conditions for the rise of a nation as a 'community bound by fate' (*Schicksalsgemeinschaft*) (Otto Bauer).[27] With a unified system of administration for the entire country and the establishment of English as a kind of *lingua franca* among the diversity of Indian languages, the British also created two other structural conditions for the nationalist discourse.[28] However, in order to have better political control over the subcontinent, the colonial rulers consciously did not interfere with traditional social fragmentations, like the caste system, or with regional and religious forms of association.[29] An important difference to European forms of establishing a nation thus consists in the maintenance or even enhancement of traditional affiliations and social structures that are opposed to the principle of an egalitarian national integration. Thus, the dismantling of pre-modern patterns of inequality in favour of a modern praxis of national citizenship based on equality was not carried out in British-India. This meant that traditional social segmentations could be transferred into the structure of the modern colonial state instead of being replaced by the latter.

Apart from its function as the structural and organizational framework for the rise of nationalism in India, colonialism was also the central point of reference for a self-definition as delineation from the other.[30] In his discussion of India's modernity Avijit Pathak[31] has made the useful suggestion that we should understand colonialism as the background for the rise of a modern collective consciousness not only as physical, or political, hegemony but that we should also examine its reality as a 'cultural or symbolic power'. In this sense the struggle for national self-determination and Independence also has to be understood as the conflict with British presence in the symbolic field and in that of culture. The earlier mentioned dual division of colonial reality into a material sphere dominated by the British and a spiritual one that was declared to be intrinsically Indian–and for which all forms of foreign interference were first rejected[31]–is part of a broad repertoire of oppositional cultural and national strategies against a colonial state that was visibly obstructing national selfhood. Given the overwhelming foreign presence in India, culture functioned as the key competence of the intelligentsia in the process of national emancipation long before concrete steps were undertaken to mobilize the masses for self-rule:

> Culture here can become a structured intellectual-spiritual activity, to mobilize the imagination of society for its self-image and activity; a work that falls mainly to the intelligentsia. . . . In India the turn to culture made it possible for the intelligentsia to go back in history to fill the resistance against colonial rule with themes and inspirations from the past.[33]

Against the backdrop of colonialism, culture is thus constituted as the first and most important terrain of national competence and, in this sense, it becomes a specific characteristic of nationalism in all colonized societies. In India, from the very beginning this dual division of colonial reality created a 'basic ambivalence'[34] in the nationalist discourse which is apparent even today and which still determines the relationship with the West. Although the focus on 'intellectual-spiritual activity' (Alam) was a conscious strategy of delineation against the Western colonial rulers, even the most radical religious nationalists in India were aware of the fact that Western hegemony could only be questioned through selective imitation in practical political terms. Delineation and imitation are, therefore, the two collaborative aspects in the history of the formation of national consciousness under colonialism as well as in independent India.

Along with colonialism as the external framework and the inner point of reference for nationalism, cultural diversity is a second specific condition. It is superfluous to mention that in comparison with all existing European nation states India has a far greater and more fundamental cultural diversity that is also an outcome of its religious diversity. The relevant question here is to what extent this heterogeneity determines, or even impedes, the formulation of a national self-image.

In order to define the problem more accurately it would help to take up a suggestion made by Stuart Hall which appears to be eminently suitable for approaching the question of cultural plurality and the (im)possibility of an Indian nation:

> We shouldn't think of national cultures as uniform entities but rather as a discursive model which represents differences as unity or identity. They are ridden with deep inner divisions and differences that are 'united' only by the exercise of cultural power. As in the imaginations of the 'self as a whole' in Lacanian psychoanalysis identities are maintained through a unified representation. . . . But this belief becomes a myth in the modern world. There is no nation in Western Europe which consists only of one people, one culture or one ethnic group. All modern nations are culturally hybrid.[35]

In this context India is different from Europe only insofar as the actual condition of becoming a nation, namely the cultural hybridism against which it has to fight, is a historically more extensive and more fundamental fact. The attempt to establish national identity in the modern sense is, in its very definition, the reduction of an essentially far more diverse reality. In all forms of nationalism this discrepancy between a 'discursive model' of the nation, which represents inner 'differences as unity', and the deeply plural social reality contains the potential for violence as an obvious consequence of the reduction of reality. India is not an exception in this regard, but rather an extreme case of the fundamental character of nationalist discourses that unfolds in a highly explosive manner in the Indian context.[36]

It goes without saying that India's cultural landscape is the second important specificity of the nationalist discourse. Stuart Hall's concept of the 'discursive model' identifies a significant characteristic of nationalism and also sheds light on its mode of operation. The nation isn't an existing entity that has to be awakened but it is, in the first instance, a construct of language which is represented culturally as a 'symbolic community' and thus becomes historically significant as a category of thought.[37] Nation as a category doesn't derive its relevance for political action from the fact of a common culture but from the belief in it,[38] or, as Claus Leggewie says, not from the fact of commonality but from the 'belief in commonality'.[39] The criterion of India's cultural heterogeneity is therefore significant for the nationalist discourse since one has to ask what strategies were used for coping with diversity to achieve political unity and how this reductionism shaped politics. However, it would be wrong to infer that nationalism is impossible in India on account of this diversity, for some forms of nationalism in India's past and present have shown themselves to be highly adaptable.

The third specificity of Indian nationalism consists in the relationship between tradition and modernity which differs from the way this is normally formulated in Western nationalisms. The theories previously mentioned which proceed on the assumption that there is a close connection between the rise of nationalism and the comprehensive processes of modernization postulate a contrast between an earlier, pre-modern phase and the later, modern-nationalist phase. Although this may, to a large extent, be true for the historical developments in Europe, it is irrelevant for a discussion of the Indian context. The view of modernity as a rupture is based, on the one hand, on its juxtaposition with tradition which, in this view, is completely replaced by modernity as the next phase of historical development. On the other hand, the concept of tradition doesn't refer only to pre-modern social forms but also to the dominance of religion in all spheres of society which is gradually pushed back till complete secularization is achieved in modernity, although religion as a marker of group identities is permitted.[40] As is indicated by Rothermund's concept of 'solidarity-traditionalism'[41] there is no clear distinction drawn between tradition and modernity in the different forms of nationalism in India. On the contrary, here it is tradition which provides the symbolic and cultural repertoire for the formulation of India's 'specific modernity'.[42] In this connection Clifford Geertz refers to the characteristic interaction and, therefore, simultaneity of essentialism and epochalism in post-colonial states. Essentialism as one of the strategies for constructing collective national identities falls back on the essences of local traditions and symbolic forms of the inherited cultural landscape and uses these elements of cultural memory according to the political needs of the times. Epochalism, on the other hand, conceives of national selfhood as a product of a shared political and economic history.[43] It is this interplay of traditional essences and historical epochs which constitutes the special form of national consciousness in the former colonies. With regard to the special forms of nationalism in India, therefore, tradition is not to be viewed as the conceptual opposite of modernity but rather as the necessary means of its reformulation.

However, the connections between nationalism and religion as an important part of tradition are far more extensive. The distinction between a civil, secular nationalism, on the one hand, and religious, cultural forms of it, on the other, is generally linked with a value-judgement. Mainly because of the tendency of politicized religion to use violent means to achieve its goals, the first, secular form is considered 'good' nationalism since it spurns religious fanaticism to establish loyalties based on equality, citizenship and freedom.[44] Cultural or religious nationalism, on the contrary, is, according to prevalent, mainly Western, opinions, oriented towards opposition to other religious communities and, therefore, more prone to violence and thus 'bad'.[45] Western theories of nationalism didn't completely neglect the aspect of religion but they generally included it in an abbreviated form.[46] Even in the West, religion played a central role in establishing the horizons of nationalist thought and action. Along with the standardization of the forms and content of education and the bureaucratization of the state[47] it was mainly the propagation of a 'religion on the pattern of Protestantism'[48] which enabled the widespread implementation of nationalism. This religion revoked the function of the priest as a mediator between god and humans thus raising every individual believer to the status of a priest. It also used a standardized language to disseminate its religious message far and wide. In this way religion became the 'midwife' of a basically secular nationalism. It provided a uniform means of communication, thus creating a political space which could shelter that very nation as a cultural unit. In many cases religion marks the external borders of a nation[49] and in the classical European view of the nineteenth-century nations themselves are divine, god-given and natural divisions of humanity.[50] This metaphysical legitimizing of the nation, in turn, affects the way rulers perceive themselves: they often interpret their function as executors of a basically superhuman mission on behalf of the nation. In the European view the relationship between the nation state and the citizen is the same as that between god, or the prophet representing him, and the believer.[51] Thus, religion is not just an element that marks external boundaries but it is also the model for a metaphysically coloured national self-image.

NOTES

1. Quoted in Ananthu, 1981, p. 1.
2. 'Formulierungsgewalt' Sloterdijk, 2002.
3. Cf. Appadorai, 1987, p. 83 who refers in this context to the differing ideological conceptions of the Indian nation put forward by V.D. Savarkar and B.R. Ambedkar. The differences also characterize the nationalism discourse in modern India on the whole.
4. Roy, 1945-58: *The English Works of Rammohun Roy*, part 4, quoted in Hay, 1992, pp. 33f.
5. Chatterjee, 1993, p. 6.
6. Vivekananda, 1928, pp. 76f.
7. Gellner, 1999, p. 17.
8. Klimkeit, 1981, chapter V, p. 1.
9. Pal, 'Reform on National Lines', 1901, in Appadorai, 1973, pp. 475-8, here p. 475.

10. Pal 1913, in Grover, 1992, p. 276.
11. Nanda, 1974.
12. Cf. Nehru, 1998, chapter 4f.
13. Ibid., pp. 532f.
14. Ibid., p. 62.
15. Nehru in 'Reality and Myth', 1934, in Gupta, 1965, pp. 26f.
16. Cf. Nanda, 1998, p. 103.
17. Nehru, 1973, p. 203.
18. Tibi, 1971, p. 48.
19. Gandhi, 1940, in Appadorai, 1976, p. 656.
20. Smith, 1999, p. 37.
21. Cf. Rogers, 1994, p. 10. Cf. for this also Deol, 2000, chapter 1.
22. Cf. Nehru, 1995, pp. 426f; 1998, pp. 62, 136f, 187f.
23. Rothermund, 1997.
24. Ibid., p. 191.
25. Cf. Hobsbawm, 1992.
26. Gellner, 1983; Taylor, 1988, etc.
27. Bayly, 1998, p. 102.
28. Cf. Anderson, 1998, pp. 63ff; Brass, 1991; Brenan, 1990; Deutsch, 1996.
29. Cf. also Buck, 1994, pp. 6f; Kapferer, 1988.
30. Cf. Wertheim, 1985, pp. 195f.
31. Pathak, 1998, p. 43.
32. Chatterjee, 1993, p. 6.
33. Alam, 1999, p. 130.
34. Tonnesson/Antlöv 1996, p. 30.
35. Hall, 1994, pp. 206f.
36. Cf. Tonnesson/Antlöv (1996), p. 23; against this Parekh, 1999.
37. Cf. Gellner, 1983 and 1999.
38. Kallscheuer/Leggewie, 1994.
39. Leggewie, 1994, p. 51.
40. Cf. Gellner, 1983; Hobsbawm, 1992.
41. Rothermund, 1979.
42. Cf. Chatterjee, 1997, pp. 263ff.
43. Geertz, 1973, pp. 242f.
44. Banerjee, 2002, p. 54.
45. Cf. also Armstrong, 1997.
46. Veer, 1994.
47. Cf. Kellas, 1998, pp. 85f.

48. Gellner, 1999, p. 126.
49. Kedourie, 1993, p. 67.
50. Ibid., p. 52.
51. Ibid., p. 40.

CHAPTER 2

Performative Nation-building: Religious Rituals in Indian Nationalism

NATION AS A SOCIAL REALITY

In order to describe the functions of religion in the political discourse of colonial and post-colonial India it would be helpful to first consider the consequences of nationalism and the establishing of a modern, in India's case colonial, administrative state for notions of society and polity. In pre-modern society local principalities and other small, i.e. non-national, political units mediated between the individual and state authority. In the modern state, on the other hand, these political and administrative intermediaries no longer exist and the centre has direct access to those now termed 'citizens' through its newly formulated and increasingly wider jurisdiction.[1] Administrative centralization, the introduction of military service, improved means of data collection which gave precise information about the number and the demographic character of its subjects as well as the establishment of a unified system of education with the accompanying national canonization of the content of education—these are only some examples of the administrative revolution effected by the modern state.[2] The implementation of modern citizenship, therefore, implies that hierarchical social structures are dismantled to a certain extent and a limited discourse of horizontal relations of equality is established:

Citizenship involves essentially the question of access to scarce resources in society and participation in the distribution and enjoyment of such resources. Whereas political theory typically considers citizenship in terms of civil and political rights of access to decision-making and the selection of government, a broader notion of citizenship involves the question of social membership and participation in society as a whole.[3]

This broader, and historically more adequate, interpretation of citizenship, therefore, not only raises the question of direct political participation in the modern state, but also of adequate participation in economic processes and access to scarce resources. Both these aspects are necessary for the process of nation-building and are causally connected, albeit mostly in a historically phased manner so that either the economic integration of previously marginalized sections of society precedes greater political participation or vice versa. These developments, regardless of their sequence, develop an almost revolutionary potential in a highly-fragmented and segregated society like that of India.

This social and political re-organization leads to a fundamental change in ideas about social spaces and social relations which modern nationalism enforces mainly in two ways. For one, this involves the idea and the internal constitution of society. For modern Europe, we can speak in this context of a phased development which leads from a vertically structured agrarian society to a horizontally structured one in modernity. In contrast to the pre-modern 'mediated-access society', in modern 'direct-access society'[4] affiliation to this larger entity, the nation, and consequently to the state is no longer mediated indirectly through affiliation with a smaller, sub-national, local entity. Rather, it is now embodied directly in the fact of personal citizenship. In this respect, the colonial state in British India was a synthesis of modern elements such as centralized administration on the one hand and non-modern elements like the incorporated princely states all over the territory, classical examples for 'mediated-access societies'. In the case of religious nationalism in India this new national culture was heavily impregnated with shades of religion. Whereas in pre-modern times the function of culture and religion in the political sense was to mark internal divisions in society with regard to class and status, in the era of nationalism they function as markers of external boundaries. Culture and religion now primarily define the Self, but also the Other as that which doesn't belong to the nation. Internally, modern society in its self-image as a nation not only makes this culture the yardstick of integration for its citizens but it also becomes the only acceptable basis of all social relations and, particularly, of methods to legitimize or question hegemony: 'Whatever may be the principles of governance that a state lays down, their legitimacy is based on the fact that members of this group share the same culture (or, as the nationalist would say, they must belong to the same nation).'[5] The rulers of a nation conceived in this manner can only legitimize their position of privilege by arguing that they are there on behalf of the national culture and, on no account, by hereditary privilege, for example. The national leadership has to justify its prominent position as the convincing representative of a culture which is basically shared by all citizens. Similarly, political authority within a nation is questioned through the re-formulation or re-interpretation of this national culture which makes the desired change at the top appear necessary for its self-image.

The second important change in the idea of social spaces and relations in modern nationalism is the idea of the nation as a whole, as a unified entity, a structure with marked borders. By focusing on cultural criteria, such as the shared culture of language and religion, the existence of the nation is dissociated from its identity as a political formation.[6] The national identity of a community is then completely independent of any political entities. From the point of view of nationalism the nation exists simply as the historically changing unity of its members, regardless of the question whether this nation has a politically unified territory or an own state. This can, however, also lead to efforts to establish a common ground between nation and political organization. The actual political force of nationalism stems from this. In Europe, this step was carried out as the separation of 'cosmology and history',[7] i.e. the idea of time became secular, religious myths of origin were replaced by the story of the nation and political structures were viewed not as given but as changeable.[8] In India, on the other hand, there is, even today, an immanent link between nation and religion although attempts were made, especially by Nehru, to clearly separate these two aspects. Hindu nationalism in particular is a form of Indian nationalism that can be understood best as 'strategic syncretism',[9] i.e. as the systematic attempt to re-interpret religious and cultural traditions and to adapt them to the task of modern nation-building.

POLITICS OF RELIGIOUS RITUALS: PERFORMATIVE NATION-BUILDING

If one wants to analyse the functions of religion against the background of these new ideas that society developed about itself, it would be useful initially to interpret nation-building as an act of communication, indeed as the process of a specifically modern form of communication between, on the one hand, citizens who are strangers to each other and, on the other, between the political elites of the nation and the citizens. The point of departure for this 'communicative' interpretation of nation-building is a three-dimensional understanding of politics. In the first dimension politics encompasses a 'strategy to set up an institutional framework' which defines those political actions 'that restructure political and social conditions of decision-making and participation'.[10] This dimension includes structural measures that reflect economic and social changes and carry them over into the political arena. Secondly, politics consists of a 'programmatic-operative strategy' which functions within the given institutional framework and tries to influence political events through individual measures. Nation-building is, therefore, not only an institutionally-oriented process that happens once, but also daily political routine which remains creative within the given political structures. Thirdly, and finally, politics is characterized by the 'strategy of cultural argumentation' to influence political culture which 'aims at communication and conviction with regard to the political decisions or political actions of citizens'.[11] Nationalism in particular recognizes the significance of this spectrum of political reality and develops its persuasive power mainly by influencing the mindset of citizens:

> The convictions developed in the processes of cultural communication constitute, on the one hand, the yardstick used by citizens to measure the legitimacy of conditions of decision-making and the success of programmes of action. On the other hand, they are used to judge the principles and orientations of their own role in order to realise the political in their lives.[12]

The second and third dimensions are, therefore, necessary extensions of a concept of politics for the analysis of nation-building as a communicative strategy or an act of communication.

In the early work of Karl W. Deutsch[13] nationalism studies found an indication of the significance of social forms of communication and their modes of operation for the development of national consciousness, especially in socially fragmented societies. Benedict Anderson[14] took up this argument in his concept of 'print-capitalism' and has called it the 'key for understanding the development of completely new ideas of simultaneity' which, by virtue of being combined with capitalist forms of production, made the widespread dissemination of canonized, i.e. unified matter possible. With regard to the role of religion it is important to note that these new forms of a broad capitalist-oriented communication don't automatically work to the detriment of religion and its influence, but they transform religion itself in their forms of organization and communication.[15] At any rate, this content-based component of nation-building opens up another important field of analysis which shows us that the development of modern material infrastructure also led to the implementation of a similarly modern mental infrastructure which forms the actual backbone of nationalism. This 'inner nation-building'[16] is concerned with the most efficient means of disseminating nationalist categories of thought and language in the political arena. These then become the basis for assessing the legitimacy or the success and failure of politics.

Nationalism, and especially religious nationalism, doesn't rely only on the re-formulation and dissemination of political content in order to achieve this goal. A purely content-based communication of nationalist world-views wouldn't be particularly convincing in politics. There are essentially three 'discursive strategies'[17] that are used in the construction of national identity, namely the content itself, secondly the strategies and, finally, the means—or forms—of implementation.[18] Looking at these three levels is particularly useful for the Indian context because they raise the concept of construction beyond the purely linguistic levels (the first and second dimensions) and also include public actions, acts of staging and other forms of performative nation-building.

In order to clarify this progress in the understanding of strategies of nation-building, the three dimensions of the discourse mentioned earlier will first have to be looked at separately in a conceptual manner. The dimension of contents defines the linguistic construction of the nation, of common ancestry and a shared future, of a common national culture as well as of demarcations both internally and externally. The second dimension of strategies refers to a level that mediates between the conceptual, purely content-oriented messages of nationalism and the means of their implementation, i.e. the active, performative transformation of national consciousness. Strategies are 'more or less elaborate plans of action'[19] which are derived from conceptual models of the nation but which already contain concrete ideas for their political realization. Strategies exist as mental schemata which are mainly articulated as views on the political *status quo*. Strategies comment on political reality either in a destructive or a constructive, but sometimes also in a conserving manner, and they develop plans either for the constructive transformation of political reality, or for its destruction, as also sometimes for its conservation. As strategies they are closely linked with questions of domination, with collective consciousness and its adequate realization.

For the first level of analysis, nation-building as a content-based event, a few, brief prefatory remarks on the essence of linguistically and politically relevant categories, such as the concept of nation, are necessary. The original Latin term *natio* initially meant origin linked with birth, tribe or lineage.[20] Later, the concept of nation denoted mainly the family or the clan.[21] What these differing usages have in common is that nation, like the concept of family or community, refers to structures of social relations in which individuals are connected with one another through mutual acknowledgement and corresponding actions.[22] Obviously, there are major differences between family and nation with regard to the socio-economic foundations of the two associations. The family, for example, is characterized in material terms by an essentially direct relationship of exchange and dependence, but, as social categories, both forms of association function in an analogous manner, i.e. they are structurally similar even if they are qualitatively different. Family, like nation, denotes order; it is a 'collective principle of construction of collective reality. It can be said without contradiction that both social realities are social fictions with no other basis than social construction, and that they really exist, inasmuch as they are collectively recognized.'[23] On no account does this statement deny the material dimension of social organization, but it points to the conscious or unconscious modes of the construction and the functioning of social categories including nation. As entities of imagination and mental organization they function both as descriptive, i.e. they describe a fact, and as prescriptive categories, i.e. they function as directives and demand certain forms of behaviour in certain situations. Their persuasive power–and in this regard nation isn't an exception but the most illustrative example–doesn't lie in their essence as the sum total of experiences but in the fact that these social categories precede experience.[24] They are the interpretive filter which rank and group different routine or extraordinary experiences and relate them to the known so that they make sense. Collective as well as individual experience is, therefore, the result of the processing of reality. Those details about the exchange between the individual and reality that, with the help of social categories, are termed positive or negative remain in the form of experience in the individual and collective memory and determine action in the present and the future. For this reason Sloterdijk's notion of 'the power to formulate'[25] is a political force which is especially important for the success of religious-nationalistic mobilization and which should not be underestimated. Those who control categories of perception and are successful in changing these in favour of their own political ideology have enormous political possibilities at their disposal. After a certain point these possibilities develop on their own since collective experiences are interpreted in the light of these categories and this, in turn, strengthens the categories themselves.

However, the existence and the efficacy of social categories such as nation aren't simply the effect of mental principles of organization, but they have to be produced first and then constantly reproduced and confirmed so that they aren't forgotten. This political work of the production and reproduction of mental categories can be termed as the 'work of institution' (Bourdieu) 'both ritual and technical, aimed at durably instituting in each member of the instituted unit feelings that will tend to ensure the *integration* that is the condition of the existence and persistence of the unit. Rites of institution (from *stare*, to stand, be stable) aim to constitute [the unit] by establishing it as a united, integrated entity which is therefore stable, constant indifferent to the fluctuations of individual feelings'.[26] The work of institution consists of public ritual action for maintaining the cohesive strength of the collective. This brings us to the third level of the discursive construction of national identity,[27] the level of the means and forms of implementation which translate the contents of nationalism into political action. The elements of the work of institution as the work of assertion are, for example, acts of creation at the beginning (a peace treaty, a decisive battle, a creation myth, etc.), or 'inaugural acts of creation' in Bourdieu's words, and their logical extensions in the numerous acts of affirmation and reinforcement (national holidays), but also the acts of change including revolutionary opposition. For decades now the Hindu right in India, for example, sings a national anthem different to the official Indian one, an anthem which lays greater emphasis on the Hindu legacy.

The existence of the nation as a 'daily plebiscite'[28] depends on these constant confirmations through public acts of assertion which are meant to guarantee the continued existence of collective identity as the political foundation of the nation. On the other hand, even alternative movements and groups, whose opposition extends to a questioning of the roots of national legitimization, must enter the stage of public assertion on the opposing side and prove themselves to be the better, i.e. more convincing representatives of another concept of nation.

The work of assertion as a programme of nationalist politics is articulated mainly in the form of rituals. Political rituals essentially lead to three developments which reveal the interdependence of nation, religion and public action. Firstly, they reproduce the mental infrastructure of the nation, i.e. they create and maintain categories of unity and difference by setting up corresponding public actions. Secondly, they make the unity and the collective cohesiveness of the nation experienceable and produce a notion of difference excluding others. And finally, political rituals legitimize hegemony and power within the nation.

Rituals and Mental Infrastructure

Let us first look at rituals as the mode of reproduction of the mental infrastructure. In order to operate with the concept of ritual it would be helpful to start with a definition to clarify its meaning. On the basis of his study of political rituals in India Jan Platvoet has developed a definition that is useful for our purposes even though it remains a preliminary one. According to him ritual is

> collective, interactive, expressive, communicative, symbolic and performative behaviour with both customary and innovative, as well as traditionalising qualities, in which multi-media forms of expression are used including aesthetic stylisation and theatrical performance, and which is implicitly or explicitly directed towards the achievement of strategic goals which are often integrative in kind but may also have, and be meant to have, explosive effects upsetting the existing balance in a given society.[29]

This definition contains numerous elements that are, by no means, self-explanatory and which, therefore, need to be examined more closely. First of all we will assume that all political rituals have a strategic purpose. They are an instrument to achieve political goals for safeguarding a group-oriented integration, on the one hand, and for an aggressive, often violence-prone, exclusion, on the other.

The language of rituals, as indicated above, is one of symbols. Through symbols man confronts the chaos of his environment and gives it order and structure which he then naturalizes and objectifies.[30] This order also includes the political sphere in which the language of symbols is used to create order through the execution and description of rituals. In complex crisis situations the importance of rituals in politics increases since they are practically the only possible means of dealing with sudden changes and transformations. Signs and symbols expressed in the rituals are 'in fact the only means that groups, unable to rationally analyse complex situations, have of dealing with such situations–through stereotyping, simplification and pacification'.[31] In these situations rituals mediate and affirm what is basically uncertain and ambiguous through a simulated imperturbability and by treating the situations as a matter of course.[32] They depict the conditions obtaining as conforming to the interpretation of reality expressed in the rituals and thus affirm this interpretive horizon as a collective way of thinking.

The strategies used by political rituals for this purpose cannot always be subsumed under the categories of the sacred or religious, on the one hand, and the profane, on the other. In practice, religious rituals as a communication with supernatural beings or as an individual dialogue with the afterlife often cannot be separated from secular, decidedly political ceremonies. Both these forms of performative communication merge into one another so that it makes little sense to maintain this distinction with regard to rituals.[33] The historical examples from politics and religion in India in the next chapter will show that this distinction cannot be maintained in a concrete political situation.

A further important characteristic of rituals in politics as the means of reproduction of social categories is their performative character. This aspect was also mentioned in the definition given earlier. To begin with, rituals are performative in the very banal sense that they seek to bring into existence what they do or say.[34] In other words, reality is born out of verbal and practical execution in the framework of a ritual. What is decisive for the ritual is, therefore, not the material result of the process in the sense of producing or changing something, but the form of action itself since this determines the success or failure of the action.[35] A ritual is actionist formalism whose purpose lies in the detailed arrangement of its execution. In this context, and with regard to nationalism, Wolfgang Kaschuba has aptly suggested the use of the term 'national movement-culture' (*nationale Bewegungskultur*).[36] Nationalism, in particular, is a political programme of performance which tries to bring the people as members of the nation onto the streets in order to activate them in the name of nation and thus ensure their direct participation in the movement.

The two aspects of the performance of rituals that have been described can be summarized in the following manner. Firstly, through a speech-act or an action the ritual leads to the production and realization of an idea, a fact, a perception or other abstract concepts. In the process of its execution the ritual constructs a reality which differs categorically from material facts insofar as it includes the latter but functions independently of it. Secondly, the ritual enables broad participation in an event and, more importantly, in a reality produced by this event.[37] It is only through active participation in the act of construction of the nation that a citizen becomes an accepted member of this nation and is thus drawn into the mental and material process of integration.

Rituals and Social Cohesion

The second important function of political rituals in the process of nation-building is their potential as a means of social cohesion, their ability to establish, safeguard and also question the external demarcations of a social unit. This process of ritual, performative safeguarding and validation consists mainly of two aspects which are closely interlinked in practice, but which are discussed separately here for purposes of clarity. For one, political and religious rituals establish a positive common identity internally. With this they lay the ground for a social co-existence that appears to be natural, giving it legitimacy and the appearance of necessity. For the other, these rituals also establish negative demarcations from the outside world. They establish difference as an essential characteristic of group identity and vehemently defend the perpetuation of this difference in order not to become redundant themselves. Let us first look at the function of internal community formation.

While commenting on the community-forming potential of religion Emile Durkheim stated that this potential unfolds mainly in the common ritual enactment of religious cosmology and that, therefore, there is a fundamental connection between the ritual repertoire of a religion and the definition of the religious community.[38] In his remarks on the religious identity of Muslims in India, Imtiaz Ahmad has further differentiated this aspect and identified three levels of community formation.[39] His starting point is that the fact of shared religious beliefs alone can be an inter-regional unifying element if the necessary material infrastructure and the means of communication are available. On a second level regional specificities of religious practice are conducive to community formation while, on a third level, elements of practical religion such as medicinal cures, saint-worship, etc., which don't derive from orthodoxy and which mark the borders with people of different faith, can, under certain circumstances, become politically relevant.[40] This idea of a positive construction of community through shared participation in the ritual—and thus in religion—can also be applied to the political sphere. A few remarks are required for this. Symbolically, rituals convey the feeling of belonging to a larger political entity like, for example, the nation. This feeling is generally open-ended and undefined and is, therefore, at least in the short-term and selectively, in a position to bridge social rifts by overemphasizing the emotional aspect of commonality. In the framework of an emotionalized fervour rituals thus point to a 'limited commonality'[41] which constitutes the lowest, if not the marginal, common denominator in a society but which, in situations of external threat, becomes the decisive characteristic of the community itself.[42] Roberto da Matta has clearly illustrated this function of rituals with the examples of the Brazilian carnival and Independence Day. Da Matta specifically emphasizes the selective nature of these temporary crossings of social borders that are otherwise characterized by extreme economic and social differences. The dynamics of a cultural event such as the carnival and the political example of Independence Day are analogous. In the short-term rituals aren't able to effectively abolish social divisions, but they can manipulate and reformulate them and give them new meaning in the framework of an overarching national unity.[43] The actual perpetuation of social differences even in the ritual is masked mainly by the appearance of enjoying a kind of privilege by participating in the community-forming ritual of the nation. This privileging of participation is particularly evident in those communities which have initiation rites and draw attention to new members of the collective through rites of admission.[44] In religions this form of privileged participation is common; in the context of nationalism, however, it depends on its ideological form. Hindu nationalism of the 1920s, for example, had an elaborate process, worked out ritually to the last detail, for re-admittance to the Indian nation as a nation of Hindus. This interweaving of religious and political initiation is typical for community-formation of religious nationalism in India.

A final characteristic of the process to construct commonality and collective identity through political rituals is the plebiscitary nature of collective performance. Mass participation in public, political ritual not only expresses the approval of nation, but it also establishes and confirms the leading position of the elites who act on behalf of this nation and in keeping with their self-image. This 'voice-vote'[45] is by no means, however, the expression of a 'non-consensual solidarity' (James W. Fernandez), it presupposes a minimum degree of agreement with the organizing and mobilizing elite. The nature of collective consent wouldn't be understood correctly if the target audience of national mobilization is interpreted as the passive recipient of political goals. The concrete version of nation as collective identity needs to be not only plausible and consistent, it must also correspond to the mental needs of the citizens and provide seemingly convincing answers to the ostensibly pressing questions of the times:

The enterprise of collective mobilisation will be unsuccessful if there isn't a minimum agreement between the mobilisers (prophets, ring-leaders etc.) and those who recognise themselves in the actions and statements of the former, especially if the desire awakened by the spontaneous, concerted action to unite is absent.[46]

A basic precondition for the success of the ritual establishment of a community is the diffusely felt need for collective organization, even if it is only for the negative reason of preventing and avoiding conditions viewed as chaotic. The participants in the ritual construction of community are responding subjects of politics, even though the individual motives for participation would have to be analysed separately.

Difference plays an important, and perhaps the most decisive, role in the construction of community. The self-image of a collective is primarily defined by the contrast to the Other and, generally, unimaginable without this. Only forms of an extremely integrative nationalism, like Gandhi's for example or that of the national-liberals of the Indian National Congress, dispense, to a large extent, with this cultural and political model of aggressive delineation from the Other. As already indicated, the ritual works like the myth to mask power and hegemony within the nation, since the mobilizers cast themselves as cultural prototypes of a nation which, in a seemingly plebiscitary manner, announces its will to the public.[47] Externally, however, difference and distance aren't masked; instead they are used to mark the boundaries of the nation and it is these boundaries that ensure the privilege of participating in its rituals. The external boundaries of the nation aren't simply imaginary lines, but they are the means of privileging, of social marginalization, of cultural minoritizing and of symbolic forms of discrimination. The aspect of community dissolution must be added to Durkheim's understanding of rituals as community-forming, since the construction of a (new, modern) collective implies the disbanding of an earlier one. Radical forms of nationalism even demand its disappearance without any trace in order to prevent a clash of loyalties. A clearly defined nation has to emphatically reject such a clash on account of its claim to exclusivity. This process of dissolution and obliteration is not only socially discriminatory, but it is prone to violence since the restructuring of mental organization and demarcation precedes the actual facts. This discrepancy between the imagined borders of the nation and social reality is often eliminated with the help of brutal measures which, in their excessive forms, include genocide.[48] Concepts of purity and organic totality undisturbed by alien elements play an important role as a conceptual backdrop. For the ritual and actionist creation of national consciousness it is important not to conceive difference and its resultant discrimination (including violence) as a given constant of social reality but to interpret it 'in interaction'.[49] Difference is not a fact which can be instrumentalized; rather it develops as a political category only in its performative execution. According to Bourdieu it is performative practice in the form of a ritual which brings demarcations into existence by saying and doing difference. With regard to the nation this ritual process and the connotation of difference isn't value-free. Rather it is a negative definition of the collective in the form of delineation which also demands its real political equivalent and thus also its potentially violent enforcement.

Rituals and the Legitimacy of Hegemony and Power

The final aspect of ritual politics which has already been mentioned is its function to legitimize hegemony and power. This function is a result of the simple fact that leading actors and directors of political *mise en-scène* are required for the 'dramaturgical arrangement of action'.[50] They offer a version of nation and its effective actionist implementation to which citizens as members of this nation can react positively, negatively or with indifference. Historically, the example of India shows us very clearly that the struggle for asserting a particular interpretation of nation is mainly also a struggle for social hegemony which is then decided by the enforcement of a specific cultural and symbolic paradigm.[51] The lines of conflict in this case aren't drawn between nation and non-nation, but between differing variants of national self-understanding and their respective representatives as political elites. However, the relationship between the formulating elites and the citizens to be mobilized shouldn't be viewed as a simple mechanism of manipulation. Rather, in the context of nation-building, it is a question of the political legitimizing of hegemony through the means of cultural intercession and representation based on a general idea of the national equality of the subjects. The contenders for the role of social and national leaders have to prove themselves to be prototypes of the collective cultural character of the nation and have to enforce their version of the mental categories of national self-understanding with actionist means:

> This doesn't mean that political myths and rituals are consciously launched by the elite in order to promote their own interests. Attempts at this kind of manipulation are generally recognised and they fail. What exists isn't deceit but the adoption of a social role, of a concept of social role.[52]

In his observations on the 'small kingdoms' in Orissa, in eastern India, Burkhard Schnepel emphasizes, for example, the link between ritual events in these kingdoms, on the one hand, and the political and economic conditions and changes, on the other. Despite this close link the economic and the ritual spheres exist relatively independent of one another with their own rules and their own modes of functioning.[53] Not only in traditional societies, but also in the context of modern nation states rituals constitute an important factor in establishing and maintaining dominance and political sovereignty. They are deeply interwoven with the economy even if they aren't on the same level.

The concept of a symbolic capital in Bourdivin sociology is a useful theoretical tool to describe this relationship more closely. The symbolic capital of a society, to begin with, differs fundamentally from economic capital, even though there are specific interactions which are decisive for its mode of functioning. Symbolic capital is the socially granted, individually or collectively accumulated 'capital of recognition' that allows its owner to 'exert symbolic influence'[54] both in the form of inconsequential and non-committal recognition as well as in the form of obedience and submission. The individual bearer of symbolic capital is distinguished by prestige and its resultant power to act recognized and granted by other members of the society on the basis of common yardsticks and categories. Secondly, symbolic capital can also be the common property of all members of a group:

> Since it is a being-perceived, which exists in the relations between properties held by agents and categories of perception (high/low, masculine/feminine, large/small, etc.) which constitute and construct social categories (those above/those below, men/women, large/small) based on union (alliance, companionship, marriage) and separation (the taboo of contact, of misalliance, etc.), symbolic capital is attached to groups—or to the names of groups, families, clans, tribes—and is both the instrument and the stakes of collective strategies seeking to conserve or increase it as well as individual strategies seeking to acquire or conserve it, by joining groups which possess it (...) and by distinguishing themselves from groups which possess little or are destitute (stigmatized ethnic groups).[55]

In this sense nationalism can also be understood as the collective accumulation of symbolic capital which is valorized against a colonial power through the formulation of a glorious past or spiritual superiority and thus equipped for the political and economic confrontation.[56] Naturally, there is a close connection between the form of capital and the material conditions of a society which determine the basic structures of supremacy and subordination. With regard to the rules and the individual modes of functioning, however, symbolic capital is relatively autonomous:

In short, each 'credit' of legitimate social recognition and appreciation epresents symbolic capital which, with respect to the logic of its constitution, is independent of the objective, of economic and cultural capital. *De facto*, however, it is mostly encountered only in association with the other forms of capital and is in a position to increase their existence and efficacy.[57]

In other words, with regard to the economic conditions, symbolic capital can ensure the expansion of economic and material dominance by imposing descriptions whereby social distinctions are accepted as legitimate and natural.[58] Under certain circumstances, therefore, symbolic capital is an instrument for masking real conditions. It doesn't allow one to see the material foundations of social differences in the form of privileging and discrimination. For this very reason, however, symbolic capital can also work against the logic of the material-economic since it basically grants recognition and prestige autonomously and can thus consciously counteract material privileges. Sometimes, persons or groups with a high symbolic status can effectively limit the social importance of material leaders by using their symbolic credit to impose sanctions. This is possible chiefly because it is not only material power or raw power which is required to achieve social domination but also the widespread establishing of what Bourdieu–as a consequence of symbolic capital–calls 'symbolic power':

Domination, even when based on naked force, always has a symbolic dimension, and acts of submission, of obedience, are acts of knowledge and recognition which, as such, implement cognitive structures capable of being applied to all things of the world, and in particular to social structures. These *structuring structures* are historically constituted forms (...) and it is possible to retrace their social genesis.[59]

The symbolic aspect of power thus creates the distinction between power in itself and a legitimate power, and it is essential for the continual maintenance of this power.[60] Symbolic power is, therefore, that dimension of rule which doesn't occur at the level of physical control but which appeals to knowledge and the search for meaning and from this tries to derive the recognition and legitimacy that rulers strive for.

Coming back to the significance of rituals in the context of nationalism, the Bourdivin concept of symbolic capital gives us a conceptual model that describes the interaction between socio-economic conditions and differences in a society, on the one hand, and the mode of functioning of symbolic-ritual behaviour, on the other, without revoking the specific nature and the specific mode of functioning of each of these fields. With regard to nationalism it is important to recognize the legitimating character of rituals and to interpret public 'staging' as the main testing-ground of nationalism. Obviously, nationalism functions, as Ernst Gellner has pointed out, as the necessary, alternative state ideology of a social elite that emerges from and is constituted in the process of modernization. This, however, only describes one aspect of its mode of functioning and it is, by no means, the only aspect. The understanding of the chiefly ritual dimension of nation-building must be extended through the above-mentioned details in order, particularly, to emphasize the reciprocal nature of economic and social transformation.

CONCLUSION

The relationship between nation and religious rituals can be described, in conclusion, with four concepts which, taken together, constitute the ritual aspect of nationalism. These four modes of functioning of nationalistic rituals that shape nation-building and thus translate the ideological and abstract concept of the nation into a concrete, tangible and participatory reality are the modes of standardization, synchronization, emotionalization and, finally, the mode of traditionalizing. Through these modes political rituals establish the concept of nation as a historical constant with more or less definite external borders, whose collective consciousness and memory determine the action-paradigms for the future and legitimizes its representatives.

Nationalistic political rituals have a standardizing effect because they canonize the behaviour of all concerned, i.e. they establish binding standards and thus bring about a conservative codification of culture and tradition. Even in those historical moments when nationalism effects an unprecedented mobilization that creates and accompanies upheavals and changes, it does this through explicitly conservative models of action and the rhetoric of perpetuation.[61] These standards create the appearance of order and planning in what is actually a chaotic situation, and they then function as the new criterion of orientation on the way to becoming a nation. The means for this is ritual repetition which brings a familiar model into play in every changed context, thus creating the impression of continuity. Repetition as the 'focus of performative processes',[62] however, need not always be present in a literal sense in politics. The Indian example will show that political rituals are often only conceived for a particular situation and aren't repeated later. But even in this case repetition is present in a secondary manner through the analogy with the daily rituals of religion which are borrowed for a political staging.

Secondly, performative nation-building is characterized by a synchronizing effect. Ritual as a 'motor-driven activity in which the participants team up symbolically for a common purpose'[63] not only coordinates the form of political action (standardization) but it also organizes political community-formation as a convincing event through simultaneity. After the aspect of formal accord the synchronization of symbolic actions is the second important community-creating function of the political ritual which has a lasting effect on the creation of nationalist politics. In contrast to the essence of the nation which, as a political collective, must have a more enduring existence, rituals concentrate only on a momentary phase of 'national history'. However, as against other forms of public gatherings which remain limited to a one-time occasion or a singular cause, within nationalistic logic the momentary gathering is seen as paradigmatic for the existence of nation as a historical constant and is interpreted as the moment of revelation of a fundamental truth. It is not only in this regard that simultaneity is important. As Evon Z. Vogt and Suzanne Abel have shown through the example of

Mexico, the time of execution of the political ritual is also important.[64] Not only does a synchronization of the actions of those involved mediate the nationalist message but also the time chosen: national holidays or the historical reference to a decisive event with regard to nation are signifiers in ordinary time which also mark the collective self-image.

Thirdly, the ritual emotionalizes the creation of the political discourse. Although this aspect is undoubtedly an important new quality in the mediation of politics, there have only been sporadic and theoretically inadequate studies on this theme.[65] The emotionalizing of politics is essential for nationalism since the existence of nation as a politically relevant category is based more on emotional association than on ideological conviction.[66] Finally, even the oft-quoted will to nation as the decisive criterion of membership in a national entity is a pointer to the positive significance of emotion as a measure of identity. However, feelings are not only part of a positive programme; rather they are present more vehemently in the negative form of hostility against those perceived as outsiders. Political community-formation occurs to a great extent through a generally diffused feeling of fear and threat which is converted into a positive motivation for political unity. Nationalism personifies the sources of a threat in order to get a better hold on the perceived enemy and to create a concrete object for this projected fear.[67] However, it isn't only external dangers that are personified but also the internal counter-programme, the national resurrection that galvanizes a comprehensive resistance. A clear and public division of roles in the political field of nationalism identifies the representatives of the nationalist cause and they are projected in an emotionally positive manner as leaders of the nation against the external threat. Personification of national prototypes as leaders and of external danger as a means of projecting fear, on the one hand, and the emotionalizing of politics, on the other, come together in ritually implemented nationalism to create a synthesis which has far-reaching consequences. It isn't limited to a momentary outburst of feeling as an expression of national consciousness, but it demonstrates a permanent attitude based on emotions which transforms itself into political culture.[68]

Fourthly, and finally, rituals traditionalize the modern political discourse of nationalism. This function, or qualitative characteristic, of ritually mediated politics isn't a simple result of the fact of repetition and standardization,[69] but of a complex interplay with the cultural landscape of a society.

In order to understand this it would be helpful to use the concept of cultural memory which has been extensively elaborated by Jan Assmann and which, in this form, appears to suit our purpose. The cultural memory of a society is an overarching concept for the more usual catchwords such as 'construction of tradition', 'orientation to the past', 'political identity or imagination'. It defines the 'external dimensions of human memory',[70] i.e. their forms of expression and mediation in the interpersonal arena. This memory is 'cultural because it can only be implemented institutionally and artificially, and it is memory because, with regard to social communication it functions exactly like individual memory'.[71] Cultural memory isn't a given entity but a historical product that, in varying degrees, always remains open to re-formulation and provides information about the past and the future of a society. However, cultural memory not only shows us ideas about the past and the future, it also imparts practical knowledge about their implementation. Rituals play a decisive role in cultural memory, 'because they portray the traditional and the realized forms of cultural meaning'.[72] Festivals, rituals and other occasions 'ensure–through regular recurrence–mediation and transfer of knowledge that strengthens identity and, therefore, the reproduction of cultural identity. Ritual repetition ensures the coherence of the group in time and space'.[73]

Political ritual borrows from the cultural memory of a community and also from its practical strategies of reproduction. Through the conscious analogy with routine cultural and religious forms of memory politics seeks its legitimacy in the ritual, elevates its claim beyond the here and now and links itself inextricably with the substance of collective self-perception which is mainly embodied in cultural memory.[74] Ritually mediated nationalism claims not to be a political ideology of the recent, modern epoch but an expression of the cultural essence of the collective. In other words, it is the political reformulation of cultural memory which strives for a correspondence between political organization and the cultural self of the nation. The manner in which this claim is articulated and implemented is through the traditionalizing function of political rituals. It gives the new, modern strategies of nationalist mobilization the appearance of the unchanged and thus aims at cultural legitimacy resulting in political immunization against alternative versions of a collective self-understanding. Thereby the claim to exclusivity made by religious nationalism is implemented and this also accounts for its tendency towards violence against those who cannot be full members of this nation for cultural or religious reasons or because they refuse to accept this construct.

NOTES

1. Gellner 1994, Chap. 3; O'Leary, 1998, pp. 47f.
2. Cf. also Gellner, 1965, p. 159.
3. Turner, 1986, p. 85.
4. Taylor, 1998, p. 196.
5. Gellner, 1999, p. 17.
6. Taylor, 1998a, p. 198.
7. Anderson, 1998, p. 38.
8. Cf. Arendt, 2000, Chap. 5.
9. Jaffrelot, 1993.
10. Meyer, 1994, p. 56.
11. Ibid.
12. Ibid., p. 57.
13. Deutsch, 1966, esp. Chap. 4.
14. Anderson, 1998, p. 39.
15. Cf. Veer, 1994, p. 78.
16. François/Siegrist/Vogel, 1995, p. 13.
17. Hall, 1994, pp. 137-79.
18. Wodak et al., 1998, p. 71.
19. Ibid., p. 75.

20. Geertz, 1996, p. 43.
21. Cf. Hegel, 1989, p. 338.
22. Grosby, 2001, p. 105.
23. Bourdieu, 1998, p. 66.
24. Cf. Bourdieu, 1997, pp. 59ff; Bourdieu, 1998, p. 67.
25. Sloterdijk, 2002.
26. Bourdieu, 1998, pp. 67f.
27. Cf. Wodak et al., 1998, p. 71.
28. Renan, 1990, p. 19.
29. Platvoet, 1995, p. 220; cf. also Platvoet, 1995, p. 41.
30. Kertzer, 1988, pp. 4f.
31. Edelman, 1990, pp. 35f.
32. Cf. Moore/Myerhoff, 1977, p. 24.
33. Cf. Goody, 1961, pp. 159f; Moore/Myerhoff, 1977; Platvoet, 1995, p. 219.
34. Bourdieu, 1999, p. 168.
35. Cf. Platvoet/Toorn, 1995, p. 355; Wulf/Göhlich/Zirfas 2001, pp. 10f.
36. Kaschuba, 1995, p. 296.
37. Cf. for this also Tambiah, 1985, pp. 128f.
38. Durkheim, 1981, pp. 61f.
39. Ahmad, 1984, pp. 12f.
40. Cf. Madan, 1984.
41. Moore/Myerhoff, 1977, p. 6.
42. Cf. Sirinelli, 1995.
43. da Matta, 1977, p. 263.
44. Cf. for this Kertzer, 1988, p. 17; Platvoet/Toorn, 1995, p. 354.
45. Ben-Amos, 1995, p. 248.
46. Bourdieu, 1999, p. 111.
47. Cf. Edelman, 1990, p. 15.
48. Cf. Spencer, 1990; Tambiah, 1997.
49. Fuchs, 1999, p. 142.
50. Müller-Dohm/Neumann-Braun, 1995, p. 10.
51. Gellner, 1999; Kertzer, 1988, p. 175.
52. Edelman, 1990, pp. 16f.
53. Schnepel, 1995, pp. 160f.
54. Bourdieu, 1998, p. 102.
55. Ibid., pp. 103f.
56. Cf. Bourdieu, 1976, pp. 334f.

57. Schwingel, 2000, p. 91.
58. Cf. Audehm, 2001, p. 108.
59. Bourdieu, 2000a, p. 172.
60. Schwingel, 2000, p. 115.
61. Goody, 1977, p. 33.
62. Wulf/Göhlich/Zirfas, 2001, p. 13.
63. Edelman, 1990, p. 14.
64. Vogt/Abel, 1977.
65. Cf. François/Siegrist/Vogel, 1995, esp. Sirinelli 1995.
66. Cf. Renan, 1990.
67. Edelman, 1990, p. 118.
68. Cf. Sirinelli, 1995, p. 393; Tambiah, 1985, p. 133.
69. Platvoet, 1995, p. 29.
70. Assmann, 1999, p. 19.
71. Ibid., p. 24.
72. Ibid., p. 21.
73. Ibid., p. 57.
74. Cf. Tambiah, 1985, p. 60; Trevithick, 1990.

CHAPTER 3

Beginnings of Performative Nation-building: Gandhi's Method of Political Communication

The following chapters will illustrate the preceding theoretical reflections on religion and politics through historical examples taken both from colonial as well as independent India. The aim is not to offer a chronology of modern Indian history—such an attempt would go beyond the present framework—but to look at selected aspects of religious rituals and their concrete methods of functioning in the political discourse as characteristic examples.

TRANSFORMATION OF THE INDEPENDENCE MOVEMENT AFTER 1918

When we look at the political history of modern India before it gained Independence in 1947, the 1920s prove to be a formative period in which significant organizational and structural directions were formulated. It was also a period in which the qualitative and conceptual configuration of the political discourse of the future, especially with regard to relations between religious communities, gained new directions. Not only did the constitutional reforms of the political system in British-India of 1920 have far-reaching consequences for practical politics and, therefore, also for the work of nation-building, but different attempts to formulate and visualize an Indian nation and its self-image also underwent a sustained reform and a qualitative change in comparison with previous efforts. Along with this qualitative transformation of the political discourse and the political-administrative structure of the colony, the social spectrum of participants in the national struggle for emancipation from colonial rule also changed—both those in prominent positions within the nationalist elite and those who took active part in the broad-based campaigns for mobilizing the colonized masses.

The reforms in the political system in British-India announced in 1917 by the India-minister in London, Edwin Samuel Montague, together with the Indian viceroy, Lord Chelmsford, came into effect in 1920. The reforms envisaged an Indian-British diarchy at the provincial level whereby individual ministries such as local self-rule, education, agriculture, industry and health would be transferred to ministers who would be accountable to the legislative council of the province. Since the reforms also carried out an expansion of the provincial councils, which led to a majority of elected Indian councillors in almost all provinces, this transfer of ministries meant a *de facto* sharing of power with future Indian members of government at the provincial level. Along with this power-sharing in selected and—with the exception of education and agriculture—relatively insignificant portfolios the reform also meant a shift in political events as such and, thus, in the dynamics of political competition for power and influence among the different Indian players. Prior to 1920 the contest to ensure extensive spheres of influence took place only on the local and urban level. Now the provinces became the terrain of—at times—massive controversies and conflicts for safeguarding the political constituency that constituted the power-base in a semi-democratic system. The province was no longer a consensual field of different social groups and religious communities against the British, but was now included in the local power-dynamics through a division of the electorate. With this 'provincialization of Indian politics', provided for by the reforms, religion attained a new and qualitatively different relevance for political events, becoming an often-used yardstick for mobilization in the contest for political power. The 1920s saw a reorganization of Indian politics with a growing tendency towards communalization from 1922 to 1928 and, in the end, hostilities between religious groups shaped the political landscape. In the words of an observer of these times:

The 1920s bring a change—with the growing politicization of both communities and more communal violence and rioting. It is in this period that Hindu and Muslim communal organizations grow in importance and that Congress leaders begin to characterize communalism as the antithesis of nationalism—the result of colonial manipulation which will only disappear with the coming of independence.[1]

The discovery of the importance of religion in marking the borders of one's political constituency from 1920 onwards was not completely new. The Hindu right-wing, especially, used a similar strategy in numerous movements and campaigns at the end of the nineteenth and the beginning of the twentieth century in order to widen participation in the nationalist programme,[2] but through the structural reforms introduced by Montague and Chelmsford communalism became the fundamental characteristic of political organization itself. Thus, religion brought about a radicalization which effectively changed the face of Indian politics and created an enduring counter-pole to the integrative efforts of the Congress. This counter-voice stridently demanded its place in the constitutional formation of the nation.

Along with this substantial change in the political discourse resulting from structural reforms in the political system, the participants of nationalist agitation as well as its organizers and leaders changed:

> The 'masses' entered the organized national movement on an unprecedented scale. Congress leaders and workers got drawn into the villages as never before. The participation of peasants and workers in nationalist activities, and their appropriation and reinterpretation of nationalist symbols and slogans, greatly increased. Consequent upon all this, the demands of the disprivileged came to be voiced on nationalist platforms far more insistently and concretely than in the past.[3]

The decisive conditions for the success of nationalism as a theoretical anti-colonial programme were essentially present long before the 1920s. In the nineteenth century comprehensive and semi-autonomous newspapers already existed which basically made the rise of nationalism as an ideology possible, even though waves of repression by the British against such activity could be expected.[4] The rise of newspapers in local Indian languages as lively and versatile organs of the nationalist discourse forced the British to engage in an elaborate and costly control through translations, but this could not prevent the further development of the nationalist programme and the rise of different forms of pan-Indian debates and the exchange of views. Even the emancipation of the political-nationalist leadership from the more traditional, i.e. mainly religious, authorities of Indian society had already taken place in the nineteenth century and the process had been largely completed by the end of the First World War.[5]

The qualitative change that took place in the decade between 1920 and 1930 with regard to the spectrum of mobilizers and the mobilized can be illustrated through the example of the Swadeshi movement of 1905 to 1908 and the reasons for its failure. The Swadeshi movement is significant insofar as it is a direct predecessor of the campaigns in the period after 1920 and thus demonstrates the changes that characterize India's political history in the 1920s. At this early juncture Bengal already had a very lively nationalist scene consisting of various camps ranging from moderate liberals to radical, nationalist extremists who called for an uncompromising stand against the British. The nationalist camps regarded the division of their province in 1905 as the operative factor for a vehement opposition to the British who, for their part, had used this administrative manoeuvre to weaken the oppositional camp through the systematic protection of Bengal's Muslim population. Established and widely accepted political and social leaders like Surendranath Banerji, the writer Rabindranath Tagore, or Sri Aurobindo, initially tried to articulate their protest through moderate methods such as press-campaigns, public meetings and petitions to revoke the division. When it became apparent that these methods had no effect on the British other forms of protest emerged such as the boycott of British goods in 1905. The possibility also of civil disobedience against unjust laws, used successfully by Gandhi later, and the religiously motivated national resistance of 'abiding by the truth' were already built into the programme of the movement. Initially, the boycott of British goods was actually successful, but it died out quickly due to the lack of a substantial social and political content. Even Tagore's extensive reputation in Bengal wasn't sufficient to widen mobilization. His failure to formulate clear goals of action led, in fact, to a decrease in mobilization. The stronger methods of protest such as *satyagraha* or civil disobedience were rendered ineffective on account of the unresolved contradictions between the moderate and the extremist camps of nationalists. The ideas about the form of the anti-colonial movement were too disparate. Therefore, the Swadeshi movement remained a programme of the elite who were unable to communicate their concerns beyond the small circle of those directly involved in it:

> Above all, elite action postponed efforts to draw the masses into active political struggle, which in turn would have involved conscious efforts to link up national with socio-economic issues through more radical programmes.[6]

Not only were the lower classes in the city and the countryside unaffected by the movement, but the urban middle class of officials in the colonial administration also didn't take part in the protest. Those leading the boycott were divided and could only be brought together selectively by the relatively ineffectual figures of integration heading the movement.

At the end of the First World War there was a massive economic and political upheaval in India. A rapid rise in prices, food scarcity which led to the acute threat of famine in 1919, the continued use of special laws enacted during the war and aimed at controlling political activity among the Indians, a significant decrease of loyalty to the British among the Muslims as a result of British action in the Bosporus which had threatened the existence of the caliphate—all this created favourable conditions for a synthesis of political, anti-colonial agitation and the socio-economic concerns of the colonized which was necessary for the successful broad-based mobilization of the Indian population, and the lack of which had led to the failure of the Swadeshi movement. In this scenario M.K. Gandhi proved to be an extremely adept and far-sighted player who drew several lessons from the Swadeshi movement and used them successfully for a broader mobilization. Especially in the first two years of the decade under consideration–from 1920 to 1922–Gandhi functioned firstly as a leading figure of integration at the head of the campaign for non-cooperation. Gandhi's effectiveness was not only apparent in the manner in which he planned and conducted the campaign, but also in the fact that he was an integrative factor among the ideologically disparate camps within the Congress. His exoteric political programme, his method of struggle based more on persuasion than on force and his disarming political charisma, which he consciously demonstrated even in his outward appearance, helped to overcome those internal contradictions of the movement for Independence which had led to the failure of the Swadeshi movement.[7] Secondly, Gandhi was very aware of the fact that clearly recognizable and unambiguously formulated goals were required for a long-lasting political commitment of broad sections of the population.[8] In the Swadeshi movement Tagore and his, partly also radical, comrades-in-arms tried to create this necessary condition through a programme of protest and boycott that wasn't far-reaching enough and then had to accept that they hadn't been successful in bridging the ideological divides. Gandhi's concept of self-rule (*swaraj*), more or less formulated by this time, and his identification of the evils of colonial rule–repression and economic control–combined with explicitly religious themes gave political mobilization a clear direction in which everyone could participate unconditionally. Thirdly, and finally, the anti-colonial opposition found in him a widely accepted and recognized advocate against the colonial power who knew how to articulate the country's interests and behind whom the ranks could close in the name of nation.

Gandhi's entry into the active creation of a broad-based mobilization brought about a 'symbolic revolution'[9] in the course of which not only his role as an integrative factor but also the political power of the Congress grew significantly. In addition, Muslims could be won over for active participation in the movement. Through the politicization of broad sections of the population the conditions were created for bringing nationalism as a political ideology to every individual citizen of the colony. This transfer of anti-colonialism from the elite to the masses and, chiefly, from the city to the villages meant that the end of colonial rule had been structurally initiated. Under the weight of progressive concessions the ruling power found it increasingly difficult to legitimize its present in the subcontinent.[10] Gandhi's dominance was, however, cyclical and initially limited to the early years of mobilization. After 1922—and especially after the failure of the civil disobedience campaign that had degenerated into violence—Gandhi realized that he had to share the political arena of the Independence movement with extremist groups in whose programme nation was essentially conceived in connection with religion. Their style of leadership, based on exclusion and separatism, replaced Gandhi's attempts at integration and established that form of religious nationalism which then went on to become the most vehement form of opposition to the Congress leadership under Gandhi, Motilal and Jawaharlal Nehru.

KHILAFAT AND NON-COOPERATION: GANDHI'S MASS MOBILIZATION

The first political problem Gandhi faced in 1919 and which he had to resolve in the interests of broad and committed participation in a mass campaign was the increasing division within the Independence movement between the Congress as an anti-colonial platform on the one hand, and the growing, separatist Muslim group-identity, on the other, which had been institutionalized through the formation of the Muslim League in 1906. The trend towards separatism had, however, set in much earlier. Whereas between 1885 and 1892 the proportion of Muslim delegates in the annual meetings of the Congress had been on an average 13.5 per cent, this figure sank in the period between 1893 and 1905 to 7.1 per cent.[11] The increasing withdrawal of Muslims from a non-partisan and inter-religious Congress did not alarm the leadership till the organized separation of Muslim interests finally took place in 1906. On the other hand, the Congress itself, or rather a religiously-oriented group consisting mainly of Chitpavan-Brahmins from Maharashtra around B.G. Tilak, ensured that this trend was enforced within the Congress:

> While denying religious identification and asserting secular orientation, the Congress relied upon Hindu symbols and traditions of its legitimization. Tilak, Aurobindo Ghose and Lajpat Rai maintained that the Hindu masses could only be aroused through the use of religious predispositions, the popularization of national historical myths, and the celebration of Hindu festivals and decided to blend Hinduism with nationalism.[12]

By combining non-cooperation—a specific Gandhian method—with the concern about the caliphate of the Ottoman Empire Gandhi worked towards resuming concerted action between the Congress and the Indian Muslims, or their legitimate political representatives. In the history of the Indian Independence struggle the theme of the caliphate was, by no means, Gandhi's invention. In fact, Gandhi could hark back to an already established and widely debated theme of Muslim identity and anti-British resentments. The caliph was mentioned for the first time in India during the unrest of 1857 when, at the behest of the British, he strongly condemned the revolt against the colonial rulers and called for a general solidarity with them.[13] In the 1870s and 1890s donations were collected all over India to fund refugee camps in the domain of the Ottoman Empire after the wars against Russia and Greece, thus contributing to the preservation of and cooperation with the caliphate.[14] Later, when the Ottoman Empire entered the war on the side of the axis powers, the question of a possible defeat and the resulting loss of Ottoman control over the holy places of Islam made the Indian Muslims speak out for the preservation of the caliphate. In 1916 M.A. Jinnah again took up the theme of Muslim solidarity and declared that the fate of the caliph as *Amir-al-Muslimeen*, as the leader of the believers, as 'viceroy of the Prophet' and 'defender of the holy places of

Islam', was the crucial question defining the religious and political identity of Indian Muslims:

Of the many delicate questions there is none that requires a closer attention and study by the Government and the Ministers of Great Britain than the question of the Caliphate. The sentiments and feelings and the religious convictions, not only of the Mussalmans of India but of the Mussalmans of the world, are not to be lightly treated. The loyalty of the Muhammadans of India to the Government is no small asset. . . . May I, therefore, urge that the Government should have regard for their dearest and most sacred religious feeling, and under no circumstances interfere with the question of the future of the Caliphate. It should be left entirely to the Mussalmans to acknowledge and accept their own Caliph.[15]

Obviously, Gandhi's intention of linking the question of the caliphate with the campaign for civil disobedience was welcomed by the Muslim orthodoxy. On the other hand, liberal, Western-educated Muslim leaders like Maulana Abul Kalam Azad or Shaukat and Mohammed Ali as well as Jinnah himself, who later withdrew support on account of the radical nature of Gandhi's opposition to the British, hoped to gain greater access to the mass of Muslim believers, the *umma*. From the very beginning, however, Gandhi's mobilization tactics, which focused primarily on the boycott of British courts, educational institutions and, especially, universities, appeared to face a two-sided threat. Firstly, Gandhi was apprehensive about extremist circles among the Muslims giving the action a radical twist, which is why he appealed to his Muslim allies to moderate the statements they made after the All India Khilafat Committee had been constituted in February 1920.[16] In its four-point programme the Committee had attempted to integrate the various issues around which mobilization could occur. Along with the question of the caliphate as the centre of the Muslim world and freedom of the Arab world from all kinds of non-Muslim control, the programme also provided for the goal of self-rule for India and for an improved organization of Muslims in the interests of their religious, social and economic development.[17] The first All India

Khilafat Day on 17 October 1919 already displayed an impressive balance sheet of mass public meetings and boycotts which had mobilized, for example, 20,000 Muslims and Hindus in the Madras Province and 50,000 in Delhi. This heralded an intensified and fast-growing inclusion of wider segments of the Hindu and the Muslim population in the political agenda. The action, however, threatened to get out of hand given the fact that it had been prepared in a very short time and was organizationally not yet fully in place. The second Khilafat Day on 19 March 1920 already took place amidst signs of increasing radicalism which had mainly penetrated the local units of the *ulema* and brought forth a rhetoric of violence that went against the interests of Gandhi and his supporters. Time and again the slogan of *jihad* was raised against the infidels, directed initially against the British and calling for a boycott of their goods. In this context the *Independent* in Allahabad warned its readers: 'Take great care that the control of the Khilafat movement does not fall entirely within the hands of theologians and divines',[18] a warning that would largely go unheeded. Gandhi's most important allies, the Ali brothers, Maulana Azad and Zafar Ali Khan, continued to remain faithful to their moderate line and did not view the explicitly pan-Islamic concept of the Khilafat movement as a contradiction to their allegiance to an Indian nation and its Independence.[19] Rather, they conceived the Islamic renaissance in the framework of a strengthening of the Indian nation within which Islam and its followers would have an important role to play. At the level of local mobilization, however, radical voices increasingly made themselves heard, which also caused the Indian viceroy, Chelmsford, to comment upon the need for secularizing the atmosphere in July 1920. In a 'Proclamation to the Muslims of India'[20] Chelmsford tried to interpret the peace treaty of Sevres signed in May by the Allied Powers with Turkey as a 'milestone of history' and emphasized that neither the war itself nor the peace treaty had anything to do with religion. In the same way, he said, the Indian Muslims had understood four and a half years ago that the Ottoman Empire's entry into the war on the side of the Christian Axis Powers had no religious implications. The Viceroy further urged that the exclusively secular consequences of the war be kept in mind and requested that it be strictly separated from all religious concerns.[21] For the leaders of the Khilafat movement, however, it was clearly evident that this treaty meant the ultimate disintegration of the Ottoman Empire.

Several times in the spring of 1920 Motilal Nehru expressed personal reservations against the decidedly religious programme of the Khilafat, but he continued to follow the course set by Gandhi, not least on account of the zeal displayed by his own son, Jawaharlal, for the radical attempt of non-cooperation. Those who were less acquiescent were Lajpat Rai, the most important Congress leader in Punjab, B.S. Moonje, Annie Besant and Pandit M.M. Malaviya, who strongly criticized the Mahatma for this active promotion of Muslim interests, even though the Home Rule League, led by Besant, put its infrastructure at the disposal of the Non-Cooperation movement.[22] Remaining largely oblivious to all this, the main initiators continued their work for *swaraj*. After Gandhi had formally inaugurated the movement on 1 August, he along with Shaukat Ali and Saif-ud-din Kitchlew, another leading Khilafat activist, visited the Madras Province in south India in August 1920 to enlist support for the organizational development and the further spread of their movement. The three of them not only delivered speeches and addressed public meetings in Madras and Bangalore, but they also visited the coastal Malabar region.[23] The visit was closely monitored by the British government since this region, more specifically around the village Pukottar, had already witnessed unrest and small riots against the colonial rulers and the landlords who were their allies.

The solidarity among the Muslims evoked by the Khilafat movement was used here to present a united front against the Hindu landlords and to deal with them in an increasingly violent manner including the use of weapons such as swords, spears and clubs.[24] Despite this, the opinion of the government in Madras was positive: 'The Madras government's deliberate opinion was, that little harm was done by the visit.'[25] In September the Congress officially approved the programme of non-cooperation, even though C.R. Das, the most important leader of the Congress in Bengal, was opposed to the boycott of the provincial legislative council and the upcoming elections. However, by December, at the annual meeting of the Congress in Nagpur, he had not only given up this opposition, but it was he, in fact, who introduced the resolution for non-cooperation.[26]

This change in the attitude of one of the most important critics within the Congress had already become apparent in November when Das, along with Bipin Chandra Pal and Pandit Malaviya, campaigned for active support to the non-cooperation movement among students of the Hindu University in Benares who were one of the main groups targeted in the campaign. Mohammed Ali demanded that university studies be abandoned, and even Motilal Nehru campaigned for non-cooperation as a 'spiritual war' that required mentally armed combatants.[27] Even in Bombay, the most important commercial centre of the colony, enthusiasm for the boycott spilled over to the schools. Apart from the closure of shops, a movement under the leadership of Yusuf Ali took severe action against Muslims found consuming alcohol who were immediately given the punishment of beating by an enraged crowd. According to a report by the British authorities Ali also spoke against the consumption of tea as a non-Islamic drink.[28] In Delhi, Mohammed Ali organized a meeting of over 250 Muslim clerics who signed a joint resolution for non-cooperation as well as a collective *fatwa* which used religion to condemn the political hegemony of the British.

This trend towards the active involvement of religious leaders would increase in 1921, and there is a critical reference to this in Nehru's autobiography. He was sceptical about the strong religious flavour of the campaign, even though his consent for non-cooperation remained firm and uncompromising:

> Owing to the prominence given to the Khilafat movement in 1921 a large number of Moulvies and Muslim religious leaders took a prominent part in the political struggle. They gave a definite religious

tinge to the movement, and Muslims generally were greatly influenced by it. . . . The Ali brothers, themselves of a religious turn of mind, helped in this process, and so did Gandhiji, who paid the greatest regard to the Moulvies and the Maulanas. Gandhiji, indeed, was continually laying stress on the religious and spiritual side of the movement. His religion was not a dogmatic, but it did mean a definitely religious outlook on life, and the whole movement was strongly influenced by this and took on a revivalist character so far as the masses were concerned.[29]

Gandhi's role in actively involving and instrumentalizing religion as a means of communication with the masses, on the one hand, and as a way to constitute the substance of the campaign, on the other, is also reflected in his use of language. In April 1921, for example, Gandhi called self-rule *dharmaraj*, the rule of the (Hindu) law of the world. He also called on women to take active part in the non-cooperation movement by comparing them with Sita, the wife of the mythological Hindu divine King Rama, who had resisted the overtures of the demon Ravana while in captivity. In this manner, the women of India should renounce the temptations of British luxury goods and replace them with hand-spun yarn. The rule of the demon (*Ravanaraj*) could then be overcome within a year.[30]

In December, the annual meeting of the Congress in Nagpur officially adopted non-cooperation in the form of a resolution. At this point of time there was no longer any noteworthy opposition among Congress leaders to Gandhi's methods. In the United Provinces, in keeping with Gandhi's aims, only about 33 per cent of the electorate voted in the elections to the legislative council. Among the urban Muslim population this figure stood at a meagre 9 per cent, in the countryside at 28 per cent, but among non-Muslims it was still 35 per cent.[31] This interim result of non-cooperation shows that Gandhi had come closer to his goal of including a broad section of Muslims, who had hitherto been difficult to mobilize, and this could not have pleased the British.[32] Gandhi himself, partly supported by the Ali brothers and Maulana Azad, travelled in December to large parts of Bihar, Orissa and Bengal and was able to mobilize additional support with the help of the politically attractive slogan 'Swaraj within nine months'. At the same time, even at this early stage of the campaign, the first localized spots of unrest emerged as a result of the religious underpinnings of mobilization and led to hostilities between Hindus and Muslims. In Nagpur, in the Bombay Province, Lala Lajpat Rai had organized a conference in December, parallel to the annual meeting of the Congress, to demand protection for cows considered holy by the Hindus. In his speech as president of the conference Rai pointed to the close connection between protection of the cow and the attainment of Independence. True independence for Hindus, he reiterated, meant their own state in which the ban on cow-slaughter would be applicable to all Indians. Hindus, Rai thundered in the direction of Muslims, were not afraid of any kind of opposition in this matter and no one would dare come in their way as far as this question was concerned.[33] This caused fierce controversies in the press regarding future co-existence between Hindus and Muslims in an independent state. The reactions came initially from Muslims, but then also from Hindus in the form of counter-reactions. In the Punjab, numerous Muslim newspapers strongly protested the attempt by some city administrations to ban cow-slaughter and they used this to interpret the unity of Hindus and Muslims propagated by Gandhi as a trap set by the Hindu majority to dominate the Muslims.[34] The *Gulzar-i-Hind* in Punjab accused the Mahatma of ruining Islam by trying to bring Hindus and Muslims together in one nation. His blatant overtures to the Muslim minority through the Khilafat movement, they said, only served to strategically co-opt the Muslims.[35] The *Al-Fazl* (*Quadian*) commented that Lajpat Rai's speech and efforts to ban cow-slaughter should open the eyes of all Muslims who insisted on believing that Muslims would actually gain freedom through united action with the Hindus to attain Independence and that they would be able to restore the former 'Muslim territories'.[36] Finally, in March, Lajpat Rai himself reacted to the mired but fundamental and far-reaching debate with an article about the difficult relationship between religious and national affiliation. In this article Rai emphasized that no one could be a good Hindu, Muslim or Sikh before first becoming a good Indian: 'We cannot obtain Swaraj so long as we preach to the three communities that their political and economic welfare and interests lie in keeping themselves aloof from one another.'[37] In order to gain Independence and sovereignty, he said, it was imperative to go beyond the idea of a separate identity as a religious community: 'We should cultivate the spirit of unity and good will, should so perform our duties and administer the country as to make it impossible for any foreign nation to interfere with us.' Although, with the reference to inner weakening through inter-religious rivalries, Lajpat Rai had introduced a convincing counter-argument, voices suspicious of the political alliance of Hindus and Muslims were not silenced, and they came back with renewed vigour after the campaign for non-cooperation was discontinued in 1922. Their fundamental reservations in the form of a basic mutual distrust had, however, been sown much earlier and could only be temporarily contained by the Mahatma's religious and political integrative abilities as long as the programmatic force of the campaign was still effective.

THE MAHATMA AS A RELIGIOUS MESSAGE

Another important—albeit unintended—aspect of the function of religion in the Khilafat movement concerned Gandhi's person itself. After support for Gandhi's campaign increased significantly at the beginning of 1921, especially in the countryside, the Viceroy had to report this in his bi-monthly reports to the India minister in London. With reference to the Mahatma's extensive travels and appearances at public gatherings, especially in north and east India, the Viceroy remarked that large masses of peasants regularly attended the Khilafat meetings,

> but this fact by no means indicates that the majority of the persons present understood or approved his [i.e. Gandhi's] policy. Most of them were attracted by the reverence undoubtedly widespread, which his reputation for holy and unworldly conduct has inspired, but so

little do his hearers understand what he desires that at Arrah his meeting was actually beneficial to recruitment for the Army.[38]

Clearly, this reference to the holy aura of the Mahatma helped the British to underplay the relevance of the actual concerns articulated by the movement. Yet, the Mahatma in his personal physical appearance embodied an important aspect of the message itself that had probably not been calculated in this form. The Mahatma personified almost messianic and religiously inflated expectations of deliverance which synthesized well with his political programme of *swaraj* and thus established his persuasive power at least in the short term. In this sense Gandhi was not simply another political leader, but a supernatural saviour-figure—an image that Gandhi himself provoked by linking nation and religion. For the first time in April 1921 rumours surfaced in several places in Bihar and Orissa about the 'divine powers' of the Mahatma accompanied by political rumours that self-rule had already been achieved and that an independent Indian government was to be established in the neighbouring provinces.[39] On 20 May of the same year the district-administrator of Surat in the Bombay Presidency reports:

There is apparent by a concerted attempt to spread stories of 'miracles' performed by Gandhi, of good which flows from a remembrance of him in difficulty, of evil which happens to people who do not believe in him. All the vernacular papers are now full of such stories. The idea is clearly to impress the ignorant masses. I heard a rumour that when Gandhi came to Surat he was put in prison but the doors flew open and he came out again. As Gandhi does nothing to give the lie to such stories about himself, it may be supposed he allows them to spread as a help of his propaganda.[40]

The conclusion that Gandhi actively supported this religious inflation cannot be historically validated. He was probably not even aware of these outgrowths of his religiously formulated political programme.

Another example from the newspaper *Swadesh* published in Gorakhpur (Central Provinces) clearly shows what forms the discourse on nation and its right to self-determination could take in the context of religious everyday life. The example is reproduced in detail in order to demonstrate the integration of nationalism as a theoretical and abstract political ideology in the expectations and experiences of the nationalist subjects, i.e. of every individual Indian as the addressee and potential participant in the cause of the nation:

A temple is being repaired by an anti-non-cooperator who had ordered a fine of Rs. 5 to be imposed on the sympathizers of Mahatma Gandhi throughout his taluqa.[41] On the 4th of April at 11.30 a.m. a man 21 feet in length and with four arms was seen to be strolling on the temple platform. The *chaukidars*[42] and labourers were terrified and informed the *zamindar*[43] of the incident. The zamindar came to the spot with armed attendants and saw the same four-handed figure who asked the people not to be alarmed. Then the figure went to another temple close by the zamindar's house. The zamindar ordered two or three hundred men to proceed to that spot, but the figure soon returned to the first spot and said 'Do not be afraid; Do not be afraid'. On being repeatedly asked to disclose its identity, the figure said 'I am the person whose name is on the lips of every male and female in India'. The figure asked the zamindar to speak the truth and cease oppressing people. After this the figure was transformed into [a] boy of white complexion and with a shining forehead and after some time, assuming its former shape, disappeared from view.[44]

The remarkable thing about this episode is that it essentially reproduces all the important points of Gandhi's campaign, albeit reformulated in a language inspired by mythological anecdotes which conform to the style of the miracle-story. The link with the Hindu pantheon–indicated here by the four arms and the places where the figure appeared, the two temples–is also found in other stories of this kind. Elsewhere, Gandhi was expected to appear above the river in Ayodhya, the legendary capital of Rama's kingdom. With regard to politics, the episode reproduces all of Gandhi's central concerns. Out of a sense of personal superiority, expressed in his super-human size, and out of an almost divine distance, he remains completely non-violent even when he is attacked. His revelation is initially directed at the simple people in the form of a message to instil confidence and trust. Only after that does the Mahatma turn to the landlord who, as a co-operator with the British, embodies oppression and the injustice of difficult economic circumstances. His call to tell the truth and to put an end to oppression is the Mahatma's goal of social reform, under whose banner *swaraj* was to be attained. The change in his form at the end is also worth mentioning. The Mahatma appears as a boy, dressed in white and with a shining forehead as the embodiment of innocence and purity which are meant to characterize Gandhi's being and demonstrate his god-like nature.

THE AMBIVALENT BALANCE SHEET OF PERFORMATIVE NATION-BUILDING IN ITS EARLY STAGE

In the meantime boycott-measures continued at the national-political level, and in January 1921 the Duke of Connaught's visit to India offered a good opportunity to articulate opposition to Britain. On the eve of the visit a meeting of important Congress leaders was held in Madras to co-ordinate the actions for 10 January.[45] The mass demonstrations and the closure of business establishments was a great success for Gandhi; more than 60,000 people participated in the protest rallies in the city.[46] In Bengal, where the Duke arrived on 28 January, Gandhi managed to achieve a near-total blockade of educational institutions by repeatedly emphasizing the slogan of 'Swaraj within one year'.[47] At the end of January and the beginning of February the meeting of the All India Congress Committee also took place here in order to promote the spread of the spinning-wheel in the villages, to gather donations for the Tilak Swaraj Fund, and to discuss the 'nationalization' of the curricula and the syllabi.[48] This nationalization basically meant three things: firstly, lessons in hand-spinning and the village manufacture of yarn, secondly, lessons in Hindustani, both in the Devanagari and in the Persian script and, thirdly, instruction for the students in methods of village organization, since the village was to represent the core unit of the independent nation.[49] The *Amrita Bazar Patrika*,[50] one of the most important periodicals in India oriented towards nationalism, called on students on its front page to report as volunteers to the Indian National Service and to help in the setting up of village-organization under the guidance of C.R. Das. Carried on the wave of the successful boycott that had started in Bengal thousands of students all over India voluntarily visited the over 800 national schools in the first months of this year.[51] The leader of this mobilization was the same C.R. Das who, only a few months earlier, had rejected the programme of non-cooperation.

Despite these successes in early 1921 other incidents also took place which would have been the source of worry rather than satisfaction for the Congress leadership. In Bihar, for example, the controversy between Hindus and Muslims regarding the question of cow-slaughter took on alarming proportions. The number of volunteers as well as financial support to the Khilafat and the Non-Cooperation movement decreased noticeably in May on account of tensions between the religious communities. The Muslim population in seven districts sent their own delegates to the Central Khilafat Committee in order to resolve the questions in accordance with Muslim ideas.[52] The Arya Samaj, a Hindu reform movement established in 1875 which mainly supported the Hindu cause at the local level from its stronghold in the Punjab, now began to express its views on national-political concerns more openly and in a correspondingly radical tone. The first voices were now heard, mainly from the Punjab, that the Arya Samaj should use its organizational and mobilizing potential in support of the religious majority 'endangered' by Muslim zeal in the countrywide controversies between Hindus and Muslims.[53] During the annual celebrations of the Arya Samaj in Lahore in December 1920 Rama Deva, a local leader of the organization, gave a speech in which he openly criticized Islam and called its followers intolerant and fanatical. This sparked off a conflict, carried out mainly in the local media, which already bore the nucleus of the violent conflicts of the coming years. When the Muslim camp reacted with unequivocal criticism, the Arya Samaj claimed for itself the right to practise its religion freely and without restrictions imposed by Muslims. It stated that even in the fight for *swaraj* this freedom would have to be granted to the religious majority. What would otherwise be the worth of an independent state, it asked, in which Hindus would no longer be allowed to practise their religion freely and speak out for themselves? The Hindus would be unable to accept self-rule if it meant Muslim domination. Although Hindus would be prepared to cooperate with Muslims in the interest of anti-colonialism, this cooperation could never be at the expense of their religion.[54]

In the first half of 1921 this religious zeal was also combined with a widespread mobilization, mainly of the agrarian population. This combination, limited to a region, not only led to active participation in the national campaign, but it also produced a partly explosive mix which was vented in individual actions against landlords or against political or military establishments of the colonial power. In the spring of 1920 Jawaharlal Nehru had already taken over as Joint-Secretary of the Congress in the United Provinces. The impressive organizational talent he displayed in this function as a *satyagrahi* at Gandhi's side helped to establish his position within the Congress for the first time independent of his father.[55] A meeting with peasants in his home-town Allahabad in the same year left a deep impression on young Nehru and it shaped his political commitment in the long run. Years later he spoke about this:

> Early in June 1920 about two hundred *kisans*[56] marched fifty miles from the interior of Partabgarh district to Allahabad city with the intention of drawing attention of the prominent politicians there to their woebegone condition. . . . They told us of the crushing exactions of the *taluqadars*,[57] of inhuman treatment, and that their condition had become wholly intolerable.[58]

During his subsequent visits to surrounding villages Nehru saw that this mass of impoverished peasants represented an enormous political potential for the anti-colonial movement. In the coming years he, therefore, transferred his mobilizing activity to the rural areas in order to win over the peasants to his cause. Already in the first months after the end of the war in 1918 a Kisan Sabha movement had been established, largely independent of the Congress, which aimed at organizing the peasants, mainly in the United Provinces, so that their concerns would be heard in the political arena. Nehru was pleasantly surprised by this movement in which peasants came together irrespective of caste and religion.[59] In January 1921 the British administration of the United Provinces had already stated that peasants were thronging to the Kisan Sabhas and that this factor would have to be considered in the future.[60]

This significantly increased degree of politicization of hitherto uninvolved sections of the population was met with a corresponding expansion of organizational and institutional structures to cater to the people in the urban and rural areas. Nominally, the Kisan Sabhas, the local Congress organizations and the Khilafat committees remained separate, but practically they could not be distinguished from one another in many cases. The Khilafat committees, especially, often merged with the local Congress cadres and served both organizations as a means of communication with their regional supporters. In 1921, the Congress, for example, by successfully conducting the non-cooperation and the Khilafat campaign, experienced a rapid growth of its organizational reach which extended to the southern parts of the country. Although reliable statistics for the extent of Congress membership do not exist, regional indicators from the United Provinces, Bihar, Bengal and the Central Provinces show that the years 1920 and 1921 brought a sharp rise. There was also a steep increase in the number of Muslims and, especially, of peasants among the delegates at the annual meetings. The proportion of Muslims, for example, rose from just 4.5 per cent in 1919 to 10.9 per cent in 1921.[61] Thus, one of the most important deficits of the Congress, namely the low proportion of Muslim delegates, was overcome for a short period. Financially too, the Congress gained significantly through Gandhi's skilful politics. The funds established by Gandhi[62] and his contacts with financially powerful industrialists, mainly in the Bombay Presidency, decisively extended the financial scope of the organization. This trend weakened only in 1922, after the failure of non-cooperation in February with the outbreak of violence in Chauri Chaura and the increase of inter-religious hostilities. At the end of the year British administrators recorded a renewed decrease of Congress activities in Punjab with a similar trend in other provinces. It was not only the financial volume of the Tilak Swaraj Fund that had decreased, but also the number of members and national workers.[63]

Three factors led to a hitherto unprecedented mobilization of the colonized Indian population which saw this as a welcome opportunity to express their displeasure at their economic and social circumstances: the first was the fact that the political sphere was religiously charged and that radical-religious leaders came forth to lead the campaign. The second factor was the politicization of the peasants in the framework of the social dynamics of oppression and poverty in the rural areas. The third, and final, factor was the countrywide organizational penetration of the colony by oppositional, non-British organizations like the Kisan Sabhas, the Khilafat committees and the Congress organizations. In addition to this, the numbers of the educated urban middle class, and even the rural aristocracy had risen considerably since the British had had to provide easier access to higher education in order to recruit young people for the Indian Civil Service, the iron framework of the Empire.[64] Given the all-too brief period of preparation for the campaigns and the extent of the changes they involved, one could have perhaps foreseen that this development could, at least at the local level, go in unplanned and undesirable directions. The ambivalent character of religion as a communicator of rather abstract political concepts such as the nation necessarily meant that Gandhi would possibly lose his contested and thus temporary monopoly of defining the relationship between the nation and religion to other, more radical leaders. Among the many small mistakes in the eyes of the initiators of the campaign, however, one incident, namely the Shuddhi movement, stood out. It grew into a violent rebellion whose bloody course would effectively change India's fate in the following years.

As a result Gandhi lost the political initiative temporarily and was able to regain it only much later.

NOTES

1. Page, 1999, p. xlii. Flynn (1974) expresses a similar view in the summary of her important study: 'With the eclipse of civil disobedience, political attention shifted from the lofty goal of self-rule to intra- and inter-party struggles for power and to local and provincial issues. The aspirations of nationalist leaders for early Swaraj had been crushed and in their place sectarian considerations became the main problem'. (11)
2. Sandria Freitag (1990) has presented an excellent study of these early forms of religiously motivated and argued-out methods of mobilization. Her study focuses mainly on the United Provinces in the north of British India. On the basis of local riots involving the movement for the protection of cows she discusses the development of interreligious hostilities in the name of an essentially religiously defined Indian nation. She also goes into the further development of this trend till the 1930s under the aspects of public space and politicized rituals. A study which goes deeper into the subject in the context of the nineteenth century, but with a theoretically similar framework is Yang (1980).
3. Pandey, 1999, p. 233.
4. Thursby, 1975, pp. 19-31 offers a good, though by no means complete, overview of the rise of this media landscape in the local Indian languages and the continuous controversies with the British administration. He mainly works out the regional differences in this development and clearly portrays British attempts to contain it.
5. Metcalf, 1992, pp. 232f points out in this context that it was mainly the explicit combination of this fact with existing, chiefly infrastructural, achievements which allowed for the rise of a new public arena that was indispensable for the development of modern nationalism. These new, quasi secular, nationalist leaders 'were people who utilized the new techniques of journalism, public preaching and debate, tract and book writing, and

organization. Acting as debaters, journalists, and publicists, they often had some education in government or missionary schools and, occasionally, were employed in schools or government offices'. (232)

6. Sarkar, 1983, p. 125. For a detailed portrayal of the movement and the historiography of its characteristics described above see Sarkar, 1973.
7. Cf. Dalton, 1977, pp. 592f.
8. Brown, 1977, p. 569. Dalton, 2002 also gives an insight into Gandhi's programme and his creative methods in this respect.
9. Rothermund, 1965, p. 162 uses this expression for the symbolic 'end' of colonial rule through Gandhi's actionist methods, especially in 1930. My use of the term refers, however, to the entire period beginning with his entry into Indian politics in 1918 and ending with the salt march in 1930. Cf. also Rothermund, 1997, pp. 247ff.
10. Aloysius, 2002, p. 91.
11. Sarkar, 1993, p. 94.
12. Hasan, 1991, p. 23.
13. Ashraf, 1985, p. 85 explains the history and the changing nature of this political theme.
14. Hasan, 1985, p. 3.
15. The speech is reproduced in its entirety in McLane 1970, pp. 113-17, here pp. 113f.
16. Minault, 1982, p. 91.
17. Regarding the problem of the representative character of the 'advocates of Muslims' who participated in the Khilafat movement, which also constituted a large part of the difficulties that the Congress encountered within this cooperative campaign after 1922, cf. Hasan, 1988, pp. 198f. who states that from the beginning of the movement, despite well-intentioned goals formulated in the interests of Indian Muslims, the political and organizational following among the Muslims themselves was, by no means, settled and assured.
18. The *Independent* (3.6.1920).
19. Cf. for this Misra, 1990, pp. 285f.
20. HD, 1920/59, Proceedings July.
21. Ibid., p. 7.
22. Cf. for this MP, 13.

23. HP (1922/17).
24. Panikkar, 2001, pp. 135-8.
25. HD (1922/17/4).
26. HDP (1921/35/12). Abul Kalam Azad (1989: 11) also refers to this about-turn in Nagpur, not only by Das but also by Lajpat Rai–two leaders who, at the meeting in September in Calcutta, had been strongly opposed to the adoption of non-cooperation by the party.
27. HDP (1921/33/1).
28. Ibid., p. 4.
29. Nehru, 1995, pp. 71f.
30. *The Independent* (12.4.1921).
31. HDP (1921/35/13).
32. In his autobiography Gandhi states in no uncertain terms that the intention behind linking Khilafat and non-cooperation was to achieve a politically effective unity between Hindus and Muslims. It was, therefore, logical that at the decisive meeting in Nagpur in December 1920 the resolution to adopt non-cooperation also led to the adoption of resolutions about the unity of Hindus and Muslims, the removal of untouchability and the spinning of *khadi*. Cf. for this Gandhi, 1982, pp. 449-51.
33. PPA (1921/5/105).
34. HDP (1921/35/16).
35. PPA (1921/1/7).
36. Cited from PPA (1921/5/105).
37. *Bande Mataram* (12.3.1921).
38. HDP (1921/35/17).
39. HDP (1921/13/12).
40. HDP (1921/46/7).
41. I.e. district
42. I.e. guards.
43. I.e. landlord.
44. HDP (1921/13/36).
45. HDP (1921/41/4-6).
46. *The Hindu* (11.1.1921).
47. HDP (1921/42/10).
48. Cf. for this HDP (1921/13/3).
49. HDP (1921/12/13).
50. *Amrita Bazar Patrika* (21.1.1921).

51. Cf. Chandra, 1989, p. 187.
52. HDP (1921/46/20).
53. *Prakash* (14.8.1921).
54. *Prakash* (9.1.1921), cited from PPA (1921/3/65).
55. Cf. for this Pandey, 1976, p. 83.
56. I.e. peasants.
57. I.e. landlords.
58. Nehru, 1995, p. 51.
59. Pandey, 1988, p. 122.
60. HDPD (1921/75/8).
61. Gopal, 1996, p. 421.
62. This included mainly the Tilak Swaraj Fund, set-up in 1920 after the death of B.G. Tilak, the Jallianwala Bagh Memorial Fund, set-up after the massacre in Amritsar in 1919, the Punjab Relief Fund and many others.
63. Cf. for this HDP (1923/25/42).
64. Rothermund, 1970, pp. 150f. argues in this context that during the war not only did the number of school children and successful graduates of English secondary schools increase, but that the colonial middle class was also given greater access to higher education. In addition, there were the Indian soldiers who had taken part in the war overseas on the British side and now returned as an important political constituency to a situation where the conditions for further employment were inadequate. The resulting dissatisfaction vented itself in Gandhi's mobilization.

CHAPTER 4

Political Rituals of Purity in Colonial India

THE SHUDDHI MOVEMENT OF THE 1920s

Mahatma Gandhi and other leaders of the Indian National Congress had initiated the Khilafat movement in October 1919 for the preservation of the Ottoman Caliphate and in order to strengthen the unity between Hindus and Muslims in the fight for self-rule (*swaraj*).[1] In accordance with Gandhi's principles, strict non-violence was the highest commandment of the movement. However, in August 1921, a violent insurgence broke out in the south-west Malabar region, which was then part of the Madras Presidency and is today in the state of Kerala. The uprising was directed primarily against two authorities: in the first instance, the resentment of the mainly agrarian Muslim population, the Mappilas or Moplahs, was unleashed against the colonial rulers whose monetary tax-system represented a heavy economic burden that resulted in excruciating repression, especially in the post-war years. In the second instance, the insurgents also protested against Hindu landlords and money-lenders who maintained the oppressive relations of dependency with the help of the British and prevented the economic emancipation of impoverished Muslim peasants.[2] The social and economic backwardness of the Muslim Moplahs also extended to the sphere of education and this contributed to a wide sense of group discrimination.

The already tense situation worsened through exaggerated reports that the insurgent Moplahs were forcing Hindus to convert to Islam. While today, the fact of forced conversion cannot be dismissed as completely false, the extent of this action was far more limited than suggested by contemporary press reports. Mahatma Hansraj who organized financial and institutional help for Hindu refugees in the Malabar on behalf of the Arya Samaj (a Hindu reform movement), and who was present in the area, reported 3,000 such converts.[3] However, he was interested in presenting this fact in as dramatic a light as possible in order to justify the commitment of the Arya Samaj to the 'rescue of Hindus'. The *Times of India*[4] reported between 1,000 and 1,200 victims of the aggressive missionary tactics of the Muslims, while the British, in their own interests, tried to play down the dimensions of conversion because of the volatile nature of the subject. They claimed that the number of affected people was between 180 and 500, although they added that many Hindus had been killed because they refused to convert. However, the British were wary about giving exact data since they feared violent repercussions against the converts from the Muslims as well as from the Hindus.[5] Regardless of the exact number of people who were forcibly converted to Islam,[6] the topic led to a controversy between Hindus and Muslims regarding fundamental questions of coexistence within a common nation which was often conducted in a very aggressive fashion.

Initially, the Hindu-camp, especially the right-wing anti-Muslim camp, reacted with a correspondingly vehement echo to this apparent threat. The following report from the *Times of India*[7] was symptomatic for the dramatic and exaggerated depiction of events in the Malabar which had the potential for effectively impairing Hindu-Muslim relations:

> Refugees narrate that, after forcibly removing young and fair Nair and other high caste girls from their parents and husbands, the Mopla rebels stripped them of their clothing and made them march in their presence naked, and finally they committed rape upon them. In certain instances, devoid of human feelings and blinded by animal passion, the Moplas are alleged to have utilised a single woman for the gratification of the carnal pleasure of a dozen or more men. The

rebels also seemed to have captured beautiful Hindu women, forcibly converted them, pierced holes in their ears in the typical Mopla fashion, dressed them as Mopla women and utilised them as their temporary partners of life. Hindu women were threatened, molested and compelled to run half-naked for shelter to forests abounding in wild animals.

And the political conclusion:

The ghostly spectacle of a number of Hindu damsels being forced to march naked in the midst of a number of licentious Moplas cannot be forgotten by any self-respecting Hindu, nor can it be erased from their minds.

Following on these reports the Arya Samaj in Punjab passed a resolution proposing a dual strategy as a counter-measure for the Hindus, namely 'Shuddhi' on the one hand and humanitarian help on the other. The latter point was based on reports that the Arya Samaj had received from the Madras Presidency and was meant to alleviate the immediate material plight of the Hindus, some of who had had their houses burnt down or had been forced to leave their homes in order to flee from violence and further threats.[8] Just as important and even mentioned first in the resolution, was Shuddhi, a ritual concept that was meant to effectively remove all traces of the religious marginalization of the converts among the Hindus.

The concept of *shuddhi* comes from the Sanskrit and is derived from the adjective *shuddh* meaning 'pure' and 'cleansed'. It has an explicitly religious connotation. The other, alternative meanings of this adjective, namely 'holy', 'unpolluted', 'innocent', 'bright' or 'white' clarify the religious-ritual context of this attribute.[9] The noun *shuddhi*, which is derived from this, has two meanings. The first is 'purity' itself, 'holiness' and 'brightness', the stage in which the object denoted by the said adjective exists. In the second instance *shuddhi* also denotes the process to reach this stage, the act of 'cleansing', 'atonement' and 'penance' which re-establishes the condition of purity and sanctity.[10] What is important is that these concepts gain sense and meaning only in the context of Hindu cosmology, in the superordinate concept of purity and impurity as fundamental principles of human interactions as well as in a religious-ritual sense. The caste hierarchy also emerges from these concepts.

In the ordinary religious world of the Hindus the concept of *shuddhi* in itself does not exist and as such it is more or less a new or a re-discovery by the political actors of the nineteenth and twentieth centuries. What exists however in Hindu practice is the concept *shuddha*, or the belief associated with it, which can be characterized in the following manner:

> The connotation of this word is conveyed by invoking images of fullness or completeness in the specific sense of perfection. It thus refers to the most desired condition of the human body or, more comprehensively, the most desired state of being. *Shuddha* and its opposite, *ashuddha*, are attributes of animate beings, inanimate objects and places with which a human being comes into contact in the course of everyday life.[11]

An unmarried woman, who is considered untouched by sexuality, water from the holy rivers of India, milk as the product of the holy cow or even Hindu temples are in themselves objects of idealized purity. On the other hand, contacts with non-Hindus such as Christians who have no rules of purity, or Muslims whose rules are completely different, with low caste Hindus, with animals other than the cow, with dead tissue such as leather, with human excrements in general, with non-vegetarian food or with specific places such as cemeteries are considered to be polluting. The contact with such objects leads to defilation and purity can only be restored ritually provided that the basic status of purity was initially present.

The rituals of the Shuddhi movement that were organized in the following months and years by the Arya Samaj and other organizations with a similar ideology were meant to fulfil two practical tasks. They were meant to carry out re-conversion, or cleanse the untouchables and low caste Hindus, and to give the people concerned the feeling and the assurance of having permanently regained their traditional place in the Hindu social structure. However, the concrete forms of the rituals had to be accepted by the 'pure' and especially by the Brahmins. This was generally ensured by integrating the pandits and other orthodox Hindus in the rituals since their position of privilege was mainly a consequence of their monopoly in administering rites. Both these requirements involved a precise and sensitive organization of the rites.[12] The form of the rituals was decisive for the social and national dimensions of re-conversion and, therefore, could not be left to the improvization skills of the local Shuddhi protagonists.

Already at the end of the nineteenth century the form of purification rituals had been the object of fierce controversies and had undergone numerous reforms and expansions.[13] These practical experiments resulted in a gradual extension of the jurisdiction of traditional experts for administering rites, namely the orthodoxy and the Brahmins. Otherwise, the rituals themselves remained simple and short. There was a great deal of uncertainty about the exact forms as we see from an example of 1889 which was documented by Swami Shraddhanand, a leading figure of the Shuddhi movement in the 1920s, and which illustrates the course of this 'ceremony' conducted by Pandit Nathuram, a Brahmin:

> Having extracted *Dakshinas*[14] from fallen men, he used to direct them to Hardwar where, after bath, they would get themselves purified by taking water made holy with cow-dung by paying Rs.5-4-0; then this gentleman would issue a certificate of Shuddhi. Times are changed today and even born Christians and Mohamedans are admitted into the Hindu fold.[15]

What is remarkable about this early example of re-conversion is the obvious combination of new elements such as the donation of money or the issuing of a certificate of ritual purity with very traditional elements of purification like the journey to Haridwar, the old place of pilgrimage on the banks of the Ganges.

The first big opportunity to use Shuddhi presented itself in the Malabar region where Hindus had been forcibly converted and had to now be brought back to a state of Hindu purity. On the basis of past experiences, the renewed acceptance and the state of purity of the victims of religious violence in the Malabar were based on the payment of large sums of money. On 20 August 1922 local authorities, priests and interestingly even the British district administrator, R.H. Ellis (Indian Civil Service), met in Calicut and passed four resolutions[16] which regulated the course of the ceremony up to the last detail in a casuistic manner. Each of the resolutions first determined the degree of impurity. This is followed by the healing or purifying procedure through which religious ignominy is made good again, enabling re-entry into Hinduism:[17]

1. *Cutting the tuft, repeating the Kalima,*[18] *earboring of women and wearing Moplah jackets*:[19] The victims in these cases are to take 'panchagavya'[20] for three days at any temple, to make whatever offerings they can and to repeat 'Narayana or Siva'[21] at least 3,000 times every day.
2. *Circumcision and co-habitation*: The remedy to be the same as mentioned above, but for 12 days the prayers are to be repeated 12,000 times a day.
3. *Eating food cooked by Moplahs*: The victims in this case are to wash their sins off in the holy Sethu and to obtain a certificate to that effect from the temple authorities or the 'Purohits'[22] and then observe the ceremonies in (1) and (2) for 41 days repeating the sacred names 12,000 times a day.
4. Sins not specified above are to be expiated by adopting the ceremonies fixed in (1) above to be continued for 21 days repeating Narayana or Siva 12,000 times a day.

In the first case mentioned here there are two categories of findings which go against the rules of purity. In the first instance the authors deem the adoption of external characteristics of the Muslim Moplahs as a case of pollution and thus react on their part to the Muslim rituals for conversion to Islam. Cutting of the tuft, piercing of the ears and wearing traditional Moplah jackets were the pragmatic markers of a new religious reality which were perceived and used socially both in a positive form as admittance to the new faith as well as negatively to demarcate the converts from their former communities. These external measures could also be seen as the rather violent monopolization of a person and they were applied independently of the will of the individual. Gandhi's reference to this conflict between Hindus and Muslims in his statement that conversion can only be valid and effective when it is undertaken freely and from the heart[23] is correct in the sense of religion as faith, but it ignores the reality of forcible conversion and its social and ritual implications. The far-reaching consequences of this act of conversion were in fact independent of the will of the persons concerned and they did not, by any means, require consent or the dictates of the heart. The status of ritual purity, which is decisive for the social and religious position within Hindu society, is completely independent of a subjective will. Whether the conversion is valid from the Islamic point of view is another question altogether since Islam as a faith presupposes a consent from the heart. From a Hindu perspective, however, the state of pollution sets in even if conversion to another religion is invalid. The external characteristics listed in the first point of the resolution are, therefore, sufficient to create an insurmountable, ritually determined distance to other Hindus who, for their part, would forfeit their own state of purity through further contact with the—apparent or real—converts and who therefore avoid them.

These dynamics of ritual purity are, naturally, very important for Brahmins who occupy the highest position in the social and ritual hierarchy of the Hindus. For the Shuddhi movement it was, therefore, all the more difficult and almost inconceivable to re-establish their lost status of the highest level of purity after a conversion. In an added clarification the above-mentioned resolutions therefore explicitly exclude Brahmins from this mode of re-conversion.[24] The second category of violations under the first point concerns a kind of creed consisting of the most important Islamic articles of faith. Even though they might have been delivered under force, the authors treat them on par with the other external characteristics regardless of the role played in it by volition.

Circumcision and living under the same roof as Muslims represent an aggravated form of violation as shown in the increased repetition of the name of the Hindu deity–12,000 times. Circumcision is a more serious external characteristic as compared to the wearing of the jacket or the cutting of the tuft because it is final and irrevocable and was also considered the classical characteristic of Muslim identity. Cohabitation in a Muslim household represented such a large number of violations against rules of purity that one had to proceed on the assumption of a fundamental pollution. The third point of the resolutions concerns the sharing of food which is considered the most serious form of pollution. The Shuddhi movement therefore imposed the highest measure of atonement on this violation and also prescribed a purifying dip in the nearby Sethu River.

In the clarifications appended to the resolutions there is a reference to the necessary and explicit consent of Hindu authorities, while the cooperation of the British administration is gratefully acknowledged. The conclusion sums up re-conversion with additional details which clearly show the above-mentioned connection between Muslim action and Hindu reaction:[25]

> Conversion–Man–bath, clean shave of the head, wearing a Moplah cap and dress, recitation of prayers from Koran called *Kalima*: then dinner with Moplahs, circumcision to be performed on a convenient date.
>
> Woman–Bath, wearing Moplah women's jackets and coloured clothes: Recitation of *Kalima*, food. Ears to be bored round the earflaps at a convenient date.
>
> Re-conversion–The convert removes his Moslem clothes: then bathes and puts on Hindu white clothes. Repeats the Gayatri and Vedic *mantras* which is recited to him by the Aryan Missionary,–and the convert is declared Hindu. For males, a shave before bath in addition.

It was not only with regard to rituals that the re-conversions in the Malabar region were creative inventions and reactions to Muslim atrocities. Even Hindu texts for re-conversion had to first be found. Vedic *mantras* and the *Gayatri mantra*[26] were widely known among the Hindus as meditative doctrines, although it cannot be assumed that the lower classes or non-Brahmins, who were the majority affected by the need for re-conversion, either knew the content of the Sanskrit verses or understood their religious substance.[27] Yet, in order to ensure the cooperation of the orthodoxy, which had reached a hitherto unimaginable intensity in the Malabar, they had to be included in the rituals. This could best be done by having the holy text recited by a Brahmanical authority suited to the occasion which would also place the Shuddhi rites within the correct traditional framework. In 1921 and 1922 the orthodoxy discovered a text called *Devala Smriti* which was several centuries old but was generally unknown. The Arya Samaj reacted enthusiastically to its discovery and immediately included the text in its ritual programme for re-conversion and reinstatement in the nation of Hindus. The special quality of this text was, firstly, its antiquity which gave the movement the historical depth it required and identified it as a truly religious and original Hindu undertaking. Secondly, the content of the text served to legitimize the Shuddhi movement *vis-à-vis* the orthodoxy. In 90 verses the *Devala Smriti* describes the rites of purification especially after contact with *Mlecchas*, or unbelievers.[28] Given the fact that Hinduism till then did not have any rituals for conversion in general, let alone for re-conversion from Islam, these 90 verses were like a comprehensive holy book for performative nation-building through *shuddhi* which initiated and established the renaissance of collective Hindu consciousness staged as a resurrection, but which was actually a modern creation in a modern political context.

SHUDDHI AND THE NATIONAL INTEGRATION OF THE ADIVASI

Another example of the ritual forms of the Shuddhi ceremony has been handed down from the work of the Arya Samaj among India's tribal population which was, and remains even today in the north-eastern states of the country, one of the most important target groups of Christian missionaries. The self-appointed defenders of Hinduism, therefore, also went to these people in order to increase 'Hindu consciousness' among them and immunize them against conversion efforts of the monotheistic religions. The undated report about the ceremony conducted among the Santals in what are today the federal states of Uttar Pradesh and Bihar, states:

> In the midst of the vast enclosure was a flaming fire which each convert had to approach as a sign of cleansing. Then round a little temple he must kneel, while the priest within read Sanskrit prayers. The aboriginals tried hard to kneel properly, and their attitude was absolutely devout, but such a lot of demonstration and copying, and pushing and instruction was necessary before they could understand all that was required of them, that they looked rather more flurried than worshipful. Nevertheless, their simplicity and grace seemed to outshine anything we or the Hindus were manifesting in our attitude towards them. They now passed in a single file into a huge marquee, in which twelve hired clerks sat to take their names. At one end, five Hindu officials sat, each in his private compartment, partitioned off from the rest, and here the mark was put on the forehead of the converts, the words pronounced, and the blessing given that constituted them Hindus henceforth. A copy of the Bhagavatgita was put into their hands, they were shepherded out of the marquee. . . . Each man was then given a small framed picture of Krishna. There followed an appetising dinner, after which a packet of cigarettes was handed to each, and they were harangued by the partly ones [?] on their duties and privileges: to pray at sunrise and sunset; to protect the Hindu temples against all enemies; to give up alcoholic drinks etc.[29]

The conversion, or the ritual purification, of the Santals differed from the resolutions in the Malabar insofar as the Santals, strictly speaking, had not been Hindus but followed tribal religions that were practised outside the caste order and did not demonstrate typical Hindu characteristics such as cow-worship or the commandments of purity between the castes and sub-castes. Therefore, theirs was not a case of re-conversion but of active initiation into Hinduism as conceived of by the Arya Samaj: primarily as a religiously and culturally defined national association with codified membership with the will to protect Hindu shrines against enemies. At the beginning of the purification ceremony for becoming Hindus the

Santals had to approach a fire which is considered to be a purifying element in the Hindu ritual repertoire. The ceremony itself was then a combination of religious rites and administrative procedures. For one, the priests (thus Brahmins) were responsible for the correct liturgical form of purification. Sanskrit prayers accompanied the actions, pictures of Krishna were handed out and the Brahmins ate at the same table with the new Hindus to signal the extent of the social and religious acceptance of the Santals. In many cases, the community meal at the end of the Shuddhi ceremony was not only shared by all but, as an expression of the unequivocal recognition of their status of purity, it was prepared and served by the converts themselves.[30]

For the other, twelve civil servants, who had been signed on, were an important part of the ritual. They entered the names of the converts and thus carried out an administrative 'naturalization'. This element represented a synthesis between the traditionalistic, religious and ritual components of conversion and a quasi-state-conducted procedure of registration, giving the converts official recognition as members of a modern collective. With regard to the ideological underpinnings of Shuddhi this collective could be identified as nation since it represented the actual frame of reference of this ritual constitution of identity. In this way the Shuddhi movement successfully carried out the practical combination of reformulated tradition and modern nation-building. It linked administrative procedures of registration akin to citizenship with the ritual demands of purification in order to carry out the ostensibly egalitarian integration—with regard to religion—in the association of Hindus.

This plan enabled, among other things, the canonization of important and typical Hindu beliefs and customs that formed the basis of this ceremony. The unity and clarity of dogma that Dayanand Saraswati[31] and the Arya Samaj[32] wanted to establish for Hinduism, since they recognized it as the chief advantage of the monotheistic religions, was inherent in the Shuddhi act. This began with the selection of texts like the *Gayatri mantra* or the *Bhagvad Gita* and proceeded via the declaration of important deities such as Rama,

Krishna, Shiva or Vishnu to the formulation of a 'Hindu' code of conduct which was the superficial construction of a Hindu ethics appended to the ceremony described above. According to this, a Hindu prays at sunrise and sunset, protects Hindu shrines from all enemies, does not drink alcohol, etc. The question about the grounds on which a person could be considered to be a Hindu preceded the ritual structuring of purification and was one which had, on several occasions, occupied Swami Shraddhanand, the spiritual father of the Shuddhi movement in the 1920s, since there were no traditional patterns to which one could take recourse. Thus, he defended the re-conversion of the Malkana-Rajputs, for example, with the comment that they did not display any 'Islamic qualities' since they did not follow Islamic rules of marriage, wore the holy thread, did not bury the dead, grew a tuft, respected Hindu festivals and Hindu deities, considered their Hindu forefathers to be holy, spoke Hindi and worshipped the cow.[33] Elsewhere, a journalist defended Shraddhanand's statement that the Malkanas are actually Hindus with the comment that they grew a tuft, preserved Hindu customs and lifestyles [*sic*], refused to eat with Muslims, did not drink water drawn by Muslims and also had Hindu names.[34] The last reference corresponds to stated ritual strategy of giving converts from other religions or tribal groups new names upon their entry into Hinduism in order to denote inclusion in the new collective and to wipe out all traces of the past.[35] These attempts at definition were an understandable exercise from a nationalist perspective to overcome the indistinct and arbitrary boundaries of Hinduism in favour of clear, convincing boundaries of a Hindu-nation which could be put into operation and which would provide the necessary framework for action in a confrontation with other religions. The rituals of the Shuddhi movement were meant as a preparation for such a confrontation and were also an attempt to stop the numerical decline of Hindus. They were meant to initiate a new, nationalistically reformulated renaissance of the collective consciousness of all Hindus. The apparatus for this was supplied by a model of initiation that would establish membership on the one hand, and a consistent commitment to the national collective on the other. At least in the short-term the Shuddhi movement could fulfil these two goals both rhetorically and ritually and in this way it effectively changed the political discourse in India.

CONCLUSION: PERFORMATIVE NATION-BUILDING, RELIGION AND SOCIAL CHANGES IN COLONIAL INDIA

The example of the Shuddhi movement as performative nation-building in India in the colonial context demonstrates three important points. Firstly, one has to study the social background of the movement and ask what lasting qualitative changes it brought about for the political sphere in colonial India. Secondly, with the focus on purity, such movements created a new nationalist paradigm which, as a basic model of religious nationalism, gave a decisive turn to India's modern history in the twentieth century. Thirdly, with an orientation towards nationalist politics Hinduism itself no longer remained a heterogeneous religious landscape. A comprehensive process of its reformulation and a new actionist mode in the public sphere set in and this became the condition for its successful instrumentalization for political goals.

Let us first look at the question of the social background and at the changes in the 1920s. Detailed studies of political organizations as well as observations on the origins of political leaders in the Independence struggle show that after the First World War there was a quantitative increase in the middle class[36] which also became more politicized. Rothermund has convincingly argued that the number of affluent graduates of higher education rose appreciably in the war years and that the economic conditions enabled these groups to gain political significance.[37] This trend precipitated the qualitative and quantitative growth of the members of the All India National Congress. Not only did the number of members increase, but the composition of the intellectual leaders among the members changed in the sense that the number of lawyers decreased proportionally to the increase of doctors, journalists and full-time workers of the

Congress.[38] This plurality at the level of the personnel engaged in the political discourse contributed to the emergence of a larger ideological spectrum, even though the person of Mahatma Gandhi at the top had an integrative effect.

Gandhi's mobilizing techniques also resulted in the politicization of hitherto politically passive sections of the population, especially peasants and untouchables who were now part of the political constituency and who had to be wooed actively. The Congress expanded its organizational network through branch offices and Khilafat committees[39] and this meant that the political monopoly hitherto enjoyed by high caste Hindus of the upper and middle class was increasingly contested by aspiring Hindus of other castes. In this political context of flux the Hindu nationalism of the Shuddhi movement functioned as an explicitly middle-class ideology of high caste Hindus[40] who were involved in the process of nationalization and of the political discourse in the sense of modernization, but who also wanted to shape the momentous consequences of this development in such a way as to avoid a loss of social supremacy. The religious reformulation of the national collective consciousness appeared, on the one hand, as modernization with a message of gradual equality and, on the other, it identified the traditional elite of the socially stratified system of castes as the new and legitimate leadership of the Hindu nation.[41] The newly-politicized sections of society like the peasants, low caste Hindus, or the untouchables were to be integrated in a national collective formed on the basis of a pseudo-reform of the caste order legitimized by religion and the nationalist discourse and headed by the old new experts for rituals and purity. The impact of the nationalist reformulation of India, which undoubtedly contained an emancipatory potential in the sense of a more egalitarian, citizenship-oriented inclusion, could thus be cushioned by a religious nationalism which would not appear traditionalistic and, therefore, anti-modern—a trend which would have failed given the dynamics of the period. In the view of many observers the reform attempts of the Arya Samaj and the Shuddhi movement, therefore, remained half-hearted, superficial and, only to a limited extent, socially integrative.[42] The ideology behind mobilizing a nation of Hindus against constructed external enemies was more in the nature of a strategy of silence about far-reaching maladies within Hindu society, even though the questions of untouchability and caste-discrimination were constantly discussed.

Even the well-meaning rites of purification did not deal with these problems seriously. Rather, these rites appeared to be a staging of a seemingly egalitarian national integration which, in social terms however, served to cement and not to question social hegemony.[43] As the driving force of politics the middle class safeguarded its symbolic capital in Hindu nationalism in order to emerge from the phase of modernization, which the politics of nationalism undoubtedly entailed, as a newly turned over yet, with regard to its caste structure, traditional elite. In the final reckoning, therefore, the middle class carried out a socially conservative transformation. These changes in the sphere of anti-colonial politics were transformative because they brought the political discourse closer to the functional logic of modern nationalism. The shape given to these changes, however, was conservative because pseudo-reformatory concerns took the place of a genuinely egalitarian model of citizenship and these only served to stabilize the hegemony of the upper castes in the new period of the nation.

The factor that triggered off this alternative strategy of mobilization was the failure of the non-cooperation campaign at the beginning of 1922 on account of violence. By calling off this campaign Gandhi halted the final thrust of this mobilization in an acutely politicized atmosphere and thus left a kind of utopian vacuum which the right-wing Hindu organizations were able to fill in their way. Given the active support of religious media in the service of politics earlier, the discontinuation of common goals also led to a vacuum which laid the ground for mutual hostilities among the religious communities. The British used this potential through structural reforms, especially at the provincial level, thus increasing the pressure to gain a political profile through religious identity. The interplay of these developments allowed Hindu nationalism a measure of success with its rituals of nationalist integration before Gandhi regained hegemony over the political agenda at the end of the 1920s.

The concept of purity as the second aspect of insights to be gained from the Shuddhi movement naturally stems from India's traditional social structure and is the key-concept for understanding caste. The entire order of permitted and forbidden interpersonal exchange is based on the idea of ritual purity and the possibility of temporary or permanent pollution with its social consequences for such exchange and communication. This mode of interaction was reformulated by Hindu nationalism as a nationalistic and collective public paradigm. Therefore, while its logic was changed, it was also reconfirmed. The separational logic of the concept of purity was transferred from caste boundaries to the external borders of the nation and its internal Hindu effect was gradually removed. Caste boundaries were meant to be overcome in favour of the larger collective of the nation. Exclusion based on the pattern of purity-pollution was reinforced, but it now functioned on an interreligious level, especially with regard to Muslims. The traditional pattern was thus handled in the same way as culture in the framework of nationalism. As already shown, culture and, with it, the pattern of purity-pollution in the nationalist context no longer functions as a marker of intra-societal differences but as a marker of difference to the world outside. In contrast to Europe, however, these two functions of culture did not represent different phases of development in the genesis of Indian nationalism, but they occurred simultaneously, overlapping and influencing each other. On the one hand, Hindu nationalism is indeed a modern ideology of integration for creating a larger, pan-Indian whole by excluding people of other faiths. However, at the same time, traditional cultural distinctions are invalidated only gradually, superficially and temporarily. This is what constitutes the actual attractiveness of this ideology for the high caste urban middle class and rural landowners.

Purity as a political concept has far-reaching consequences and it is also evident in the pillage and systematic eviction and killing of Muslims in Gujarat in 2002.[44] In India, this concept is of greater consequence since it draws its strength from indigenous ideas and forms of daily life which were established and became autonomous over the course of centuries. The Shuddhi movement translated this pattern of thought into a modern model of integration and since then it serves as a basis for religious and nationalistic acts of inclusion and exclusion.

Thirdly, and finally, the Shuddhi movement effected important transformations and reformulations of Hinduism itself while selectively re-designing religion in accordance with contemporary political requirements which were deeply modern and oriented towards the nation state. These changes of the 1920s, however, are part of a tradition going back to the nineteenth century of constructing and formulating Hindu identity on the basis of an examination of Western modernism.[45] The concept of Hinduism itself was the product, on the one hand, of the academic discourse of Western orientalists and, on the other hand, of Indian reformers of the time[46] who refashioned the portrayal by Europeans into a self-portrayal and thus mediated between the external image of India and the internal Hindu-Brahmanic tradition. The result was an ideologically argued out and a politically staged Hindu renaissance which

included a pronounced anti-Western bias. The usefulness and purposefulness of these new ideas was tested and evaluated with regard to their viability. It was by no means simply an uncritical, mechanical transfer of progressive ideas from the West, but rather a process of conflict and demarcation, of selection and adaptation of progressive ideas to the Indian situation in tune with the social character and the political-ideological attitude of those social forces that were confronted with the new ideas. The thoughts absorbed from the West were often mixed with religiously tinged nationalist, traditional and utopian ideas.[47]

The idea of conversion in the framework of nationalist paradigms is also a direct ideological outcome of these developments. For this, the Arya Samaj evidently borrowed from the monotheistic religions of the Near East and combined their religious and dogmatic profile with the requirements of modern nation-building. This 'semitization'[48] of Hinduism was closely linked with the construction of an acute threat to Hinduism from these very religions and it was also the primary motive for the imitational strategy of the Hindu reform movements. With this, the extreme plurality and fragmentation of the Hindu religious and social structure was sought to be more closely defined, first and foremost, as non-Muslim and non-Christian; it was adapted to the conditions of modern nation-building through canonization and dogmatic clarity and thus refashioned for political requirements.

The outcome of the Shuddhi movement is not that Hindus and Muslims are characterized by a fixed and quasi-organic cultural continuity[49] but rather the introduction of a modern national identity through an act of volition and through cultural appropriation in the field of religion—a hitherto unknown aspect, at least in Hinduism. 'Organized Hinduism' thus became the analogy and cultural objective of an Indian nationalism[50] which, in the name of a religiously defined homogeneity, declared the minorities to be a problem that was 'solved' in the course of the 1920s and even the 1930s with increasing determination and radicalism. Although at the beginning of the Shuddhi movement the unity of Hindus and Muslims in an independent nation had constituted the goal and the basis for religious armament, the protagonists of the movement increasingly distanced themselves from this political utopia and struggled to realize the concept of an independent state that demanded the complete and uncompromising cultural as well as religious subjugation of the minorities or, conversely, the Partition of the subcontinent in order to grant the Hindus their right to supremacy over the 'invaders' and the 'apostates'.

NOTES

1. For details see Ashraf, 1985; Hasan, 1985 and Minault, 1982.
2. Cf. for this Pannikar, 2001, Chap. 1.
3. Article by Mahatma Hansraj in *The Tribune* (23.10.1921).
4. *TOI* (Calicut, 7.9.1921).

5. Telegram from the provincial government in Madras to the home ministry in Delhi dated 10.11.1921, reproduced in full in HDP (1921/241-XII: 'Questions and Answers in Parliament Regarding the Number of Forcible Conversions of Hindus by Moplahs'/6).
6. For a summary of the controversy about the exact number of Hindus forcibly converted see also Sharma, 1941, pp. 197f.
7. *TOI* (Calicut, 7.9.1921).
8. Cf. HDP (1921/241, I-A: Moplah disturbances in Malabar/ Appendix III: 52-4). See also HP (1922/241-XIV/39).
9. Gode/Karve, 1959, column 1560f.
10. Monier-Williams, 1899, p. 1082; for the different, historically substantiated meanings see also Gode/Karve, 1959, column 1561.
11. Madan, 2001, p. 58. This study also gives an insight into the larger and more general principles of Hindu life, in whose rich cultural landscape concepts of purity probably play the most important role. Cf. esp. pp. 48-71.
12. Cf. Sharma, 1941, p. 211.
13. These early forms are discussed first-hand by Lajpat Rai, 1992, pp. 120f; in secondary form by Jordens, 1991, pp. 218-21; Jones, 1976, pp. 126f, 132-5; Ghai, 1990, pp. 44-9; Zavos, 2000, pp. 88-92.
14. I.e. donations of money.
15. Shraddhanand in Jambunathan, 1961, p. 111.
16. For the specific context which gave rise to these resolutions see the report of the then District Superintendent of Police, R.H. Hitchcock, 1983, p. 162 of 1925.
17. *West Coast Spectator* of 22 August 1922, cited from Nair, 1923, p. 117. This source represents the report of the Deputy Collector of Calicut, Malabar, who had already retired by then.
18. *Kalima'* are prayers from the Koran which contain the central articles of faith of Islam and which represent a creed. The resolution thus responds to the methods of conversion used by the Muslims in the Malabar. A report of 1921 states: 'For a man—bath, clean shave of the head, wearing a Moplah cap and dress, recitation of prayers from Koran called *Kalima*; then dinner with Moplahs, circumcision to be performed on a convenient date. For a woman—bath, wearing Moplah women's

jackets and coloured clothes: recitation of *Kalima*, food. Ears to be bored around the ear-flaps at convenient date' Gopalan, 1921 cited in Graham (1943): 508, footnote 1.

19. Widely recognized local dress of the Muslim Moplahs.
20. Literally 'five products of the cow', i.e. milk, ghee (clarified butter), yoghurt, urine and dung. These were supposed to be taken in the manner prescribed. From this one can historically presume that re-conversion was never gifted to any person.
21. Names of two important Hindu deities.
22. I.e. the family priest or the local priests.
23. Cf. *CWMG* (1966/XXI/204) as also Gandhi in *Harijan* on 25.9.1937 in *CWMG* (1976/LXVI/163f); in *Young India* (10.3.1927) and (17.3.1927), cited in Gandhi, 1942, pp. 262f and 267f; also *CWMG* (1966/XXI/203f) and ibid. (1967/XXIV/149).
24. Nair, 1923, p. 118.
25. Nair, 1923, p. 120.
26. *Mantras* are formulatories of prayer 'which produce a momentary transcendental reference in the context of worship'; Stietencron, 2001, p. 110.
27. Cf. Graham, 1943, p. 515.
28. Kane, 1968, p. 282.
29. Muriel Lester in 'My Host the Hindu', pp. 75-80, cited in Graham, 1943, p. 504.
30. Cf. for example, *The Leader* (11.3.1923): The report about the re-conversion in Agra states that the ceremony ended with a large *sahbhoj* (community meal) which had been prepared earlier by the wives and daughters of the reconverted *Chohans* (Rajputs), was served by them and was accepted and eaten by all; also *The Leader* (30.5.1923), *The Tribune* (7 and 14.10.1923), etc.
31. Cf. for example, Saraswati, 1915, Chap. 1 about the infallibility and the absolute wisdom of the Vedas, or his comparison of the dogmas of Hinduism with those of Christianity and Islam in the third edition of 1927, Chapters 13 and 14, concluding with the statement about the superiority of the Vedas.
32. Cf. the earlier mentioned efforts of the Arya Samaj to identify its dogma of self-definition in ten principles which also contain religious elements. For this see Chamupati, n.d., especially points 1-6.

33. *The Tribune* (23.5.1923), cf. also ibid. (24.5.1923).
34. *The Leader* (18.5.1923). Pandey 1993 offers a good overview of the historical attempts of Hindu nationalism to solve the question of identity with the help of different cultural yardsticks.
35. Cf. the extensively documented ceremony of the Arya Samaj in: Seunarine, 1977, pp. 45-8, here p. 46.
36. In the Indian context this term does not refer to capitalist entrepreneurs as in Europe, but to a class which is characterized by its position in the administration, by land ownership and access to higher education. This class comprised almost exclusively of families of the higher castes. As such, this colonial middle class was itself a product of colonial rule and was created by the British in their administrative self-interest. Cf. for this Misra, 1961, pp. 305f and Frankel, 1988, pp. 225-8.
37. Rothermund, 1970, Chap. 9.
38. Gopal, 1966, p. 424.
39. HDP (1923/25/42). This document also shows that by 1923 already there was a drop in this trend towards expansion by the Congress. The trend was obviously closely linked with Gandhi's mobilization campaign.
40. Cf. also Zavos, 2000, pp. 11f.
41. This assessment is also supported, on the basis of available data, by the social origins of the members of the Hindu Mahasabha or that of their candidates for the elections in 1926. Details of this in Gordon, 1975, pp. 197f. who emphasizes that the Mahasabha consisted mainly of high caste landowners and Brahmins of the urban middle class.
42. Cf. Graham, 1943, pp. 433-5; Seunarine, 1977, Chap. VI; Jordens, 1991, p. 225; Ghai, 1990, p. 121, etc.
43. Cf. for this also Sarkar, 1998a, esp. pp. 389f for the 1920s and 1930s, but also for the relationship between Hinduism and caste-reform in general in modern India.
44. Lévy, 1995, esp. part 2, attempts a philosophical approach to the connection between politics and the concept of purity on the basis of various examples ranging from Cambodia to the former Yugoslavia.
45. In his essay on the role of religion in the nationalist discourse of the nineteenth century van der Veer, 2001, Chap. 2, not only emphasizes that anti-colonialism and the pronounced use of

religion was not only a cultural questioning of British hegemony, but that the function of religion also consisted in its effectiveness as an element of the public sphere. The partly reformed entities of religious authority and its infrastructure served as structural prerequisites of nationalistic activism and thus established a quasi-organic symbiosis between modern nation-building and the traditional social order. See esp. pp. 41ff.

46. On the process of construction by Hindu reformers in the nineteenth century see Frykenberg, 1989, esp. pp. 30ff.
47. Krüger, 1989, p. 85.
48. Jaffrelot, 1999, p. 147.
49. Cf. for example Gauri Vishwanathan, 1998, p. 161.
50. Gold, 1991, esp. pp. 533ff examines the different approaches towards the constitution of an 'organized Hinduism' (Sangathan).

CHAPTER 5

Religion as a Strategy of Mobilization in Democratic India

In November 1949 India's constituent assembly adopted the Constitution of the new republic of India and thus set the country on the course of democracy which it has largely followed till now and which can be termed a success. There was only a temporary suspension of democratic norms during the 18-month period of Emergency declared by Indira Gandhi in 1975, and during this period governance was carried out through special powers independent of the normal, democratic political processes. However, even this state of emergency was based on the Constitution and allowed for legal mechanisms. Thus, one can speak of uninterrupted constitutional continuity in India since 1950 when the Constitution came into effect. The subject of the relationship between religion and politics in India will, therefore, also have to deal with the specificities of India as a democracy since these determine the character of political conflicts and the contest for power.

The selected examples mainly illustrate the political and religious strategies of a party which was formed in 1980 and which, in the period from its formation till 1998, recorded an unparalleled rise from a marginal political force to the ruling party: the Bharatiya Janata Party (BJP). What is particularly interesting about this phenomenal success is that it happened with the help of mobilizing tactics that were heavily dependent on religious and nationalist rhetoric, although the available empirical data shows that this was not the only reason for the success of the BJP. In the short-term, however, and in very specific instances, these strategies of mobilization contributed decisively to the identity formation of this new party which was then able to create its own distinctive political profile and also develop its organizational structures which form the backbone of the party even today.

The BJP constantly changed its strategies of mobilization in keeping with political requirements. At the beginning, these strategies were in the nature of protests from a party in the opposition, but in the spring of 1998 the strategies served to consolidate power after the party took over the government. In what follows, an attempt will be made to trace this development beginning from 1989, which represents an important turning-point, and ending with the events surrounding the nuclear tests which was one of the first official acts of the BJP government.

RELIGIOUS RITUALS AS DEMOCRATIC OPPOSITION: THE AYODHYA CONFLICT

The year 1989 marked a turning point in Indian politics when the BJP moved closer to the two most important Hindu-nationalist organizations, the Vishva Hindu Parishad, World Hindu Association (VHP) and the Rashtriya Swayamsevak Sangh, National Corps of Volunteers (RSS) and thus paved the way for a successful organizational coalition which would finally bring the BJP into power. In January 1989 the VHP began preparations for a large, public mobilization in order to give voice to its agenda for the formation of a Hindu nation. The angle for all religious-nationalistic actions in the subsequent years was the conflict surrounding Ayodhya, the legendary birth-place of the divine King Rama. In 1526 the Muslim ruler Babur, in order to demonstrate his worldly triumph in a sacral framework, had had a mosque built on the place where a temple had earlier marked the supposed place of Rama's birth (Ram Janmabhoomi). The VHP and the RSS took up this conflict that had its roots in the nineteenth century and staged several Hindu-nationalistic protests around this Hindu-Muslim conflict. In December 1992 they succeeded in destroying the mosque and this led to communal riots in the entire country.[1] It was not just a political event, but it was represented as a struggle for religious survival of the Hindus.[2]

At the Kumbh Mela in Allahabad, a Hindu festival in which more than a million people participate, the VHP and the committee set-up to liberate the Ram Janmabhoomi announced that a nation-wide campaign to lay the foundation of a Rama temple would begin that very year which would focus attention on the problem:

> In the past no serious efforts were undertaken to organise Hindus throughout the country. Representatives of the [Ram Janmabhoomi Mukti Yagna] samiti[3] and the [Vishva Hindu] *parishad* will traverse the entire nation in order to organise the Hindus. The liberation of Ram's birth-place will become the main theme of the elections.[4]

As had happened in 1984, the action would coincide with elections to parliament at the end of 1989 in order to ensure a wide reach for the campaign and for the ideological concerns of the VHP and the RSS.

At this point of time the BJP was engaged in maintaining a balance between its ideological and organizational closeness to radical organizations on the one hand, and its cautious tactical cooperation with V.P. Singh, a former Congress minister who had left the party to set-up a third front of secular and pro-minority groups, and who was pushing for an alliance with the BJP. In February L.K. Advani, the then president of the BJP, rejected the possibility mooted by Singh to form an organizational alliance for the forthcoming elections in order to defeat the Congress party. Advani emphasized what were for him important programmatic differences, but he left the question of a strategic partnership open.[5] Given the forthcoming elections the RSS also increased pressure on the BJP to come out with a comprehensive statement on the political situation which would also talk about the formation of an explicitly Hindu party.[6]

In the characteristic division of work at the head of the party between moderates and radicals, the leader at second position in the BJP, Atal Behari Vajpayee, then decided to force the subject of Ayodhya within the party. During the birthday celebrations of the

RSS-founder, Vajpayee argued for 'reclaiming' the Ram Janmabhoomi and asked the Muslims to give up all claims to the mosque.[7] 'Ram was born centuries before Babar and Ram and Krishna were Hindu gods, therefore Hindus were the rightful claimant of the site',[8] he thundered, pointing in the direction of the Muslim opposition and the Congress.

In March, Advani had already given the first indication of a possible political cooperation between the BJP and the RSS, but the decision was postponed initially till September.[9] In June, however, the national executive committee of the BJP met in Palampur in Himachal Pradesh and confirmed the coalition with the Shiv Sena in Maharashtra for the forthcoming elections.[10] The issue of Rama's birth-place was reflected as an independent point in the resolutions.[11] It was cynical of Vajpayee to assert that the BJP did not want to make the Ram Janmabhoomi an election issue unless the government did not permit the foundation stone of the temple to be laid and the temple to be subsequently built in Ayodhya at the Ram Janmabhoomi.[12] By June the party took on the Ayodhya controversy in a concerted manner and tried to gain a profile as a Hindu party, although it occasionally backed down from this position for tactical reasons.

In June, Moropant Pingle, a long-serving and organizationally competent member of the RSS, presented concrete details of the forthcoming mass-based actions. Sanctified bricks were to be distributed from 30 September onwards in more than 400,000 villages and cities where they would be worshipped before being taken to Ayodhya for the construction of the temple. The ceremony for laying the foundation stone would be conducted on 9 November.[13] The VHP chose this time for conducting the campaign to coincide with the *Utthan Ekadasi* festival in November at which Hindus in Uttar Pradesh, especially in the region around Ayodhya, celebrate the awakening of the gods after a nine-month's sleep to remove injustices among humans.[14]

Ashok Singhal, the general-secretary of the VHP, let it be known long before the start of the campaign that his organization aimed at collecting about 5,00,000 bricks by 9 November and that preparations were in full swing.[15] Beginning from July bricks were fired in different parts of India bearing the inscription 'Shri Ram' (Lord Rama) and, following the instructions of the VHP, Ganges-water was used along with normal water to mix the clay.[16] According to a senior functionary of the VHP, 10,000 volunteers 'who would be prepared to make any sacrifice, would guard the *Shilanyas*[17] ceremony of the temple.'[18]

Secular political forces like the Congress, especially Home Minister Buta Singh,[19] or V.P. Singh's Janata Dal pleaded that the decision about the fate of the Ram Janmabhoomi should be left to the judiciary. This was, however, rejected by the participants of the campaign who stated that the matter lay outside the jurisdiction of the courts.

The background for these political warnings was a decision of the Uttar Pradesh High Court in July to set-up a special committee to look into the release of the Babri mosque land for laying the foundation stone of the temple.[20] Ashok Singhal, however, rejected the idea of abiding by court decisions as 'gratuitous'[21] and Advani reiterated this:

A court can decide peripheral issues [*sic*] of title, of ownership, of possession etc. But it cannot adjudicate as to whether Emperor Babar did actually invade Ayodhya, destroy the temple and erect a mosque in its place, and if so, what should be done in that regard. As a matter of fact, these pertinent questions are not at all before the court.[22]

The RSS also protested against bringing in the courts and argued that in an earlier Muslim (Shah Bano) case regarding payment of maintenance the government had also annulled a decision of the courts and corrected it on religious grounds. In a resolution the organization once again pointed out that the Ayodhya-issue was a matter of national significance:

It is but proper, therefore, that all our patriotic people regard it as their sacred duty to remove every sign of such wanton aggression and construct an imposing temple commensurate with their profound faith and devotion for Shri Ram.[23]

It is remarkable that the resolution speaks so openly about the destruction of the mosque. The VHP had refrained from making such statements and had generally left the fate of the mosque open while talking about the laying of the foundation stone and construction of the temple.[24]

In order to extend the reach of the *Ram Shila pujas*,[25] especially in rural areas for which the campaign had primarily been conceived,[26] the VHP used the strategy of openly involving religious authorities. Hindu priests, holy men and ascetics took charge of organizing the prayers. In contrast to earlier campaigns of this kind, the religious players now emerged openly and, in the framework of democratic events like elections, made open political statements without any reservations.[27] On the whole, more than 1,200 religious leaders took part in the campaign thus ensuring a suitably sacrosanct atmosphere.[28] The Shankaracharya of Shringeri, for example, an important Hindu religious leader, marked the commencement of the *Ram Shila pujas* by publicly worshipping the first brick with the inscription 'Shri Ram' in an elaborate religious ceremony before handing it over for worship to the other believers.[29] The campaign began in a synchronized manner throughout India on 30 September, when the bricks, as objects of worship, were taken to more than 500,000 villages and sold there for Rs.1.25. According to the plan, the bricks would to be collected again by mid-October in no less than 6,000 centres of the VHP from where they would be transported in lorries to Ayodhya to await the foundation-stone ceremony on 9 November. The ahistorical comment of the organizers was:

> This particular method was adopted to associate as many people of this country as possible with the reconstruction of Ram Janmabhoomi temple destroyed by Moghul invader Babar for the putting up of a mosque there and for the recovery of which Hindus have fought 76 battles in which lakhs of Hindus sacrificed their lives over four centuries.[30]

Even before the campaign began the BJP brought out its manifesto for the forthcoming elections mentioning primarily two important issues. The first one concerned questions of corruption and maladministration in the government, while the second issue was the 'liberation' of Rama's birth-place. This latter issue was, however, incorporated into other concerns such as the removal of Article 370 from the Constitution granting special status to Kashmir, or the abolishment of all acts of positive discrimination of religious minorities.[31] At the end of September Advani, pointing to the VHP and speaking on behalf of the party, said:

> But let everyone understand, friends and foes alike, that the BJP's stand on this is categoric and unequivocal. The Ram Janmabhoomi site must be handed over to Hindus and a temple must be constructed there.[32]

In Mumbai, the local units of the BJP openly supported the Shiv Sena in worshipping the bricks[33] and Vajpayee suggested—at the beginning of the campaign in Mumbai—that the mosque in Ayodhya be removed 'brick by brick' and reconstructed on a less controversial site.[34] Leading members of the parliament in Maharashtra took charge of organizing the rituals. G.B. Sardesai of the VHP in Mumbai also emphasized the fact that his organization had prepared a special pamphlet providing information about the correct procedures to be followed for the ceremony and requested the believers to follow these instructions faithfully in order to ensure the validity of the ritual.[35]

In this religiously charged atmosphere the Congress too tried to profit from the widespread sense of renewal and, especially, from the rural mobilization. In his inaugural campaign-speech in Faizabad, near Ayodhya, Prime Minister Rajiv Gandhi spoke of the imminent establishment of 'Ram Rajya', the rule of Rama, in India.[36] By using this concept from M.K. Gandhi's symbolic repertoire—which had, however, in the meantime become a loaded concept—Rajiv Gandhi tried to position his party, for all intents and purposes, in proximity to the VHP campaign. At the local level, particularly, Congress campaigners used the widespread hysteria about Rama to gain political capital and they used the direction given by their party president for resorting to a religious-political rhetoric even if they could not publicly support the worship of the 'sanctified' bricks.[37]

The BJP was strongly criticized by secular parties such as the Janata Dal for this general 'Hinduization' of political practice after October 1989.[38] The leadership of the BJP, however, continued its open cooperation with and its participation in the campaign.[39] In the meanwhile, Home Minister Buta Singh requested the VHP to come to New Delhi for confidential talks. As an outcome of these talks the VHP agreed to fully cooperate with the police and the army in the further organization of the campaign and also to carry out the ceremony for laying the foundation stone on 9 November outside the actual premises of the mosque in Ayodhya.[40] Two developments constituted the background of these initiatives on the part of the home minister. For one, the special senate of the High Court in Uttar Pradesh had already decided in August that the *status quo* was to be maintained, i.e. that no construction would take place on the fenced-in premises of the mosque. By agreeing to carry out the foundation-stone ceremony outside the mosque the VHP deviated from its earlier course of refusing to recognize the jurisdiction of the courts. For the other, there had been violent clashes between Hindus and Muslims in several places during the course of the campaign, and this would have provided the government with the excuse to use the police against any mass mobilization. Especially in many places in western India it was the public processions of Rama-devotees at the beginning of October and not the collecting and worshipping of bricks which provoked resistance from sections of the Muslim population. With slogans such as '*Saugandh Ram Ki Khate Hain/Hum Mandir Wahin Banayenge*' (We take an oath in Rama's name/We will build the temple there), '*Bachha Bachha Ram Ka/Janmabhoomi Ke Kam Ka*' (All children of Rama/Work for the Janmabhoomi temple!) or '*Chahe Pant Anek Hain/Hindu Hum Sab Ek Hain*' (Even though there are many sects/As Hindus we are all one) the participants in the *Rama Shila pujas* aroused the ire of the

Muslims, especially when this happened on a Friday and during prayer-times in the mosques.[41] By 6 October, 43 people had to be arrested in Jaipur and 12 wounded persons had been admitted to hospitals. The chief minister of Rajasthan (Congress) therefore mooted a ban on the *pujas* and declared that permission would have to be sought for each procession that was part of the campaign.[42] Violence also occurred in other states in northern India which, however, were locally contained.[43]

The VHP, on the other hand, confirmed its intention of continuing its programme of mobilization for Ayodhya,[44] even though processions had been banned or their routes severely limited, as for example in Bihar[45] and in the immediate vicinity of Ayodhya.[46] A few days before 9 November, the left-wing opposition of the communist parties and V.P. Singh's Janata Dal decided to stage a counter-event in Ayodhya under the banner of communal harmony in order to defy the symbolic regime of Hindu nationalism locally.[47]

In Ayodhya itself everything was geared towards the day when the foundation stone was to be laid. On 7 November, the court in Allahabad once again reiterated its position announced in August with regard to the foundation-stone ceremony and stressed that the decision taken at that time to maintain the *status quo* not only applied to the land on which the mosque stood, but also to the extended terrain around it which followers of the VHP, some of them armed, had now occupied in preparation for the ceremony.[48] A day later, however, the Home Ministry in Delhi issued a declaration stating that the area of VHP activity did not fall within the area demarcated by the court. The laying of the foundation-stone was thus declared to be legal on the condition that law and order were maintained.[49]

From 5 to 9 November five large trains with pilgrims brought the bricks from all over India to Ayodhya where they were unloaded on the piece of land directly in front of the mosque.[50] For several weeks pilgrims from the entire country had been arriving in Ayodhya and on 9 November, the police were expecting an influx of 4-5 lakh people.[51] In fact, the concluding rally in Ayodhya stretched out over two days. At 9.30 a.m. of 9 November the VHP, led by the VHP chief of Uttar Pradesh, Sirish Dixit, as well as by the all-India vice-president, Prasad Toshnival, began the rituals to consecrate the earth (*bhoomi puja*) in which the foundation of the temple was to be laid. These rites took place in a small area of just a few square metres which the VHP had cordoned off several days earlier, and only about 10,000 VHP and Bajrang Dal activists had taken up position in its immediate vicinity. For reasons of security the rest of the pilgrims could not be allowed in front of the mosque since the situation anyway, according to eye-witnesses, threatened to become chaotic.[52] Outside Ayodhya more than 25,000 people celebrated the traditional festival of the awakening of the gods, and in Faizabad the demonstration for communal harmony organized by the left parties, in which about 15,000 people took part, went off peacefully.

The main part of the ceremony for laying the foundation stone was continued only on 10 November, and its ritual arrangement is very interesting from a nationalist perspective. Beginning from 1.35 p.m., holy verses from the Hindu Vedas, from the *Adi Granth*, the holy book of the Sikhs, and from Buddhist scriptures were recited.[53] Accompanied by the almost hysterical screams of participants two bricks were placed in the earth by a man called Rameshwar Chopal after these had been blessed and worshipped by the vice-president of the VHP, Vijaya Raje Scindia.[54] Bricks from 18 countries, among them Bangladesh and Pakistan, were also included in the ceremony in order to demonstrate the international alignment of the Hindu community.[55] It was also significant that the main protagonist, Chopal, was an outcaste from Bihar.[56] This served as an indication that the VHP rejected the discrimination of this segment of Hindu society in the name of religious-nationalist integration.

The comments and interpretations of this event by the participants themselves give us an insight into the significance of the example of performative nation-building that was staged here. In his speech Ashok Singhal, the international president of the VHP, tried to point out the importance of the laying of this foundation stone for India as a nation.[57] The ceremony to lay the foundation of the temple, he said, marked the end of a 450-year history of the stigma of foreign domination in India, especially the domination over the most important symbols of national honour and freedom. 'It is a great leap forward in the onward march of all-round Hindu renaissance', he said, which, like a wave, was washing over the entire country. 'It was a powerful expression of the eternal Hindu spirit that Bharat shall once again resurrect herself as a glorious Hindu Rashtra shedding her benign cultural and spiritual fragrance all over the world.' The moment, he said, was undoubtedly one of national achievement but, he continued, it should not induce rapture or complacency. It was, rather, a moment of self-examination and preparation for the completion of the hitherto incomplete mission of 'our national renaissance' in general and the construction of the historical shrine in particular. Ashok Singhal's speech, and this was also the basic idea behind the laying of the foundation stone, emphasized nothing less than a new actionist and ideological foundation of the nation. It was evident in Singhal's grand rhetoric that along with the foundation stone of the temple he was also trying to lay a new foundation for India and its collective self-understanding. In an analogy to Nehru's famous speech at midnight on 15 August 1947 Singhal stressed the dawn of new ideals and national freedom. Nehru had said:

> At the stroke of the midnight hour, when the world sleeps, India will awake to life and freedom. A moment comes, which comes but rarely in history, when we step out from the old to the new, when an age ends, and when the soul of a nation, long suppressed, finds utterance. . . . At the dawn of history India started on her unending quest, and trackless centuries are filled with her striving and the grandeur of her successes and failures. Through good and ill fortune alike she has never lost sight of that quest or forgotten the ideals which gave her strength. We end today a period of ill fortune and India discovers herself again.[58]

Singhal, on the other hand, emphasized the end of 450 years of oppression and meant the Mughal period of India's Muslim rulers.

But even he spoke of India as a nation in the quest for new ideals and of its new self-discovery, albeit of a completely different kind, namely as 'Hindu-rule (*Hindu Rashtra*)'. Singhal also warned against arrogance and exhorted his followers to pursue the necessary goals consistently and to bring the Hindu-nationalist mission to its completion so that it may radiate out into the world. Nehru, in comparison, had said in 1947:

> Freedom and power brings responsibility.... That future is not one of ease and resting but of incessant striving so that we might fulfil the pledges we have so often taken and the one we shall take today ... and so we have to labour and work hard to give reality to our dreams. Those dreams are for India, but they are also for the world, for all the nations and peoples are too closely knit together today for anyone of them to imagine that it can live apart.[59]

The pressing problems of poverty and underdevelopment were what caused Nehru to call for hard work. When Ashok Singhal asked his followers to get down to work he was more concerned with making India a Hindu nation and organizing politics according to the principles of Hindu nationalism.

H.V. Seshadri, one of the most important ideologues of the RSS, also called the laying of the foundation stone the 'resurrection of Hindu rule' and he pointed out that since the Khilafat movement the Hindus had to accept one setback after the other. With the help of the RSS and the VHP, he stated, the Hindus had understood that their fate lay in their own hands and that the awakening of the nation had now become reality. The ceremony in Ayodhya

> indeed portends a marked and significant turn in our national situation. It is also evident that the new turn will prove to be not only as a corrective to the self-deluding and self-destructive trend of the last several decades but also an affirmation of the Nation's resolve to stand up effulgent in the light of its pristine cultural heritage illuminating up every single sphere of its life with that inspiring vision.[60]

Balasaheb Deoras, the RSS chief, was even more unequivocal with regard to the establishment of a new Indian nation:

Even though we attained independence in 1947, we are as yet in the process of securing cultural and ideological independence. The restoration of Ramjanmasthan is symbolic for the re-establishment of our national pride just as the reconstruction of the Somnath temple was. . . . I wish the Samiti all success in its endeavours to construct the temple of the National Hero who signifies the unity and integrity of this country.[61]

The basic patterns in these dubious comments are already well known. The Muslims are portrayed along with the British as occupiers of the country, a model set out by orientalist historiography of the nineteenth century and later taken over by the religious-nationalist reform movements.[62] This model, however, suggests a little too easily that the original India, on the one hand, and modern, free India on the other are Hindu-dominated and that the country has freed itself from the chains of Muslim rule. The second pattern concerns the self-perception of Hindu society sketched out therein as a collective in which all Hindus are included. In a manner that is also familiar Hindus are portrayed as victims of history who have suffered a long stretch of oppression and religious as well as national domination.[63] The assumed role of the victim serves to legitimize the aggressive 'renaissance' of the Hindus which is meant to lead the nation back to its roots and the original essence of its being.[64] The pilgrimage of the bricks was the performative translation of this programme which—at least in the short-term—gave its protagonists and their concerns an undeniable position of dominance even in the political field. The ruling Congress party, here in the person of Home Minister Buta Singh, not only allowed the foundation-laying ceremony to take place, but in doing so it also contradicted decisions of the court and thus undermined its authority which had already been questioned by the refusal of the VHP to accept these decisions.[65] Rajiv Gandhi, for his part, tried to profit from the general hysteria about Rama's birth-place with references to Rama Rajya and by seeking the official blessings of Hindu *gurus*. This strategy would prove to be a miscalculation of voter's sympathies and, especially, of the BJP's strength.

The election results in November were clear. The most striking aspect of these results was the increase in seats for the BJP which was only overshadowed by the rise of the Janata Dal. Having gained almost 11.5 per cent (previously 7.4 per cent) of the votes, the BJP got 85 seats (previously 2) in the Lok Sabha (the Lower House), the Congress received 39.5 per cent of the votes (previously 48.1 per cent) and thus 197 (previously 415) seats, while the Janata Dal under V.P. Singh got 17.7 per cent of the votes (previously 6.7 per cent) and 143 seats (previously 10).[66] The very thing that the BJP had expected before the elections and which should have been cause for concern thus occurred: the electoral agreements with the Janata Dal had led to its rise, but its Hindu-image had not been sufficient to present itself as an alternative to the Congress in the place of the Left parties. A closer look at the results in the federal states shows that in the core areas the strategy of 'Hindu-rule' centred around the Ayodhya issue had not brought about the expected results. In Uttar Pradesh, which sent 85 members to the Lok Sabha in Delhi, the BJP got a modest 7.6 per cent of the votes, falling far short of its expectations. In Maharashtra,[67] however, the party performed much better with 23.7 per cent of the votes, and in its later strongholds in Rajasthan, Madhya Pradesh, Gujarat and Himachal Pradesh the party managed a breakthrough with 29.6, 39.7, 30.4 and 45.3 per cent respectively.[68] In the most important state, however, in Uttar Pradesh, the BJP was able to establish itself only in 1991, and its failure to do so in 1989 was a marked impediment.[69] Despite this, the party had taken a decisive step forward and it succeeded in carving out its profile in the context of the crisis in the INC.[70] Looking back, the elections in 1989 were the decisive event which not only provided a motivational support but, even in social terms, represented the point of departure for the party's rise. The ritual politics appealed especially to high-caste Hindu voters who made the significant growth of the BJP in north and west India possible, and this trend continued in the elections of 1991.[71] By gaining the support of the highest castes the BJP had won back its most important political constituency which could now be used to attract other segments of the electorate, again with the help of performative strategies. This time around, however, the BJP no longer stood on the sidelines of the VHP, but it became the director and the main protagonist of an action-based religious and cultural nationalism. This meant that the campaigns had to be transformed in accordance with political necessities. L.K. Advani, who was still the president of the BJP in 1989, proved to be eminently suitable for this difficult but publicly effective task.

POLITICS AS MYTHOLOGY: ADVANI'S RATH YATRA

The government that was formed at the beginning of 1990 under Prime Minister V.P. Singh was an extremely fragile coalition which brought together not only ideologically heterogeneous parties, but also very diverse political programmes. The immediate common goal of overthrowing the Congress was the only programmatic bond that was strong enough to temporarily bridge the extreme contradictions between the coalition partners.

BJP president Advani decided to follow a two-pronged strategy. While extending support to the government, on the one hand, he also tried, on the other, to give his party a sharper Hindu profile under the banner of nationalism. Immediately after the new government had been sworn in, the VHP declared that it would continue its campaign for building the temple at the Ram Janmabhoomi in Ayodhya[72] and in a ninety-minute meeting with Prime Minister V.P. Singh the leaders of the organization warned him against any interference in these 'matters of religion'.[73] At this point of time, in the summer of 1990, the VHP's concern was certainly justified since the course set out by the prime minister was explicitly against the formation of a united Hindu society in order to ensure the political career of his party beyond the short-term success in the elections of 1989. In June, Advani announced in an interview to the RSS-magazine *Panchjanya* for the first time that a new mass campaign would be organized in case the government continued to hinder the plans of the VHP and prevent the building of a Rama-temple in

Ayodhya.[74] The representatives of Indian Muslims called on Advani to cooperate with the VHP which, in the meantime, had announced that the construction of the temple would begin on 30 October of the same year. It was, they reiterated, the duty of the Muslims to respect the 'strong feelings of the Hindu majority' and to agree to a possible re-location of the mosque to another, nearby place.[75] At the same time Advani attacked the government for its inaction in Kashmir and criticized the systematic eviction of Hindus from the valley. The government, he claimed, was concentrating too much on the religious minorities and was neglecting the obvious threats to the Hindus. Almost 95 per cent of the Hindus, he further stated, had already been forced to leave the valley and live in camps in Jammu under unacceptable conditions.[76]

On 12 September, Advani announced that he would undertake a 10,000-km long pilgrimage through the north Indian states 'to mobilise public opinion and canvass support for the BJP's point of view on the Ram Janmabhoomi'.[77] The journey was to begin on 25 September and end on 30 October in Ayodhya, the day the VHP was to begin the construction of the temple.[78] These dates were significant and had been carefully chosen by Advani. In a speech to the Upper House in 1989 Advani had already explained at length that besides Ayodhya, Somnath was also a national shrine where—after Independence—the government under the leadership of V. Patel had used state funds to rebuild a Hindu temple which, like hundred others, had been a victim of Islamic invasion.[79] Advani based his concept of a secular state on this, namely:

> A secular state is not an irreligious state . . . secularism does not mean disowning our past history or heritage or culture. . . . Yes, it may be essentially Hindu but it is Indian history, Indian culture and Indian heritage.[80]

Similarly, Advani felt that the state should take on the responsibility for re-building this 'national heritage' in Ayodhya or, at least, not prevent the VHP from carrying out this task. Somnath, therefore, was to be the starting-point of his Rath Yatra, the pilgrimage with the war-chariot, in order to further instil Hinduism in the collective consciousness of the nation and to gather it around the holy places.

The BJP's association with the government was thus fundamentally called into question. Although Advani emphasized in the press conference on 12 September that the BJP would continue to honour its agreements with V.P. Singh and that it was also in the party's interest to have the government complete its term in office,[81] the beginning of the Rath Yatra was interpreted in RSS circles as the beginning of the end of the government.[82] The Yatra essentially offered Advani two kinds of advantages. Firstly, if, from a BJP-perspective, the government remained un-cooperative it gave the party a welcome excuse to overthrow it and, secondly, the long-term enterprise of constructing a distinct identity for the BJP could be carried out in order to reap political profits in the next elections.

While Advani was carrying out his preparations, the VHP also began to get its cadres ready for the imminent confrontation with the government. In June itself the *Dharma Sansad* of the VHP, the parliament of religious authorities, met in Haridwar and formed the Shri Ram Kar Seva Samiti[83] that was meant to coordinate and guide the construction of the temple.[84] On 1 September, the VHP-Committee for the Liberation of Rama's birth-place' began to distribute 'Rama-lamps' in Ayodhya and subsequently in the entire country as traditional Diwali oil-lamps which are lit in every house at this time. In this way the VHP wanted to clearly mark the start of the third large campaign in the name of Rama.[85] In addition, more than 250,000 volunteers of the organization were expected to arrive in Ayodhya by 30 October in order to participate in the ceremony to mark the beginning of construction.[86] For the VHP the beginning of construction itself was an incontrovertible fact that had to be staged at the time announced and it was not going to brook any delay in this matter.

During a three-day internal party meeting in mid-September in Bhopal the BJP once again reiterated its 'disappointment' with the Janata Dal government. At the same time, however, Vajpayee emphasized that the only reason for not withdrawing their support to the government and thereby causing its premature end was the possible public reaction to this de-stabilization which could adversely affect the BJP.[87] Accordingly, Advani's Rath Yatra was also understood as an attempt to create a suitable and sufficiently emotional reason for such a move against the government so that the BJP's position could be further strengthened in the ensuing elections and it could become the new ruling party. At this meeting the party cadres at all levels were mobilized to ensure their commitment to the campaign. Prior to the campaign, however, Vajpayee, the future prime minister, denied all political and electoral intentions: 'Our decisions on all issues, including the temple, have been totally delinked from the vote. For us the temple issue is linked with national pride.'[88]

The visual arrangement of Advani's 'war-chariot' is interesting with regard to political rituals. An eye-witness, who saw the chariot entering south Delhi on 15 October, describes his impressions in the following manner:

> The chariot was an extended DCM-Toyota van redecorated as a strange looking chariot. On the sides of the truck, sweeping cut-out patterns rose up to provide a small roofed space above and behind the driver's cabin. On the raised platform behind the driver stood five men, with L.K. Advani . . . standing centremost and addressing the crowd through loudspeakers mounted on the roof of the driver's cab and atop the rear cabin.[89]

The two sides of the Toyota were decorated with two large lotus flowers, the party symbol of the BJP which is also found on the ballot papers to enable illiterate voters to recognize the candidate.[90] The design of the motorized chariot recaptured Arjuna's chariot (*rath*) from the *Bhagavad Gita* and resembled the chariot from the popular TV serial on the *Mahabharata* which, a few years earlier, had brought this mythological story to Indian houses every Sunday and had contributed decisively to a further popularization of the stories surrounding Krishna and Rama.[91] The person responsible for producing Advani's chariot, Shanti Dev, a well-known, commercially successful artist and a BJP-follower from Mumbai, used the collective memory of the TV serial and constructed visual analogies to this in order to place Advani in the corresponding mythological framework.[92] The reproduction of this event of performative nation building was ensured with the help of a video shoot along the entire route of the Yatra and this video production was also used in the elections of 1991. The result of these efforts was a perfectly staged and organized campaign, arrangements for which resembled an election campaign, even though it was not explicitly political. The borders between politics, religion and mythology were very cleverly diffused in Advani's Rath Yatra and it allowed the BJP to appear apolitical while translating the story of Rama into the political imagination.[93] Therefore, the intention of this campaign was by no means, as Advani tried to emphasize, the avoidance of all forms of theatricality,[94] rather theatricality became the primary medium and content of politics since it made nationalism, as it was understood by the BJP, attractive and tangible.

Accompanied by a large crowd from the local population and an impressive contingent drawn from participating organizations like the BJP itself, the VHP, the Bajrang Dal and the youth-organizations of the party, Advani began his journey on 25 September 1990 in Somnath. Witnessed by an audience of about 20,000 people Advani and his wife Kamala visited the famous temple of Somnath, invoked the blessings of the gods and carried out, visible to all, a ritual in which they made an offering of 101 lotus flowers and coconuts to the Shiva-lingam. The religious act was followed by a political one, namely paying obeisance to the statues of Deen Dayal Upadhyaya, whose birth anniversary was being celebrated, and Vallabhbhai Patel, on whose initiative the Somnath temple had been rebuilt.[95] Representatives of tribal groups presented Advani with a bow and arrow, the traditional weapons of Rama; the priests of the temple gave him a saffron flag, while the Gohil Samaj, a Kshatriya organization, gifted a sword to the BJP president. Pramod Mahajan, an important BJP politician, remarked on these obvious military gestures at the beginning of the yatra: 'If we are to use all the weapons presented to us, we can liberate the Ram Janmabhoomi in a day. But in a democracy the most powerful weapon is the mass awakening. And it is for this that the Rath Yatra has been undertaken.'[96] In his speech Advani also emphasized that the Yatra was being undertaken as a 'crusade for the strengthening of national unity' and 'for the promotion of nationalism in this country'.[97] He stated further: 'We want to restore the pride of this country by building the temple in Ayodhya, an act which would represent the second nationalist renaissance after independence.'[98] Therefore, according to Advani, it was not in the interests of the Yatra to create unrest and discord between Hindus and Muslims. He also remarked that he had wanted to underscore this fact by choosing a young Muslim man called Jahil to drive his 'chariot'.[99]

Certain fundamental characteristics of the Yatra became evident during its first phase in Gujarat, and these images accompanied the journey through north India. Wherever the procession halted, the local population, encouraged by the Bajrang Dal and the VHP, presented Advani with traditional weapons like tridents, swords, bows and arrows or machetes.[100] Slogans that were familiar from the *Ram Shilas* (Ram-bricks) campaign and the militant speeches of Vijaya Raje Scindia[101] were instrumental in creating a charged atmosphere along the route of the Yatra. The resonance from the people living along the route was initially very satisfying for the organizers who were very pleased when they were greeted in Ahmedabad by 50,000 people along with all 10 BJP ministers in the state government.[102] Critical voices were, however, heard from the coalition partner in this state, the Janata Dal minister Karamshibhai Makwana complained that the BJP was misusing state property and government infrastructure, such as jeeps, to carry out the Yatra. The police were also unhappy with weapons being displayed so openly in such a sensitive region and felt that these were not effective means of carrying out political propaganda. They stated that Gujarat had seen far too much communal violence and that they could not fulfil their responsibility of ensuring peace between the religious communities when leading politicians were contributing publicly to a militarization of the situation.[103]

The throngs of people witnessing the Yatra, however, continued. Even in the smaller cities that Advani visited in the beginning like Chotila, Nadiad, Anand, Karamsed, Baroda and Fazalpur[104] local party cadres along with those of the VHP and the Bajrang Dal ensured that the BJP president was met by an ever-increasing crowd of onlookers who were following the programme of the Yatra with great interest. Fireworks, traditional dances of the local population and ritual offerings, carried out at the Toyota-'chariot', made for a political spectacle which found a good echo and, generally, enthusiastic assent in the local print media.[105]

Encouraged by the positive resonance to his undertaking Advani used a sharper tone against the government in New Delhi. In Baroda he stated that it was very possible that the BJP would withdraw its support to the government far earlier than expected. On the other hand, however, Advani ruled out the possibility of forming an alternative government with the Congress. This meant that any such political step taken by the BJP would result in new elections.[106] In an interview with the *Organiser* Advani once again stated that the aim of his undertaking was to educate people about the vandalism of foreign invaders and that the national integration of all Hindus would have to be promoted and supported.[107] The actions of the prime minister, he continued, would only encourage separatism among the Muslims and would endanger national unity.

The first high-point of the Yatra, the stop in Mumbai, was organized in close cooperation with the Shiv Sena. Witnessed by a large crowd of onlookers Advani's 'chariot' entered the metropolis on 30 September. In front of the Shiv Sena Bhavan, the headquarters of the party, Advani and the Shiv Sena chief, Balasaheb Thackeray, faced an enthusiastic crowd of thousands of people. In his usual manner Thackeray first gave an aggressive speech saying that all those who were against the shifting of the mosque in Ayodhya, i.e. mainly the Muslims, did not deserve a place in this country. He then told Advani to remove the small green stripe from the BJP flag and make it entirely saffron.[108] Advani was then somewhat more reserved but yet unequivocal. The 'pandering' to religious minorities in the country and the resultant weakening of Indian nationalism in the last 40 years would have to stop, he stated. In contrast to earlier times, leading politicians of the country, he said, were afraid to speak on behalf of the Hindus and, as a consequence, there was a general, national degeneration in India, which came from denying its identity.[109]

On his route through Maharashtra, Advani subsequently only stopped in larger towns like Pune, Nasik or Nagpur where the BJP had earlier received a lot of encouragement from the voters and where branch-units of the RSS were also strong. The enthusiasm continued in Madhya Pradesh, the next state that the Yatra crossed. Here, innumerable onlookers gathered even in the rural areas and often waited for hours to catch a glimpse of the novelty of Rama's chariot, rumours of which had quickly spread.[110] Muslims repeatedly asked the government to stop the Yatra, and the first voices were soon heard demanding a fitting reply to Advani's provocations.[111] Advani himself refused to be affected by all this, he stressed that the Yatra would continue[112] and he openly stated that it had been a political mistake from the very beginning to have supported the V.P. Singh government.[113] On the margins of this political show there was an outbreak of communal violence between Hindus and Muslims in Karnataka leading to President's rule in this state.[114] In Rajasthan, a state which in the past had often witnessed outbreaks of violence between the two religious groups, emergency was declared in a number of cities where the Toyota-procession was due to arrive and strict restrictions were placed on public gatherings.[115] Even in Uttar Pradesh (UP), which lay ahead on the route, preventive measures were taken, partly politically motivated, to prevent violence and to control Advani in Ayodhya. By 20 October, the police in this state had arrested about 15,000 activists of the concerned Hindu right-wing organizations, among them also leading BJP-politicians like Kalyan Singh.[116] On the orders of Chief Minister Mulayam Singh Yadav, a vehement political opponent of Advani, the borders of the state were closed for large-scale migrations and mobilization in the vicinity of Ayodhya was banned.[117] In Meerut 43 activists of the BJP, the VHP and the Bajrang Dal were arrested, in Kanpur 275 people were taken into custody for fomenting unrest and in Allahabad Asad Ansari, the general-secretary of the Muslim Youth Conference was also jailed for violent agitation.[118]

In the meantime, Advani himself arrived in Delhi. Contrary to the actual circumstances of his campaign Advani stated in an interview in the capital: 'I am particularly gratified that all the prophets of doom who said that the journey would leave behind a trail of destruction and riots, have been proved wrong.'[119] Advani emphatically warned the government against stopping him or even arresting him.[120] In Delhi, the BJP also prevented an all-party meeting slated for 17 October that had been organized in order to find a consensual solution for Ayodhya. In a personal meeting with the prime minister, Advani and Vajpayee reiterated their position that the Yatra had been too successful so far for them to enter into negotiations.[121]

In Bihar, the next and the second-last state on the route, the Yatra was more or less peaceful, even though for political reasons the chief minister, Laloo Prasad Yadav, continually warned of the threat of violence between Hindus and Muslims.[122] In UP itself, the preventive measures that had been carried out for several weeks were continued. Hundreds of volunteers of the VHP, the RSS and the Shiv Sena who were pouring into the state and into the vicinity of Ayodhya were arrested and prevented from reaching Ayodhya.[123] Advani himself left no doubt about his intention of visiting UP and successfully ending the Yatra there as planned.[124]

When Advani was finally arrested on 23 September while entering UP in Samastipur the participants in the procession there reacted violently and the police had to resort to a lathi-charge.[125] On the same day the BJP handed over a letter to the President of India withdrawing its support to the government and Prime Minister V.P. Singh was forced to face a confidence-motion in parliament.

In accordance with Advani's wishes, however, preparations for the construction of the temple continued. Vajpayee now took over the initiative in the BJP and, in addition, he increased coordination efforts with the VHP. In Mumbai, the Shiv Sena organized a wave of protests against Advani's arrest during which state property was also destroyed. In West Bengal, Rajasthan, Madhya Pradesh, Uttar Pradesh, Gujarat, Karnataka, Orissa, and in the rest of Maharashtra communal clashes claimed innumerable lives.[126] The VHP, however, continued its efforts to bring its volunteers into Ayodhya. The party stated that around 30 October around 65,000 VHP activists were still waiting to enter UP.[127] Vijaya Raje Scindia and Atal Behari Vajpayee were also taken into custody before the date set for the start of temple construction in order to prevent them from taking part in the event. On 30 October, the VHP succeeded in marking the beginning of construction through a symbolic act without actually being able to start the work of construction.[128] The massive deployment of police prevented the organization from doing this and five volunteers of the VHP died in the attempt to break-through the barriers set-up by the police and paramilitary forces. Another hundred were injured in a lathi-charge, six government jeeps were set on fire and ten buses were burnt down.[129] Chaos reigned in Ayodhya and communal violence broke out in north and central India.

The political campaign of the Rath Yatra had established a new nationalist and culturally defined geography which portrayed India as a sacred territory[130] with its umbilical point in Ayodhya, the holy place of pilgrimage (*tirtha*). In Hindu popular belief the characteristic of such a place is that it represents a meeting-point between heaven as the seat of the gods and earth as the sphere of humans, and it is from here that pilgrims can look from one world into the other. Combined with the BJP's nationalistic programme Ayodhya became the cosmic birth-place of the nation of Hindus.[131] The BJP and VHP rhetoric of beleaguerment and oppression gains its logic only in the framework of this elevation of Ayodhya to a geographically sacred space. The prototypical and decisive character of the 'liberation' of the Ram Janmabhoomi can only be derived from this and then staged as a key political question. In this politicized cosmology Ayodhya as a profane place somewhere in north India becomes hierophantic, a medium of the encounter with the sacred and culminating point of the national, collective awakening. In the context of this framework Ayodhya, the legendary birth-place of Rama, establishes a modern, national community which gains its identity from Ayodhya, is reflected in it and becomes its point of departure and return.[132] In Advani's campaign Ayodhya became the political myth of the origin and the future of the nation of Hindus headed by one who, in the tradition of Rama, fights with a bow and arrow for the liberation of an apparently 'oppressed majority'.

This interplay of nation and religion, however, also denied the diversity of the Hindu religious landscape and formulated a sense of national and cultural belonging which was meant to establish a new and powerful membership in the nation.[133] Ayodhya thus not only became the site for the re-birth of the nation, but loyalty and active participation in 'Rama's liberation' also became the decisive yardstick for integration in the new 'Hinduized' India. This left out not only the religious minorities, who were opposed to this marker of loyalty, but also the southern parts of the country which, for historical reasons, did not participate in this tumult around Rama.

The Congress under Rajiv Gandhi had also tried to defy the BJP in October by organizing its own Sadbhavana Yatra,[134] thus trying to achieve another goal, namely communal harmony, through similar means. This action was also primarily motivated by the politics of democracy. In the course of his Yatra Rajiv Gandhi visited Varanasi, Fatehpur, the constituency of Prime Minister V.P. Singh, Channopatna in Karnataka which had recently witnessed severe unrest, Madras, and surrounding villages in Tamil Nadu in order to speak against the discrimination of the dalits.[135] On 12 October, Rajiv Gandhi's route led him to Ayodhya and Faizabad where he suddenly began to promote his programme of national integration and where he criticized the Hindu nationalists for their religious exclusivity.[136] At the end of October, however, the Congress Working Committee again expressed the view that the symbolic actions of the VHP in Ayodhya should be allowed,[137] which meant that there was no unequivocal rejection of the Ayodhya campaign by the Congress party. Rajiv Gandhi was thus unable to come out of the ideological shadow of the BJP and his party again disappeared behind the religious-nationalistic bluster of the Hindu right-wing.

After the fall of the V.P. Singh government on 16 November, the BJP had to ensure that the crest it was riding on was also reflected in terms of democratic politics, i.e. it had to bring its support-base from the streets into the polling booths.

Immediately after the end of Advani's campaign the party began a wide distribution of videotapes among the urban middle class, and in the villages it showed this video-material of the Rath Yatra and the worship of Rama in Ayodhya with the help of video-equipment mounted on a car.[138] The newly-elected BJP president, Murli Manohar Joshi, soon sketched out the election manifesto of his party which, he said, would focus on the failure of the Nehruvian state and foreground the new national identity with regard to culture, economics and politics.[139] Regarding the question of Hindu nationalism Joshi was even more resolute than his predecessor Advani. Joshi interpreted Hindutva, i.e. the political version of Hindu culture, not only as the backbone of the nation, but also as a 'geo-political concept' which, in his opinion, extended from Afghanistan to Indonesia and was based on a common culture and a shared ethos.[140]

Vajpayee, however, expressed his concern that by aligning itself so strongly with the question of the Ram Janmabhoomi and with Hindu nationalism his party could be narrowing down its prospects.[141] The plenary meeting of the party in February 1991 in Jaipur finally agreed to take up the question of Kashmir as the second substantial issue in the coming elections along with Ayodhya.[142] The BJP wanted to foist the image of a more secular nationalism on the controversy surrounding Kashmir in order to make itself more acceptable to voters, especially in south India.

The BJP manifesto for the elections in June mentioned, along with a number of other points, both Ayodhya and Kashmir as two central concerns of the party, albeit to a far more modest extent than earlier discussions had led one to expect. With reference to Ayodhya, the BJP stated that the construction of the temple was a 'symbol of the rehabilitation of our cultural heritage and of national self-respect': the 'Babri-construction' would, therefore, have to be shifted.[143] The word 'mosque' was avoided as far as possible. In the context of Kashmir the party regretted the continuing violence in the valley, promised free elections and demanded that Article 370 of the Constitution be scrapped which granted special rights to the state of Jammu & Kashmir.[144]

The broad party-organization in the form of local cadres and branch-offices, especially in north and west India, along with the help of the ideologically related VHP and RSS contributed in making the BJP campaign effective as never before. According to conservative estimates, almost 2 lakh volunteers of the RSS alone were campaigning for the BJP in May 1991.[145] The VHP also organized processions carrying urns with the ashes of those killed in Ayodhya, thus keeping alive the memory of those events.[146] Even actors, especially those who had played the role of Rama's wife, Sita, and of the demon Ravana in the TV serial *Ramayana* mentioned earlier, campaigned with the BJP for Rama—and naturally also for a lucrative seat in parliament.[147]

The gains made by the BJP in the elections to the Lower House (Lok Sabha) were especially impressive in contrast to the decline of the Janata Dal. This decline made it possible for the BJP to become the second most important political force in the country. The proportion of votes for the BJP rose from 11.4 to 20.0 per cent, and its share of seats in the Lok Sabha increased from 85 to 119. The proportion of votes for the Congress went down to 36.6 per cent, but its 227 seats represented a small gain. The Janata Dal, however, the second largest party in 1989, won only 11.8 per cent of the votes, and its share of seats shrank from 143 to a mere 56.[148] A comparison of the election results with the route of the Rath Yatra shows that Advani was correct. To a large extent, it was he who had strengthened the effect of the party's upward trend in its strongholds. In Gujarat, for example, the proportion of votes for the BJP rose from 30.4 to 50.4 per cent, in Madhya Pradesh from 39.7 to 41.9 per cent, in Uttar Pradesh from 7.6 to 32.8 per cent, in Rajasthan from 29.6 to 40.9 per cent, and in Delhi from 26.2 to 40.2 per cent.[149] Despite this, the party's success cannot be attributed solely to Advani's Yatra. In Maharashtra, for example, which had been a focal point of the campaign, the BJP's share of votes decreased from 23.7 to 20.2 per cent. In Andhra Pradesh, the southernmost point of Advani's Yatra, the BJP had gained significantly (9.5 per cent) in comparison to 1989 (2 per cent), but even this result fell far short of their expectations.[150] In the core areas, however, especially in UP which has the largest number of seats in the Lok Sabha, the BJP strategy had been successful and it had become a political force to be reckoned with.

In the elections held in 1996 the BJP was able to become the party with the largest share of votes but it was unable to form a ruling coalition. Till it was finally able to form a government after a new election victory two years later, the party and its allied Hindu-nationalist organizations carried out several similar campaigns to remain in the focus of attention. The echo this time was far less than the resonance received in the 1980s and early 1990s and there was nothing new in the concrete shape given to these further campaigns. The rise of the BJP as the most important and, on an all-India level, only opponent of the old Congress party is a complex process that took place against the backdrop of far-reaching social transformations. India's growing inclusion in international economic developments led to social changes which also affected the political landscape of this democracy. It would, therefore, be inappropriate to interpret the above-described events only as a result of better strategies of mobilization and of the clever use of a religious discourse. These were, however, a sufficient condition for success and the BJP did indeed owe a significant part of its political potential to the clever combination of theatrical staging and democratic demands.

RELIGIOUS NATIONALISM AS STATE CHAUVINISM

When Atal Behari Vajpayee (BJP) was sworn in as the new prime minister in March 1998 it was the first time in India's history as a democratic republic that the post was occupied by a person who had never belonged to the Congress. One of Vajpayee's first official tasks, which became known after the event, was to order the nuclear tests that were carried out in May by scientists of the Homi Bhabha Atomic Research Institute.[151] A few hours after the powerful explosion in the Rajasthan desert the prime minister appeared before the press and read out the following statement in a sober manner but with evident satisfaction at the success of this politically decisive act:

> Today, at 15.45 hours, India conducted three underground nuclear tests in Pokhran range. The tests were conducted with a fission device, a low-yield device and a thermonuclear device. The measured yields are in the line with expected values. Measurements have also confirmed that there was no release of radioactivity into the atmosphere. These were contained explosions, like the experiment conducted in May 1974. I warmly congratulate the scientists and engineers who have carried out these successful tests.[152]

With this India officially became a nuclear power and repositioned itself among the international powers.

An almost humorous aspect of the events of May 1998 was the reaction from the USA that the CIA had known nothing about the preparations in the desert, not all of which would have taken place underground.[153] This is all the more surprising since the signs for this consequential event had been fairly clear. During the entire 1980s and the early 1990s there had been a lively debate in India about the possible realization of the 'nuclear option' and leading politicians from diverse camps had repeatedly spoken about the likely possibility of using nuclear resources especially with regard to the threat from Pakistan.[154] Besides this, the BJP had already stated in its election manifesto of 1991 that the military should be equipped with 'nuclear teeth' to meet the threat from neighbouring countries.[155] In April 1993, while commenting on the BJP's position if it came into power, Advani had also said:

> I think we have no option in this regard. With Pakistan going nuclear and China having been a nuclear power for many years, India, in order

to have its dealings with these two neighbours on a level ground, simply must become nuclear.[156]

In the election manifesto of 1998 point 2 of the sub-chapter on 'External Security' had also clearly expressed the BJP vision in the form of an imperative: 'Re-evaluate the country's nuclear policy and exercise the option to induct nuclear weapons!'[157] Finally, the programme of the coalition government headed by the BJP also contained a reference to the priority of external security which included the nuclear option.[158]

Although there were some mild and localized protests which opened up debates about the consequences for India such as US-sanctions,[159] the enormous follow-up costs of the nuclear status,[160] or the expected arms-race with Pakistan,[161] the general mood, especially in the capital city, was one of joy and enthusiastic jubilation about the 'super-bomb'.

In contrast to all serious discussions about the diverse and negative consequences of this political decision for India, the BJP tried in the following weeks to stage the nuclear test as an event for nationalist elation and thus it continued its methods of mediating political contents. In this context the nuclear tests became the showpiece of Hindu nationalist megalomania. It was only long after the tests, and almost exclusively with regard to the negative economic consequences of US-sanctions, that a paralysed political opposition found words of protest.

Vajpayee's 'Hindu-bomb'[162] was referred to as an achievement in armament politics when the BJP was called on to form a government for the second time after the failure of 1996. The ideologically and politically extremely fragile coalition gained a measure of stability and political discipline through this patriotic-nationalist adventure. The nationalism of the bomb united the members of the coalition temporarily and the compromised opposition, which could have gained political laurels for this same act, could only look on in silence.[163]

The BJP linked the first tests with a national holiday so that their supporters would have enough time to celebrate the event in a befitting manner.[164] In Jodhpur and Pokhran in Rajasthan, in the direct vicinity of the test site, the BJP staged a celebration coinciding with the 540th anniversary celebrations of the city of Jodhpur. The Commissioner of Jodhpur, Lalit Pawar, in whose area the test site was located, stated: 'The people of Jodhpur, which was the capital of West Rajasthan, could not have got a better gift. It is a memorable day for us.'[165] After the second series of tests was completed on 13 May, the prime minister travelled to Bangalore in order to celebrate the 'moment of fame' in a large event organized by his party. Venkaiah Naidu, the then General-Secretary of the BJP, announced to the entire country: 'The BJP appeals to all patriotic people to join us in the celebrations. The nation is rejoicing, it is not mere party issue.'[166] Ironically, local BJP members from Rajasthan started sending out the 'holy earth' of Mother India from the vicinity of the test site in Pokhran throughout India, so that 'patriots' from outside Rajasthan would also be able to worship the blessed earth. The problem of radioactivity that had occurred even in these underground tests, despite all statements to the contrary by the prime minister,[167] was not taken into consideration. Vajpayee had to intervene personally and put an end to the distribution of radioactive soil.[168] On 20 May, the prime minister visited the test site where, in the company of scientists of the nuclear programme, he presented himself and other members of the government as the men of India's nuclear future.[169] On 30 May, the prime minister repeated these demonstrations of power and appeared before a large gathering, including the media, with a sword in his hand to be felicitated as the most powerful potentate of the hour.[170]

The episode of radioactive soil from Pokhran being distributed all over India as a traditional object of worship and the combination of the nuclear tests with Vajpayee's appearance carrying a sword demonstrate the context in which these tests were perceived and celebrated. These archaic gestures of worship and admiration appear to be completely inappropriate for the actual event in Rajasthan and seem to be without any understanding for the significance and the character of an atomic bomb. In personal conversations too

Indians confirmed that a nuclear awareness was completely absent, even in the urban population. The opinion-survey carried out by the *Times of India* in eight cities on 26-7 May confirms this impression.[171] Eighty-one per cent of the respondents, all of them from large cities, welcomed the government's decision to test the bomb and 69 per cent agreed that they 'felt good' about India's new status as a nuclear power.[172] The survey also showed that a large majority of the urban population was happy with Vajpayee's declaration and did not agree with the opposition's criticism of the tests. Sixty-five per cent felt that the tests were in the national interest and 73 per cent regarded the tests as absolutely necessary for the country's security. However, only 35 per cent agreed with the defence minister's statement[173] that the People's Republic of China was the first and most important opponent in India's neighbourhood. Comparative figures about Pakistan in this context are, however, not available.

It was only on 27 May that the prime minister made an appearance in the Lok Sabha in order to justify his decision and to explain his intentions. The tests, he felt, had given India 'a renewed sense of national pride and self-confidence'[174] and had brought the country 'on the path of self-determination, independent thought and action'[175] and were based on a broad national consensus:

> The rationale for the Government's decision is based on the same policy tenets that have guided us for five decades. These policies have been sustained successfully because of an underlying national consensus. It is vital to maintain the consensus as we approach the next millennium.[176]

What is interesting about this speech is primarily the fact that in it Vajpayee did not abandon the goal of nuclear disarmament, but that he now wanted to achieve this goal through India's status as a nuclear power:

> In 1988 we put forward an Action Plan for phased elimination of all nuclear weapons within a specified time frame. It is our regret that these proposals did not receive a positive response from other nuclear states. Had their response been positive, India need not have gone for

the current tests. This is where our approach to nuclear weapons is different from others. This difference is the cornerstone of our nuclear doctrine. It is marked by restraint and striving for the total elimination of all weapons of mass destruction.[177]

It was L.K. Advani who finally spoke up more clearly. On 18 May already—and thus before the tests in Pakistan—Advani asked the fraternal state to take note of the changed conditions and to give up its enmity with India. In Parliament, Advani, now the home minister and thus responsible for internal security, sketched out the threat from Pakistan in a historical and contemporary perspective:

Jammu and Kashmir may be the target of their 'operation TOPAC' but overall as Pakistan has taken a decision to become a nuclear weapon state our concern should be to become a nuclear power state, to take care of our security needs and to gain a prominent position in the world. Besides, our policy is to oppose some countries which are practising the policy of nuclear apartheid in the world. Pakistan's nuclear policy is India-specific. It is directed towards India and that too Jammu-Kashmir specific.[178]

The tests, conducted on the instructions of the BJP as the ruling party, constituted the end of a series of actionist strategies of mobilization which started at the beginning of the 1980s and set a corresponding re-formulation of national self-consciousness in motion. With the events of 1998 a far-reaching process of political transformation was brought to an end which, through new means of mass mobilization, mediated and communicated new versions of state and society. The result was a very male-defined, exclusively Hindu collective which produced and staged modern self-visions with traditional and, occasionally, archaic vocabulary. The conditions and structural prerequisites of these processes were varied and often linked with international developments. The campaigns also did not constitute a linear rise of the BJP. The party had to accept setbacks and wrong assessments while constantly fine-tuning its strategies in accordance with the given context. But the interplay of religion, politics and nationalism constituted the matrix of its difference, especially with the Congress party, and informed its new concepts of state and society in which, in end effect, the global hegemonic claims of a militant Hinduism were established.

The hitherto discussed examples of religion and politics in modern India have shown different methods and strategies of filling spaces and discourses in the political-public sphere with varying messages and ideologies. What has not been discussed, however, are the changes in the nature of this sphere itself. Since discourses on politics and religion are generally geared towards maximum public response, the questions about the structure of the public space, the media-related possibilities and the channels of communication become decisive. The strategies of political communication must be worked out in accordance with the structure of this public sphere if they are to be successful. In the last two to three decades there have been fundamental changes in this sphere in India which will be analysed in the following chapter. The focus will also be on social reasons for the rise of the BJP which took place mainly in urban spaces in the framework of increasing globalization. The picture that emerges is anything but homogeneous and clear, but all the more interesting because of the availability of empirical data which gives rise to surprising results.

NOTES

1. Gopal, 1991 offers a good overview of the various facets of the Ayodhya controversy before the destruction of the mosque; for the consequences of the events of 1992 see McGuire/Reeves/Brasted, 1996.
2. Cf. Katju, 2003, pp. 57f.
3. I.e. the Committee to liberate Rama's birth-place.
4. *The Indian Post*, Bombay, 18 January 1989.
5. Interview, *India Today*, 15 February 1989.
6. Cf. *The Telegraph*, 5 February 1989.
7. *The Indian Post*, 7 April 1989.
8. *Indian Express*, Bombay, 7 April 1989.
9. *The Indian Post*, 20 March 1989.

10. Cf. a later interview with Advani cited in Jaffrelot, 1996, p. 382.
11. BJP 1989, pp. 14, 15, 17.
12. *India Today*, 30 June 1989, p. 61.
13. *The Telegraph*, 18 June 1989 and *Frontline*, 5-18 August 1989, p. 27.
14. Datta, 1991, p. 2524.
15. *TOI*, Bombay, 29 July 1989.
16. *Organiser*, 23 July 1989.
17. I.e. *shila*, the Hindi word for brick.
18. *Organiser*, 23 July 1989.
19. In August, for example, the home minister tried to point out how absurd the campaign was by stating in a report that a god such as Rama did not need to be 'liberated' since he lived in people's hearts. In addition, law and order were to be maintained under all circumstances and this meant that the decisions of the courts were to be respected. Cf. *Indian Express*, Bombay, 8 August 1989 and *Frontline*, 28 October–11 November 1989, p. 18.
20. For the very complex history of the legal battle for the Babri-mosque land and also for the various historical and archaeological arguments and counter-arguments see Mishra 1991. Noorani, 1991 offers a purely legal perspective on Ayodhya.
21. *TOI*, Bombay, 29 July 1989.
22. Advani, 1989, p. 4, also reproduced in *Organiser* 27 August 1989.
23. *Organiser*, 30 July 1989.
24. During a press conference Moropant Pingle had once spoken for the RSS about the destruction of the mosque which had led to a huge outcry (cf. *The Telegraph*, 18 June 1989), but VHP leaders remained cautious about making such statements. In August, Deoki Nandan, vice-president of the VHP, stated: 'The VHP has no immediate plan to demolish the present structure where the Ramlila idols . . . are installed'. Cf. *Organiser*, Independence Day Special 1989.
25. Literally 'Prayers to the Rama-bricks'.
26. Blom Hansen, 1999, pp. 161-5 describes an illustrative case for the rural direction of the campaign and analyses the organizational expansion of the VHP, especially in rural areas, as a direct consequence of the *Rama Shila pujas*.

27. Van Dyke, 2002, p. 144.
28. *Organiser*, 20 August 1989, cited in Jaffrelot, 1996, p. 385.
29. *The Indian Post*, 26 August 1989.
30. *Organiser*, 8 October 1989.
31. Cf. BJP, 1989a.
32. *The Telegraph* 26 September 1989. For the support given on the national level by the BJP to the VHP see also *The Indian Post*, 26 September 1989 as well as *The Telegraph*, 30 September 1989.
33. *TOI*, Bombay, 3 October 1989.
34. *The Indian Post*, 2 October 1989.
35. *TOI*, Bombay, 1 October 1989.
36. *The Telegraph*, 5 November 1989. Cf. also Lochtefeld, 1996, p. 105.
37. Upadhyaya, 1992, p. 845.
38. Cf. *TOI*, Bombay, 4 October 1989.
39. *The Telegraph*, 6 October 1989.
40. Ibid. See also *The Telegraph*, 6 October 1989.
41. *Indian Express*, Bombay, 11 October 1989.
42. *TOI*, Bombay, 9 October 1989.
43. Cf. *TOI*, Bombay, 27 October 1989 and 1 November 1989.
44. *The Independent*, 20 October 1989.
45. *The Telegraph*, 4 November 1989.
46. *The Telegraph*, 5 November 1989.
47. *The Hindu*, 6 November 1989.
48. Cf. for this Hasan, 1998, p. 202.
49. *The Telegraph*, 9 November 1989 and *TOI*, Bombay, 9 November 1989. Cf. also *The Independent* 18 November 1989.
50. *TOI*, Bombay, 2 November 1989. A few months later it was discovered that the bricks of the Rama Shila Yatra were, for static reasons, not suited for the construction of a temple. Cf. for this *Sunday Observer* 1 July 1990.
51. *Frontline*, 28 October–10 November 1989, p. 19.
52. Cf. *TOI*, Bombay, 10 November 1989.
53. *Business Standard*, 11 November 1989.
54. *The Independent*, 11 November 1989.
55. *TOI*, Bombay, 11 November 1989.
56. *Frontline*, 25 November–8 December 1989.
57. Speech reproduced in *Organiser*, 19 November 1989.

58. Nehru, 1985, p. 135.
59. Ibid., pp. 135f.
60. Seshadri, 1989.
61. *Organiser*, 26 November 1989.
62. Romila Thapar (1975) has presented an extensive and fundamental study of the developments and mistakes of colonial historiography that is still valid. Pandey's study of 1999, Chap. 2, takes a similar direction. Chatterjee (1995) describes the reception of these historical models by religious nationalists and goes into their explicit 'Hinduization' of history. Chatterjee also gives an extensive portrayal of the historiographic model of Muslim rule as 'foreign rule'. Cf. esp. pp. 122-5. For the falsification of history in general and for the idealized concept of a 'golden era' before the advent of Islam see Thapar, 1989, esp. pp. 214ff and Chakravarti, 1998, esp. pp. 227f.
63. Neera Chandoke has used the word 'victimization' for this phenomenon (lecture at the University of Mumbai, 13 December 2001). This does not mean the actual oppression or discrimination of a community or a religion, but the concrete process by which a group takes on the role of a victim.
64. In this context Blom Hansen, 1993, p. 2271 uses the very apt expression of 'Kshatriyaization' for the militant verbal, physical and action-oriented rearmament of Hindus—an expression that derives from the warrior-caste of the Kshatriyas. With this term Blom Hansen especially refers to the above-cited image of the 'angry Hindu' who has stopped putting up with what is meted out to him and is now ready to strike back.
65. Cf. for this Subrahmaniam/Gupta, 1989.
66. The percentile division of votes taken from Singh 1994, p. 30; the division of seats from Chiriyankandath, 1992, p. 269.
67. Blom Hansen, 1998, pp. 129f. emphasizes in this context that the results of the election in Maharashtra constituted a breakthrough since they came about through an alliance with the Shiv Sena and because there was a general feeling that enthusiasm for the 'saffron wave' was on the rise.
68. Singh, 1994, pp. 27-9.
69. For the career of the BJP in UP cf. Zoya Hasan, 2001, p. 4403.
70. Chiriyankandath, 1992, pp. 68f. portrays the so-called 'Rama-

factor' in the gains of the BJP by showing that most of the electoral constituencies from which the BJP won in 1989 were within or near those regions that had witnessed communal clashes during the bricks-campaign.

71. Kumar, 2001, p. 68.
72. *TOI*, Bombay, 27 January 1990.
73. *The Statesman*, Calcutta, 9 June 1990.
74. *The Telegraph*, Calcutta, 30 June 1990.
75. *Indian Express*, Bombay, 14 August 1990. For the suggestion made repeatedly by Advani to relocate the mosque see *Organiser*, 2 September 1990.
76. *The Hindu*, Madras, 13 June 1990.
77. *The Telegraph*, Calcutta, 13 September 1990.
78. 25 September was the birth anniversary of Deen Dayal Upadhyaya one of the main ideologues of the BJP and its predecessor parties. Cf. for this *The Hindu*, Madras, 13 September 1990 and *Organiser*, 7 October 1990.
79. Parliamentary Debates 1989. Rajya Sabha, *Official Report*, vol. 151, no. 16, New Delhi, column 258ff.
80. Ibid., column 259f.
81. *TOI*, Bombay, 13 September 1990.
82. Cf. *Organiser*, 26 August 1990; also the caricature in *Organiser*, 30 September 1990.
83. Literally: the Committee of Rama-volunteers.
84. Sankar, 1991, p. 14.
85. *Organiser*, 16 September 1990.
86. *TOI*, Bombay, 17 September 1990.
87. *TOI*, Bombay, 19 September 1990.
88. *TOI*, Bombay, 24 September 1990.
89. Davis, 1996, p. 28.
90. Cf. photo in *Frontline*, 13-26 October 1990, pp. 20f.
91. For the parallels between the TV serials and the Rath Yatra cf. Farmer, 1996, esp. pp. 102-8; for the effect of the TV serials *Ramayana* and *Mahabharata* see Dalmia-Lüderitz, 1991, Malinar, 1995 and Thapar, 1989a. Mankekar, 2000, esp. Chapter 4, offers a good empirical study of the reception of these serials by Hindu viewers. Kapur, 1993, pp. 105-7 discusses the serials in the context of a general radicalization and politicization of the iconography of Rama. Rajgopal, 2001, Chapter 2, analyses

the visual codes of the serial, especially with regard to the political-nationalist message of the staging which effected a special form of synthesis between religion and nationalism.

92. *The Week*, 30 September 1990, p. 30.
93. Cf. for this Pollock, 1993.
94. Interview, *The Independent*, Bombay, 25 September 1990.
95. *TOI*, Bombay, 26 September 1990.
96. *Organiser*, 14 October 1990.
97. *Organiser*, 7 October 1990.
98. *TOI*, Bombay, 26 September 1990.
99. *Organiser*, 7 October 1990.
100. *Organiser*, 14 October 1990.
101. In one of her speeches in Gujarat V.R. Scindia stated that the Yatra would basically be peaceful. If, however, she added, anyone were to oppose it Hanuman (patron of the militant and aggressive Bajrang Dal) would be there to take care of the problem. Cf. *TOI*, Bombay, 27 September 1990.
102. *TOI*, Bombay, 27 September 1990.
103. Cf. interviews in *Sunday Observer*, 30 September 1990.
104. *TOI*, Bombay, 29 September 1990.
105. For the reception of the Yatra in the local as also in the English press cf. Rajagopal, 2001, pp. 193-5.
106. *TOI*, Bombay, 29 September 1990.
107. *Organiser*, Deepavali Special 1990.
108. *Financial Times*, Bombay, 1 October 1990.
109. *TOI*, Bombay, 1 October 1990.
110. *TOI*, Bombay, 8 October 1990.
111. *Hindustan Times*, New Delhi, 7 October 1990.
112. *TOI*, Bombay, 7 October 1990.
113. Interview, *Sunday Times of India*, 14 October 1990.
114. *Frontline*, 27 October–9 November 1990, pp. 35-41.
115. Cf. for this *Indian Express*, Bombay, 12 October 1990 as well as *Sunday Observer*, 14 October, 1990, which reports about curfew being imposed in Udaipur. For Rajasthan in general see the portrayal by Padmanabhan/Sidhva, 1990, p. 60.
116. *TOI*, Bombay, 10 October 1990.
117. *Frontline*, 27 October–9 November 1990, pp. 11f.
118. *TOI*, Bombay, 15 October 1990.

119. *Organiser*, 28 October 1990.
120. *The Telegraph*, 16 October 1990. Advani was reacting to a statement given by Home Minister Subodh Kant Sahay in Delhi saying that, if necessary, Advani would have to be arrested if he were to carry out his programme, as planned, in Ayodhya. Cf. *TOI*, Bombay, 14 October 1990.
121. *TOI*, Bombay, 17 October 1990. Cf. also *India Today*, 15 October 1990, pp. 34f.
122. *TOI*, Bombay, 19 October 1990.
123. *Sunday Observer*, 21 October 1990.
124. Ibid.
125. *TOI*, Bombay, 24 October 1990.
126. For a detailed documentation of these excesses see the reports in the *TOI*, Bombay between 24 October and 27 October 1990.
127. *TOI*, Bombay, 27 October 1990.
128. *Economic Times*, 2 December 1990.
129. *TOI*, Bombay, 31 October 1990.
130. Deshpande, 1995 points out to the role of geography, i.e. to the significance of space as a category in Hindu nationalism.
131. For Ayodhya's character as 'tirtha' see Veer, 1997, pp. 58-65 and Veer, 1987, p. 285.
132. Cf. Shri Ram Janmabhoomi Nyasa, 2001; Dubashi, 1992, esp. p. 55; Singh, 1993, esp. pp. 6, 18.
133. Nandy, 1996, p. 73.
134. This 'mission of goodwill' was announced by Rajiv Gandhi in September when Advani's plans for the Rath Yatra had been finalised. Cf. for this *The Telegraph*, Calcutta, 15 September 1990.
135. *TOI*, Bombay, 6 October 1990.
136. *The Telegraph*, 16 October 1990 and *TOI*, Bombay, 13 October 1990.
137. *The Independent*, Bombay, 1 December 1990.
138. *The Daily*, Bombay, 20 December 1990. Cf. also *TOI*, Bombay, 27 December 1990. Kulkarni, 1991 also provides extensive documentation of the use of visual media by the BJP on the basis of videos used in this election campaign. Manuel, 1996, p. 131 shows that the politics of videotapes was first used by the Congress in 1983 and was taken over only later by the BJP.

Basu et al., 1993, pp. 82f. analyse the contents of video-cassettes used by the VHP.

139. Interview, *Sunday*, 23 February 1991, p. 12. Cf. also Interview, *Sunday Observer*, 13 January 1991.
140. Interview, *Organiser*, 3 February 1991.
141. *TOI*, Bombay, 4 February 1991.
142. *Frontline*, 16 February–1 March 1991, as well as interview with L.K. Advani, *Daily Telegraph*, 14 February 1991.
143. BJP, 1991, pp. 1 and 5.
144. Ibid., p. 7.
145. *India Today*, 15 May 1991, p. 26.
146. Veer, 1996, p. 170.
147. *Sunday*, 19-25 May 1991 under the title 'In the Name of Rama'. Rama himself, or rather, the actor who portrayed the divine king, had already campaigned for the Congress party in 1988.
148. Percentile distribution of votes from Singh, 1994, p. 49. Distribution of seats from Chiriyankandath, 1992, p. 269.
149. All percentile details of the distribution of votes taken from Singh, 1994. Tables of the elections in 1989 and 1991, pp. 25-49.
150. Cf. Manor, 1988, pp. 168f. for the possible causes of the problems faced by the BJP in the south.
151. Wallace, 1999, pp. 22f states in this context that Vajpayee took this decision even before the 'National Security Council' could be re-constituted after the elections and that this decision had also not been placed before the cabinet for its vote. The prime minister, therefore, took this far-reaching decision only in consultation with a close circle and, till two weeks after the test, he left the public completely in the dark about the background and the motives for the test.
152. *TOI*, Bombay, 12 May 1998.
153. Cf. *International Herald Tribune*, 15 May 1998, p. 4.
154. Vanaik, 1995, esp. pp. 1-18 and Bidwai/Vanaik 2001, pp. 63-75 give a good overview of the discussions in the 1980s along with a historical perspective going back to 1945.
155. BJP, 1991, p. 37.
156. *Pioneer*, 17 April 1993.
157. BJP, 1998, chapter 'Our Nation's Security', sub-chapter 'External Security', para 2.

158. Cf. *Der Standard*, 19 March 1998.
159. One of the most active groups that offered resistance was organized around the writer Arundhati Roy who called for protest marches in Delhi. Cf. for this see her essay in *Outlook*, 27 July 1998.
160. Cf. for this the document about the costs using information from the defence ministry and from renowned physicists quoted in Ram, 1999, pp. 31-3. Also Bidwai/Vanaik, 2001, pp. 159-67.
161. *International Herald Tribune*, 20 March 1998, p. 5.
162. This term clearly places the decision to carry out the tests in the ideological context of the Hindu right-wing which had been demanding the bomb for a long time. Cf. for example, Golwalkar, 1974, pp. 71, 105, 174; also Sarkar, 1998, pp. 1726f as a secondary source. For the origin of the term 'Hindu-bomb' see Maaß, 2000, p. 248.
163. Mulayam Singh Yadav, the defence minister in the previous government, said, for example, that the bomb would have been ready for the test even in October of the previous year after he had sanctioned large amounts of money for the preparatory phase. Cf. *TOI*, Bombay, 16 May 1998.
164. Corbridge, 1999, p. 244.
165. *TOI*, Bombay, 13 May 1998.
166. *TOI*, Bombay, 15 May 1998.
167. The writer Amitav Ghosh, 1999, pp. 6-13 gives an impressive report about the local conditions directly after the tests.
168. *TOI*, Bombay, 20 May 1998.
169. *Frontline*, 19 June 1998, pp. 4f.
170. *Frontline*, 19 June 1998, p. 15.
171. The survey was conducted against the backdrop of the prime minister's speech in parliament on 27 May which will be discussed later. The respondents comprised 2177 adults in the cities of Bombay, Delhi, Calcutta, Madras, Bangalore, Ahmedabad, Lucknow and Patna. The results can be see in *TOI*, Bombay, 31 May 1998.
172. *Times of India* gives a comparative indicator in this context, according to which 90 per cent agreed with the tests immediately after they were carried out. This means that in the following weeks concurrence with the government's decision decreased even though, as shown above, it was still very high.

173. Cf. *Lok Sabha Debates*, Twelfth Series, vol. 2, no. 1, 2nd session (12th Lok Sabha), 27 May 1998, New Delhi, column 335.
174. Ibid., column 278.
175. Ibid., column 284.
176. Ibid., column 280.
177. Ibid., column 285.
178. Ibid., column 340f.

CHAPTER 6

Transformations of the Public Sphere: Religion, Politics and Globalization

In contrast to the 1920s and 1930s there is more precise and empirically verified data available for the most recent political developments that led to the rise of the BJP. This data gives us an impression of the changes that have occurred and are still occurring in this enormous demographic space encompassing more than a billion people. In all this, the size of the country is in direct proportion to the complexity of events, and in what follows it will only be possible to go into some of the characteristics in a cursory manner.

THE BJP's CONSTITUENCY

Extensive social profiles of voters are available in which preferences are categorized according to different criteria but which give us a general picture of the typical BJP-voter in the second half of the 1990s. At the same time, we must remember that in some statistics the BJP is not identified as a single party along with other national parties but as a strategic block in the framework of broad coalitions that the BJP entered into before each of the elections in 1996, 1998 and 1999. Not only were not all the coalition partners associated with the Hindu-nationalist spectrum, but even the composition of the coalition varied considerably in each of these elections which meant that the social profile of the voters also changed.[1] Some of the parties that joined the BJP coalition in 1998 were the AIADMK, a regional party in Tamil Nadu with a large base amongst peasants, the Akali Dal from Punjab, supported mainly by Sikhs, or the Telugu Desam Party from Andhra Pradesh. The social target groups of these parties are very different from those of the BJP.

Keeping these points in mind, the empirical material that was gathered during these key elections for the BJP in 1996, 1998 and 1999 gives us the following picture. Compared to all other national coalitions the voters for the BJP and its political allies are, to a large extent, male. This trend became apparent in the 1996 elections when 26.8 per cent of the men, but only 23 per cent of the women voted for the BJP. Two years later the trend became stronger when 36.3 per cent of the men gave their vote to the BJP as compared with 29.2 per cent of the women.[2] Even in 2004 when the BJP and its allies lost the elections to the coalition led by the Congress party, this male dominance remained.[3] There is a strong probability that the BJP-voter comes from an urban setting rather than from an agrarian-based rural background. In 1996 only 22.6 per cent of the rural voters gave their vote to the BJP as compared to 32.2 per cent in the urban areas.[4] This trend continued over the next two years. Although the gap between urban and rural voters initially became narrower (31.8 per cent in the rural areas, 36.3 per cent in urban areas), it widened again in the elections of 1999.[5] The urban concentration had not materialized to this extent at the beginning of the 1990s when the BJP campaigns had focused mainly on rural areas. This does not mean, however, that the BJP did not have a political base in the rural areas at the end of the 1990s. In 1999, of every 100 voters 73 came from rural areas, a number that was only marginally lower than that of the Congress party.[6] With regard to the age of voters we see that the BJP is almost equally strongly represented in all age groups, less however, among those above 56[7] while it is significantly more popular among those between 18 and 21.[8]

While discussing the question of the socio-economic background of BJP voters it is necessary to make a distinction between caste and class affiliations. These criteria for social divisions are not identical, but they display points of contact and intersections mainly at the upper and lower ends of the scale. In other words, the probability of material prosperity increases with affiliation to a high caste and vice versa, even though this cannot be generalized.[9] If one initially looks at these two determining characteristics for a person's position in society separately it becomes apparent that with respect to caste it is the high-caste voters who are the BJP's main clientele. A local study conducted in the agrarian-dominated district of Jaunpur in western UP in 1993 and 1994 had already shown that the BJP is primarily a party of the higher castes and that its voters are, to a large extent, Brahmins.[10] In the 1996 elections 33.6 per cent of the higher castes (Dwijas) voted for the BJP; two years later the figure had increased to 38.5 per cent. In 1996 only 23.6 per cent of the Other Backward Castes (OBC), a numerically important political group, voted for the BJP, but this figure went up in 1998 to 34.6 per cent. Obviously, the BJP was able to make inroads into this important group in the intervening years.[11] Although even in 1998 more than half the BJP voters were from the highest castes, the party was able to win over sections of the lower castes as well. Even among the lowest castes, or among the casteless and the tribal population, the BJP was able to increase the number of its supporters. However, these numbers remained modest in comparison to the proportion of voters from the highest castes.[12] In 1998 about one-fourth of the Scheduled Tribes (ST) and about one-fifth of the Scheduled Castes (SC) voted for the BJP.[13] One can, therefore, assume that the party conducted special campaigns in small towns and in rural areas to build-up their support base in these social classes and that they were partially successful.

Christophe Jaffrelot's detailed empirical studies[14] on the caste-affiliations of BJP candidates reflect these voter-trends, even though they show that till 1999 Brahmin-dominance among the politicians of this party was far greater than the hegemony of the upper castes among the voters. The proportion of the highest castes among BJP members of parliament who were re-elected to the Lok Sabha in 1999 was still almost 38 per cent. However, this figure represents the lowest ratio since 1989 and constitutes the temporary end of a continuous decrease.[15] In 1998 almost 55 per cent of the National Executive Committee of the BJP, the highest policy-making organ of the party, consisted of members of the upper castes.[16]

Regarding the question of the economic profile of BJP voters, i.e. their class affiliation, all available sources point to a direct connection between income, on the one hand, and the probability of voting for this party, on the other. If the voters at the national level are divided into four classes, the proportion of BJP voters increases with the level of prosperity.[17] Even in 1999 the poorest sections of Indian society gave the BJP only one-third of the votes that it got from the upper classes.[18] The voter-analysis of 2004 showed that this position had not changed. The defeat of this party and its coalition in 2004 was, therefore, not the outcome of a decrease in its support-base but of better coalition-formation on the part of the Congress party with regard to the economically weaker sections of Indian society. The BJP therefore remains the favoured representative of the upwardly-mobile, economically prosperous sections.[19]

This electoral attitude corresponds to the profile of the voters with regard to education and occupation which, in turn, depends on income and prosperity. The higher the educational level and the higher the professional status, the greater is the preference for the BJP. If one then combines the criteria of caste and class and tries to establish a pattern it is clear that both these criteria influence one another when it comes to the probability of voting for the BJP. Firstly, the BJP draws its support predominantly from prosperous, high-caste Hindus who live mainly in urban areas and are male. Secondly, the probability among the lower castes to vote for the BJP rises with increased prosperity.[20] The upwardly-mobile urban social strata, and partly also those in rural areas who do not belong to the traditionally privileged section of Hindu society on account of their caste, is drawn to Hindu nationalism when its economic status improves. An example can serve to illustrate this. If the entire electorate is divided on the basis of economic background into two camps of which the upper, more prosperous, segment comprises about 45 per cent of the voters, while the lower consists of roughly

55 per cent, then the BJP wins about 69 per cent of its votes from the economically well-off upper 45 per cent and the rest from the lower segment.[21] The BJP voters are, therefore, a social block comprising those who, in the context of economic liberalization and increasing internationalism, could profit from their existing advantages in traditional society and become the new middle and upper class. Further, the block consists of those segments of the lower castes who want to join the middle class and who can aspire to this on the basis of their new-found upward mobility. Finally, the block also contains a considerable proportion of the socially underprivileged who are increasingly feeling the pressure of these social changes or who are not in a position to exploit the new economic possibilities.

With reference to the political-religious mass campaigns of the BJP the empirical material gives us some interesting insights, even if one cannot directly derive their exact effects on the political landscape. We know that voters with a higher level of education, a high economic status and a high-caste background, as well as men and urbanites have a marked interest in political campaigns and are, therefore, increasingly targeted by and involved in these campaigns.[22] Since this clientele also constitutes the primary support-base of the BJP and since the party's campaigns were, in most cases, also election campaigns, it can be assumed that through these forms the party had found the appropriate means to communicate politics and ideology in order to address and mobilize its support-base.

A look at individual cases confirms this conjecture. In 1998, when the BJP ordered the nuclear tests and, subsequently, staged this event as a grand national resurrection, it remained unnoticed by large parts of the rural population despite wide media interest in the event.[23] In a survey conducted one year after the elections 46.5 per cent of the respondents, who were drawn from all parts of the country, stated that they had never heard about these tests. The remaining 53.5 per cent, who knew what 'Pokhran' (the test site) was associated with, came mainly from urban areas.[24] A large number of those who had heard about the tests, namely about

30 per cent, welcomed the government's decision as compared to 10 per cent who stated that the tests had been a mistake.[25] A look back at the year 1993 is also interesting in this context, a year in which the nation was rocked by the aftermath of the destruction of the Babri mosque in Ayodhya. Although the elections in that year did not go in favour of the BJP, the empirical data shows clear trends which allow us to draw conclusions about the effect of such political-religious campaigns. A survey conducted by the Delhi-based 'Organisation for Socio-Economic Systems' among almost 800 voters showed that 34 per cent of the Hindu respondents approved of the destruction of the mosque as compared to 6 per cent of the Muslim respondents. Fifty-three per cent of the Hindu respondents also supported the idea that those responsible for it should go unpunished as compared to 18 per cent of the Muslim respondents. The majority of all respondents, however, did not consider the BJP to be the author of this destruction and instead named the central government in Delhi which was then a Congress government. Forty-seven per cent of the Hindus and 73 per cent of the Muslims agreed that Prime Minister P.V. Narasimha Rao's administration bore responsibility for the catastrophe.[26] The survey also showed that support for the destruction of the mosque was greater among educated, male, high-caste Hindus in corresponding professions in UP than among other Indian voters.[27] Data collected on this topic a few years later contradict these findings to some extent,[28] but the party preferences of the respondents show that over 40 per cent of BJP voters welcomed what had happened in Ayodhya.[29] Another source from 1993 mentions the concurrence of 66 per cent of the BJP voters.[30] With the passing of time criticism of the event seems to have increased. Despite this, it is evident that while a large section of the voters and even sympathizers of the BJP did not approve of the chaotic and violence-prone situation created by the destruction of the mosque, they displayed significant sympathy for the concerns of the campaign in Ayodhya.

The data cited above can neither provide a linear explanation for the rise of the BJP nor can it answer all remaining questions. However, a basic pattern of the kind of following it gained emerges—a pattern that unites contradictory elements. These contradictions, such as the role of Hindu nationalism as the ideology of the upwardly-mobile in the middle and upper classes on the one hand, as well as a valve for the economically weaker lower middle and lower classes directly affected by increasing internationalization are, however, responsible for the success of the party; a success which also consists in representing different things to different groups of supporters. The social block of voters as a manifestation of these contradictions is, however, a temporary one, limited by time and, therefore, prone to disintegration.

CHANGES IN THE POLITICAL PUBLIC

The higher-than-average educational level of BJP voters leads to another factor that is important for understanding the functioning of the party, namely the question of the media and the fast-changing and far-reaching changes in the structures of the political public. Data from the year 1999 shows that more than any others, BJP voters were exposed to the discourse of the mass media and they used this to arrive at their political opinions. All voters were divided into four categories ranging from 'not exposed to the media' to 'very exposed' and were questioned accordingly. Of those who stated that they followed the media very closely, 26.6 per cent were BJP voters, 24.1per cent voted for the Congress party, while 6.9 per cent and 1.0 per cent were Left Front and Bahujan Samaj Party voters respectively. 31.9 per cent of all BJP voters stated that their contact with the media was very intense, 28.5 per cent identified themselves with the second category and 24.2 per cent stated that they did not keep up with the political media. Among Congress voters, on the other hand, only 20 per cent followed media debates closely, 27.1 per cent belonged to the second category and 31.6 per cent had had no contact with the political media.[31]

The question of changes in the composition and distribution of media is, therefore, very relevant, especially for the political rivalry between the BJP and the Congress party. Here, it is mainly the years from 1983 to 1998 which are interesting, i.e. that period when the BJP, along with its Hindu-nationalist allies, advanced from a marginal position to the centre of the political stage. The fastest developments in this period occurred in the Indian television market.

These 15 years brought about an enormous increase in television's penetration of the country and this, in turn, increased the instrumental repertoire of politics. According to the Ministry of Information and Broadcasting in New Delhi, the first quantitative leap in this sector happened between 1984 and 1985, i.e. in the year when Indira Gandhi was assassinated and her son Rajiv Gandhi succeeded her as prime minister after an emotionally-wrought election campaign. Indira Gandhi herself had initiated the ambitious expansion plans which materialized after her death. From March 1984 till May of the following year the reach of the state monopoly television, Doordarshan, among the Indian population rose from 30.4 to 56.2 per cent, and television's service area increased from 17.5 per cent of the country to 36.5 per cent. This trend continued in the following years and in December 1993 83.6 per cent of the population and 64.5 per cent of India received Doordarshan.[32] Six years later, in 1999, these figures had grown further to 86 per cent of the population and 68 per cent of the territory.[33] The reach of cable and satellite networks also went up quickly after the opening of the Indian market in 1991. Whereas in 1992 only 7.8 million households were connected to this international network, in 2000 the number had gone up to 19.1 million.[34] These figures are meaningless if the population cannot receive the programmes due to lack of TV sets. But, even here, there were fundamental changes in this period on account of economic progress and the quantitative expansion of the urban and rural middle class. Between 1985 and 1993 the number of television sets in India rose from 6.75 million to a little more than 40.3 million.[35] Present figures prove that the average number of television sets in relation to the number of households is much higher in urban areas than in the rural ones. However, we must remember that, as with newspapers, where there are fewer television sets there are probably a higher number of users per set.

Even though television's penetration of urban households in India is not very high when compared with Sri Lanka,[36] in Delhi, for example, already 86.5 per cent of households owned a television set in 2001. In the cities of the north Indian states Haryana, Punjab and Himachal Pradesh this figure was 82.3 per cent, in Maharashtra and Goa it was 76.4 per cent and in Gujarat 71 per cent.[37]

These changes obviously had repercussions for national politics. As is evident from the figures quoted above, already in the second half of the 1980s Rajiv Gandhi had access to the majority of the Indian electorate through state television. Towards the end of his term in 1988/9 Rajiv Gandhi used this exclusive access to the opinion-forming channels of Doordarshan in order to project himself. This 'Rajivdarshan', as the opposition called it, did not, however, help him very much in ensuring a majority in parliament. Rajiv Gandhi's visual campaigns on television were, at this point, still too amateurish and exaggerated.[38] The political profit that the Congress party could gain from this new media was, therefore, correspondingly modest. However, the massive control of the visual media by the Congress party, which was the ruling party at that time, continued for a few years, so that the opposition's, and thus also the BJP's, access to mass-media multipliers was severely restricted for a long time.

On another level, however, television began to unfold a new, indirect political relevance which benefited the religious-nationalist forces and helped the BJP to project itself as a party of the Hindus. To begin with, television changed the nature of cultural production in India:

> With the boost given to consumption by Rajiv Gandhi's government, the increasing prominence of the media signalled an industrialisation of not only material goods but also of 'culture' in general. The things people used, as well as the ideas and images they received, were more and more part of a single circuit of consumption, relayed by industries that for all their differences, were engaged simply in the business of business. The unprecedented centralisation of cultural production makes understandable the circulation of similar narratives in different fields—

economy, polity and culture, as social discourse increasingly begins to pass through a small number of interconnected channels.[39]

This uniformity of discourses thus not only affected the sphere of cultural production. Even politics and its versions of society, of the future, or of national self-understanding could, as a result, be reformulated and homogenized more effectively, more directly and more quickly.

This trend towards a uniformity of ideas and images was determined by those who controlled the production of meaning. However, they did not always do it consciously or systematically. A decisive event for the new direction in cultural production was the telecast of the television serials based on the Hindu epics *Mahabharata* and *Ramayana* from 1988 onwards.[40] These serials were an unprecedented success in India. Analyses have shown that as a result of the telecast of the *Ramayana*, Rama, the legendary king of Ayodhya and an incarnation of the god Vishnu, was converted in the collective imagination of Hindus from a legendary to a historical figure. Even the mythological Ayodhya, symbol for a just and benevolent rule, was equated through the serial with the actual city in north India, and it could become a political factor only on the basis of this popularity.[41] The serials not only unified and standardized the different narrative traditions of this religious theme both visually and with regards to its content,[42] but they also propagated, in social terms, a very problematic image of the quasi-ideal society under Rama's rule. In the various stages of the *Ramayana*, Rama's wife was always shown as subservient and obedient,[43] and the basic social tenor of the serials was extremely conservative. Rama's life became an analogy for the presumed fate of India as a nation as well as for the lives of many viewers. A man from a great family is done out of his throne, he has to go into exile from where he returns in triumph through his strength and courage.[44] With these mythological-religious instruments the serials created a uniform image of the causes for the unsatisfactory condition of the Indian nation in present times especially when compared with the idealized 'past' in Rama's kingdom, in which justice, prosperity and religious unity reigned.[45]

Rajiv Gandhi initially tried to gain political mileage from the people's enthusiasm about the serials. Even in the election campaign in 1988 the Congress party showed that it had the support of the actor who played Rama in the serial.[46] The actors who played Sita, Rama's wife, and the demon Ravana were won over by the BJP for their campaign in 1991.[47] What was far more important and decisive, however, was the fact that visually Advani's Rath Yatra was modelled on the television serials and that the people along the route of his journey could experience the continuation of the serials live on the road. In 1989 already, during an India-wide campaign, the followers of the radical VHP had used the collective memory of the serials and often dressed like the main actors.[48]

On the whole, the serials helped in extending the 'visual vocabulary'[49] with which the nation of Hindus could enact and portray itself politically. The BJP clearly exploited these new possibilities in the most skilful manner and translated the cultural and religious trends towards centralization and homogenization among the newly created audience of the mass-media into political strategies. Especially in urban areas, the serials created a 'Hinduized' public which demanded a commitment to the 'great heritage of our forefathers' from everyone. Rama was the most dazzling figure of this heritage which hardly featured any women. The new Hindutva rained down on the Indian population from all media channels. A member of the Shudra caste describes the situation in the following manner:

> Suddenly, since about 1990 the word 'Hindutva' has begun to echo in our ears, day in and day out, as if everyone in India who is not a Muslim, a Christian or a Sikh is a Hindu. I am also told that my parents, relatives and the caste in which we were born and brought up are Hindu. That totally baffles me. In fact, the whole cultural milieu of the urban middle class—the newspapers I read, the TV that I see—keeps assaulting me, morning and evening, forcing me to declare that I am a Hindu. Otherwise I am socially castigated and my

environment is vitiated. . . . I do not know how I can relate to the Hindu culture that is being projected through all kinds of advertising agencies. The government and the state themselves have become big advertising agencies. Moreover the Sangh Parivar harasses us every day by calling us Hindus.[50]

The executive committees of the state television, Doordarshan, who were close to the Congress, initially tried to boycott the BJP-campaigns. After the election campaign of 1984 L.K. Advani commented on what he perceived as the exclusive right of the Congress party to use the national television network. He also complained about the one-sidedness of the news coverage and the political colouring of the programmes. At that time itself Advani propagated a liberalization of the media which Rajiv Gandhi was naturally opposed to.[51] During the Rath Yatra in 1990 it was mainly the local, non-English language press which reported extensively about the progress of the journey while Doordarshan in Delhi limited itself to the most basic information about it.[52] During the next BJP-campaign in 1991 (Ekta Yatra) the then BJP president, Murli Manohar Joshi, commented on the meagre coverage that his campaign was receiving in state television:

What hasn't surprised me at all is the role of television and Doordarshan. The medium is being misused to spread disinformation, and though we had met Doordarshan officials in New Delhi, there was no proper coverage of such a major event.[53]

The first steps towards economic liberalization in 1991 also resulted in some initial reforms in the media sector. In January of that year CNN reported about the Gulf War in Iraq, initially from hotels and other central locations. In May, Rupert Murdoch's Star TV went on air, while ATN and Zee TV followed in 1992.[54] In the space of a few years these developments accrued an impressive balance sheet. By 1999 already more than 18 million households were connected to the private cable and satellite programmes.[55] It was mainly the younger generation which was increasingly making use of the rich variety of visual images on offer.[56]

With reference to the BJP and its campaigns these developments changed important prerequisites for access to a correspondingly large viewership. In an internal memo circulated in 1993 the BJP pointed out that it was counting on the help of the cable television networks to reach more households with news of its new political campaign:

> It is the medium on which the government has absolutely no control, though it is trying to have it lately. This network can be used as an instrument to fight Doordarshan's official propaganda, which is always favourable to the ruling party even during elections. . . . It is tomorrow's electronic network and the BJP will have to take separate and special cognizance of this new organ of the electronic media.[57]

Later campaigns such as the 'Swarna Jayanti Rath Yatra' in 1997 were conceived mainly with reference to the viewers of private television networks and local newspapers in order to bypass the monopoly exercised by Doordarshan.[58]

The strategies of performative nation-building used by the BJP since 1990 were an effective means of circumventing those channels of publicity that were more or less controlled by the government, and of creating alternative forms of publicity for the party's campaigns with the help of the local and also the English language press.[59] With the beginning of liberalization in the media sector the BJP discovered better conditions for their entry into the mass media since the private television networks functioned exclusively on market principles and, therefore, welcomed any political show offered to them which would draw viewers. The BJP recognized this internal logic of the new media landscape and reacted to it accordingly.

NOTES

1. For this phenomenon of regionalization of the party landscape and the consequences for national politics in India cf. Basu/Mukhopadhayay, 2000 and Rothermund, 1998.
2. Cf. the tabular list of the results in Mitra/Singh, 1999, p. 134. For the data of 1996 see also Singh, 1997, p. 60.

3. Yadav, 2004, p. 5389. Nayar, 2004 and Desai, 2004 interpret the results of this election.
4. For a possible sociological explanation of this phenomenon cf. Patel, 1993.
5. Ibid. For the data of the 1999-elections see Yadav/Kumar/Heath 1999, p. 39.
6. Yadav/Kumar/Heath, 1999, p. 39.
7. Mitra/Singh, 1999, p. 134.
8. In September 1999 *India Today* published the results of a survey among 3,200 Indians in this age group. The BJP was, by far, not only the most popular party, but A.B. Vajpayee turned out to be the greatest bearer of hope for the young voters. Cf. Malik, 1999.
9. For the relations between caste and class see Gupta, 2000, pp. 139-47 as well as Lieten, 1996, p. 137. Rudolph/Hoeber Rudolph, 1984 give very illustrative historical examples for the same.
10. Lieten, 1996, p. 139.
11. Singh, 1997, p. 60 and Mitra/Singh, 1999, p. 134. Cf. also the graphs in ibid., pp. 136f.
12. Cf. for this Yadav/McMillan/Chandra, 1998, p. 49.
13. Cf. ibid., p. 50.
14. Jaffrelot, 2003.
15. Ibid., Table on p. 469.
16. Ibid., p. 470.
17. Mitra/Singh, 1999, p. 135.
18. Yadav/Kumar/Heath, 1999, p. 38.
19. Yadav, 2004, p. 5392.
20. This conclusion corresponds to the discussion about the rise of Hindu nationalism and the role of the middle-class in India in Desai, 1999, pp. 703f.
21. Yadav/Kumar/Heath, 1999, p. 39.
22. Singh, 1997, Tables 2.3 (p. 16) and 2.5 (p. 19).
23. Cf. also Yadav/Heath/Saha, 1999, p. 46.
24. Cf. for this also Kantha, 1999, p. 360.
25. CSDS-Data, Post-Election Survey, Lok Sabha Elections, 1999.
26. Chhibber/Misra, 1993, p. 667.
27. Ibid., p. 669.

28. Mitra/Singh, 1999, Table 4.7 (p. 146).
29. The results for other parties in comparison: Congress (16.5 per cent), National Front (24.1 per cent), Bahujan Samaj Party (27.3 per cent).
30. *India Today*, 15 January 1993, p. 18.
31. CSDS-Data, Post-Election Survey, Lok Sabha Elections, 1999.
32. Government of India, Ministry of Information and Broadcasting 1995, Table 21 (p. 186).
33. Farmer, 2000, p. 266.
34. K.J. Kumar, 2000, Table 7.1 (p. 114).
35. Government of India, Ministry of Information and Broadcasting 1995, Table 24 (p. 189f).
36. Cf. for this Page/Crawley, 2001, Table 3.2 (p. 101).
37. Ibid., Table 3.5 (p. 103).
38. Cf. Rudolph, 1992, pp. 86f.
39. Rajagopal, 1994, p. 1660.
40. Varadarajan, 1999, pp. 189-94.
41. Rajagopal, 2001, pp. 99-117.
42. Thapar, 1989b, p. 23.
43. Dalmia-Lüderitz, 1991, pp. 224f.
44. Cf. for this also the analysis by Mankekar, 2000, pp. 188f.
45. Arvind Rajagopal points to this interpretation. Cf. Interview, *TOI*, Bombay, 27 August 2000.
46. Thapar, 1989b, p. 23, fn. 73.
47. *Sunday*, 19-25 May 1991 under the title 'In the Name of Ram'.
48. Rajagopal, Interview in *Frontline*, 18 August 2000, p. 79.
49. Freitag, 2001, p. 35.
50. Ilaiah, 1996, p. xf. Cf. for this also Varadarajan, 2002, pp. 73-7.
51. Interview, *Organiser*, 11 August 1985, p. 7.
52. Rajagopal, 2001, pp. 193f.
53. *Sunday*, 22-8 December 1991, p. 31.
54. Government of India, Ministry of Information and Broadcasting 1995, Table 29 (p. 193).
55. Page/Crawley, 2001, Table 3.2 (p. 101).
56. Ibid., Table 4.1 (p. 123).
57. *TOI*, Bombay, 3 November 1993.
58. Cf. *Business Standard*, Calcutta, 24 May 1997.

59. Muralidharan, 1991 gives a good analysis of the manner in which the English language press dealt with the destruction of the Babri mosque in Ayodhya.

CHAPTER 7

Terrorism and Religious Violence in South Asia: The Performative Politics of Fear

TERRORISM IN MODERN SOUTH ASIA

The history of terrorism in modern South Asia goes back to the nineteenth century. India, Pakistan and Bangladesh, which will be the focus of the following observations, not only share a common past of conflictual relations with each other in which time and again terrorism played an important role, but a common colonial experience as a unified state under British rule till Independence in 1947. The beginnings of terrorism as a political strategy lie in British-India. The historiography of the Indian freedom movement is marked—for historically obvious reasons—by the dominance first of the liberal camp within the Indian National Congress (INC) established in 1885, and later of Gandhi. This historiography emphasizes the constitutionally-oriented, more or less consistently non-violent tradition of political struggle against British rule, but this was by no means the only form of resistance. From the beginning, a violent mode of opposition also existed in South Asia which seldom operated openly, but which did influence the course of history through its very existence. The more radical members of the INC planned to include the existence of these groups in their political strategy and to use the possibility of a violent, terrorist alternative to the direct negotiations with the moderate camp of the Independence movement as a means of pressurizing the British.[1] Indeed, terrorism as an anti-colonial method indirectly, but sometimes also directly, played an important role in convincing the British rulers to negotiate structural reforms and gradual political participation even before First World War. Terrorism in colonial South Asia was, therefore, first and foremost an indirect means of coercion which functioned as a tactical addition to the strictly non-violent leadership of the Independence movement.

After Independence in 1947 the young Indian republic and Pakistan, which till 1971 consisted of West and East Pakistan, the latter being today's Bangladesh, were confronted with numerous forms of terrorism, including religiously motivated forms, which not only called in question the political systems as such but also national integrity. The Kashmir-conflict was initially one between two countries, and it was only in the 1980s and 1990s that the conflict developed into a front for religious-fundamentalist terror groups. In Punjab, a strong Independence movement had existed since the 1940s, which sought to establish a separate state for the Sikhs. At the end of the 1970s networks developed in this region which, from 1982 onwards, carried out selective attacks, initially against the administrative establishments of the state, but later also against those of civil society like public transport.[2] In 1984 this conflict led to the storming of the Golden Temple, the most holy shrine of the Sikhs, by troops of the Indian Army, since leaders of the movement had barricaded themselves inside the temple. The north-eastern region of India is another traditionally violence-prone area. A strong autonomy movement arose in this mainly Christianized region already in the 1950s. With logistic and military help from China and Pakistan the movement began its opposition to the government in Delhi.[3] Today there are over 30 organizations in this region which operate against the Indian state and which are also active beyond national boundaries, namely in Bhutan and Bangladesh.[4] In central India Maoist groups have been reacting since the 1960s to the catastrophic economic and social conditions, especially in rural areas, using these conditions to justify attacks on state institutions. In Pakistan, with a tradition of political Islam going back to the 1930s, there has been a spread of religious-fundamentalist networks in the last two or three decades[5] which has a strong influence on the internal politics of the country and, in the meantime, also on political developments in the entire region. In Bangladesh, the deficits of democracy in the history of the country as an independent nation since 1971 has led to an authoritarian structure which, for some years now, has been encouraging the spread of Islamic-fundamentalist organizations with links to Pakistan.[6]

South Asia is, therefore, a region where terrorism is, by no means, a new phenomenon. It was and is a region where numerous forms of terrorism with varying motivations have originated, which have gained a new dimension in an era of global networking. With regard to religiously motivated terrorism, which is our concern here, South Asia was and, now particularly, is a key region in the global perspective where organizational and ideological forms with an international bearing were and are being developed. A look at processes specific to the region therefore allows insights into developments in 'transnational terrorism'.[7] In what follows, the theoretical perspectives on performance, religion and politics will be carried forward and discussed in the context of this final example.

TERRORISM AND RELIGIOUS VIOLENCE AS A TRANSFORMATION OF SOCIAL REALITY

It is necessary to first look at the term 'terrorism' in order to understand the use of this concept which originated in Europe. Particularly in the context of globalizing processes which manifest themselves in an increasing internationalization of production, trade and other forms of social interaction, categories are often used which are meant to help understand apparently analogous developments all over the world. Terrorism is one such global category whose use in political debates masks its historical origins and the fact that it is, therefore, selective.[8] I proceed on the assumption that, with reference to South Asia, the use of the term 'terrorism' can be a useful epistemological tool. The problem, however, is to clearly distinguish the forms of violence associated with it from other forms of religious violence. This not only concerns the phenomenology of violence, i.e. its form and structure, but also the probable underlying causes of violence. It, therefore, needs to be emphasized at the outset that in South Asia religious terrorism and other forms of religiously motivated and religiously justified violence are inextricably linked and that religious terrorism cannot be understood adequately without taking this interdependency into account. This entails choosing a definition for terrorism in South Asia that is, on the one hand, concrete enough to be meaningful, i.e. it can be distinguished from other forms of religious violence, but, on the other, is open enough to allow the regional context to be thematized.

Terrorism is here taken to mean, very broadly, a strategy of violence that is used exclusively by people not linked with the state in order to create an atmosphere of fear in society as a whole or among sections of this society, in other words, to spread terror. Political goals are thereby set in accordance with a self-chosen world-view. The method used in this strategy is to work underground and act without any warning in order to reduce the predictability of actions as far as possible. A necessary precondition for terrorism is, therefore, the existence of such a world-view which legitimizes terrorism as a strategy. In the case of religious terrorism it is religious fundamentalism which constitutes this framework. It not only justifies violence itself, but also the overarching context in which acts of terrorist violence gain their significance. Conversely, however, the interdependency between fundamentalism and violence cannot be reduced to terrorism because, with reference to India for example, Hindu fundamentalist excesses also lead to other forms of violence. Examples of this are religious pogroms against minorities, genocide-like attacks which result in mass murder and mass-displacement, or selective campaigns which provoke quasi-spontaneous violence against people of other faiths.[9] In the context of relations between different religious communities in South Asia terrorism and other forms of religious violence enter into a correlation pregnant with consequences which has to be taken into consideration in order to understand terrorism better. In the following examples given from South Asia's contemporary history it therefore becomes clear that religious terrorism and other forms of religious violence not only exist alongside each other, but that they also interact with one another and have to be mostly interpreted in direct connection with one another.

The earlier specification of actors not associated with the state does not exclude the state as the direct point of reference, or as the actual actor, in the context of terrorism. In South Asia the state emerges, on the one hand, as the target of religious terrorism, since it is the enemy of religious-fundamentalist groups, especially Islamic ones. On the other hand, however, the state itself is, as will be shown, the direct initiator of other forms of religious violence such as pogroms against religious minorities. These forms cannot be termed terrorist although they undoubtedly spread terror. Both groups of actors, whether associated with the state or not, are thus initiators of religious terror which does not necessarily stem from terrorism.

Religious terrorism as a strategy in South Asia functions mainly in two ways. Given the connection between the world-view of the individuals or the organizations, on the one hand, and terrorism as a method, on the other, it can be understood as a specific strategy of communication that compels those directly targeted and the larger public to take note of the message.[10] Contemporary forms of regional and transnational terrorism especially function within the framework and in accordance with the structural prerequisites of an 'economy of attention' which, like the financial capital of classical economy—often also an important aspect of the terrorists' plans—revolves around attention-capital.[11] This form of capital, however, does not exist and function solely in its own interests, but in a close interaction with political power for example, which too increasingly defines itself through attention. In this economy of attention terrorism is an extremely effective strategy of capital accumulation which, in turn, regulates the access to political power. Terrorist activities that succeed in gaining a high degree of attention over a long span of time automatically gain political relevance regardless of the state's reaction, even if this reaction normally determines the success of the provocation. However, to deduce from this that the act of violence 'primarily has a symbolic significance' since it is the 'bearer of a message' which says that 'this could befall anyone'[12] would entail a functional reduction of the act of terror and does not do justice to its mode of functioning which actually goes far beyond this.

Terrorism is by no means only the mere communication of a message, but the effect of the message is also intrinsic to its functioning, and this effect is capable of changing reality itself, or, at the very least, the perception of reality. What is decisive, therefore, is how the attack is received by the broader public, and this experience is incorporated in the plan itself. In addition to the act of communication through a radical act of violence terrorism influences the paradigms of self-perception of a society or of certain groups within it.[13] Basic assumptions about the constitution of society such as the function of the state to protect its citizens, the guarantee of public safety, or even the self-understanding of Indian society, for example, as the co-existence of different religious groups, are directly questioned through the act of terror and can lead to a breakdown in the structure of a society.[14] Following J.L. Austin one can also interpret terrorism as a 'speech-act' which not only communicates something but which, in the act of execution itself, already changes reality and must therefore be closely related to its context in order to be understood and to be effective.[15] This change concerns individuals, especially those who, as potential victims, are directly affected by the act of terror, but also collectives, whose social imagination changes.

However, terrorism is context-bound also in another sense. It tries to create a political situation which seeks to narrow down, as far as possible, the scope for reaction by the state or by other opponents. Naturally, terrorism can never completely narrow down the options for reaction to its provocation, but through the context and the kind of attack, or the goal it selects, it is sometimes able to leave its opponent with no political alternative other than a vehement counter-reaction. This, in turn, focuses attention on the terrorists and gives them political significance. Terrorism as a political strategy in India, Pakistan and Bangladesh takes place in an already existing, highly sensitive atmosphere of tensions between these countries, on the one hand, and between groups not associated with the state on the other. Its effect then unfolds within this scenario.

The direct reference to the region with its social and political specificities is, therefore, a decisive prerequisite for an adequate discussion of this topic. In what follows, answers will be sought chiefly to two questions, namely the reason for religious violence or religious terrorism in South Asia today and how its mode of functioning can be understood in the present context through the use of performative approaches.

STATEHOOD IN SOUTH ASIA: HISTORICAL CAUSES OF TERRORISM AND RELIGIOUS VIOLENCE

Terrorism and religious violence in South Asia cannot be traced back to a single cause or a particular development. Since the 1980s the region is going through an accelerated transformational process through which sections of its societies are becoming part of the internationally active elite, while for large sections of the population this process only means the continuance of their precarious existence. South Asia is thus in the process of a comprehensive and highly complex transformation which, with its social and economic consequences, also affects the co-existence of different religious groups. One of the decisive factors and also the cause of religious violence in South Asia is the historical legacy of statehood, i.e. the varying formations of the post-colonial states in India, Pakistan and Bangladesh. This not only affects the relations between these states but also relations between religious majorities and minorities, in other words, mainly between Hindus and Muslims. The constitution of statehood thus becomes the point of departure for anti-state terrorist violence even if it cannot completely explain the causes for religious terrorism.

After the chaos of Partition in 1947 the political elite in India around the first prime minister, Jawaharlal Nehru, made an effort to establish a political system which would allow for increasing democratic participation and for the peaceful and prosperous coexistence of all sections of society within a national project of modernization. The relationship of the state to religion was ambivalent from the beginning. On the one hand, the young republic pledged itself to secularism and, especially, to social modernization. State authority was interpreted as an instrument to counter separate religious identities and mobilization on such platforms in order to establish and maintain national integrity.[16] The political institution for this task was the centrist party of consensus (the Congress party) which had brought together the most diverse ideological camps within its fold and which thus represented a hegemonic block that ensured the continuity of the nation in the framework of democracy while consolidating the new state.[17]

On the other hand, however, an attempt was made in the first decades to actively influence the organization of religion through the state. The state undertook an active role in ensuring religious plurality by financing religious infrastructure or by handing over civil jurisdiction to religious communities, especially in the case of the Christian and Muslim minorities.[18] The result of this ambivalence towards religion was, however, that it did not allow an adequate political instrument to be created which could include the socially very relevant factor of religion in political mechanisms of control.[19] The institutions of Indian democracy thus did not have the means to integrate religion in the processes of consensus-formation and to deal with the issue of relations between Hindus and Muslims, for example, in a politically effective manner. The logic of modernization and secularization of the post-colonial state in India ensured that religion as a social force was always interpreted and sanctioned from a position of superior authority and thus gained the nimbus of the pejorative and the polemical. The state's ambivalent relationship to religion became evident in the crisis of the 'Congress-system' in the 1970s when the party that had once dominated experienced a crisis of authority. Indira Gandhi and the Congress leadership tried to overcome this crisis by 'Hinduizing' politics in an attempt to establish a democratic majority by mobilizing the Hindus. This model found followers in the 1980s and 1990s and brought forth Hindu nationalism as an independent political movement.[20] It brought about a shift in the character of political culture in India which exposed religious minorities to a considerable amount of pressure and even to state-sponsored inter-communal violence. The politicization of the Hindu majority was a paradigmatic break with the traditional political understanding of the republic, and the state could not counter this move on account of its own, largely unclarified, relationship with religion. The result is an atmosphere of interreligious hostility, especially towards Muslims and Christians, including persecution similar to genocide. Islamic religious terrorism is reacting to this changed context through 'counter-measures' which target civil and religious institutions of the Hindu majority. The state is, therefore, under a dual threat: from a politicized Hinduism, on the one hand, which is opposing the secular character of the country, and, on the other hand, from terrorism which is trying to undermine the functioning of the state.

The aspect of statehood in the context of religious violence and terrorism presents a completely different picture in Pakistan. The aim of this state, its foundation-myth, was to give the Muslims of British-India a home, and this was justified on the grounds that Muslim interests were not adequately represented by the Indian National Congress. The Muslim League became the political organ that governed Pakistan after Independence. In contrast to the Congress, however, it did not develop any democratic mechanisms within the party with a corresponding mass base, but remained an elitist movement that used Islam as a tool for mobilization.[21] This character of the Muslim League was also transposed onto the nation, Pakistan, which, directly after 1947, was governed by an elite that had not, however, come from the Muslim majority provinces of British-India and was only able to develop weak institutions. Although Mohammed Ali Jinnah, the first Governor-General of Pakistan, had stated before the constituent assembly that religion and faith had nothing to do with the state, Islam, even in the 1950s, increasingly functioned as the central marker of collective national identity.[22] A broad Islamization from 1979 onwards, which affected mainly the education sector and basic political consensus in Pakistan, not only encouraged the rise of Islamic groups in Pakistan, but it also aggravated the interreligious conflict between the country's Sunni majority and Shia minority since the thrust of Islamization was oriented towards a fundamentalist theology of Sunni-Islam.[23] Other religious minorities like Christians or Sikhs traditionally occupy a marginalized social position which exposes them to the hostility of the religious majority especially during crises of the state. From the beginning Pakistan as a state, therefore, had to struggle with the problem of its social legitimacy which was aggravated by the weak representational character of its political institutions. This was compensated in turn by the importance of the military and the administration. This historical legacy creates, on the one hand, favourable conditions for terrorism and, on the other, it is also a structural prerequisite for political relations and networks in the region especially with regard to India. The character of the state is, in any case, a decisive criterion for explaining the contemporary situation.

Bangladesh as a nation is the result of the futile efforts made by Pakistan to realize an effective national integration. Islamabad's excessive centralism and the politically repressive hegemony of West Pakistan accompanied by a complete disregard for the demographic relations between both parts of the country led to the formation of Bangladesh in 1971. The new state initially set out to establish a democratic and secular foundation. India's role in bringing Independence to Bangladesh meant that the new nation also took its political orientation from India and aspired to a similar political system. The pragmatic politics of Sheikh Mujibur Rahman's government, however, failed to establish the requisite democratic institutions of the state which would have provided the structures required for this goal.[24] These deficiencies in the framework of the state led to increasing disintegration and to the emergency in 1975 which gave the government special powers to carry out an authoritarian rule. After the lifting of emergency in 1977 General Zia ur-Rahman had the principle of secularism and the ban on religious political parties removed from the constitution in order to extend his power-base.[25] This trend of the Islamization of politics continued in the 1980s and it also led to an increase in the number of Koran schools in Bangladesh—a development that mirrored the one in Pakistan.[26] The social situation of the minorities gradually worsened and the Hindus especially, who constitute roughly 10 per cent of the population, faced increasing hostility which was fuelled by attacks on the Muslim minority in India. Today, Bangladesh is a country divided between the spheres of influence of two dominating parties which are trying to establish political supremacy in the framework of democracy by catering to radical-Islamic forces. Although assessments about the progress of Islamization differ radically from one another, it can be said that the process is being continued—with support also from the Arab countries and from Pakistan—and this is gradually changing the character of the state.[27]

These current changes in the South Asian states are based on historical developments and post-colonial conditions which are almost analogous in the case of Pakistan and Bangladesh. Both states were unable to set-up functioning systems and democratic institutions after they were established. Both states have tried to compensate these deficits through authoritarian rule and alliances with religious-extremist organizations and parties. In India, the state continues to be more efficient and, therefore, also more visible, but even here its character is undergoing change with the crisis of the post-colonial process of modernization. The current development with regard to religious fundamentalism and terrorism is characterized by the fact that the nationalist religious movements opposed to the state in South Asia are building networks in the framework of a 'subaltern globalization'[28] and are thus becoming regional, or even, transnational actors. The individual states in the region are finding it increasingly difficult to deal with this development. The crisis or, in the case of India, the transformation of the state is, therefore, the decisive historical condition which has made the present boom in terrorist and other violent activities possible.

VIOLENT SPEECH-ACTS: SOUTH ASIAN TERROR AND COUNTER-TERROR

The paramount goal of terrorism is to change the atmosphere of the societies it is opposed to, which leaves the governments of these states no real alternative as regards their reaction to terrorist acts. Terrorism can be termed religious when it sees its ultimate justification in a cosmological end-time struggle that takes place between good and evil with the terrorists viewing themselves as the facilitators in the completion of this struggle.[29] This fundamentalist perspective is by no means oriented only to the afterlife, rather its primary battle arena is this world itself in which the eschatological reign of god has to be established.[30] From the point of view of its arena religious terrorism is worldly, but its basic dimension is cosmological. Terror itself thus becomes not only a moral commandment but the advent of the actual history of salvation.

If one looks at this framework of action it becomes clear that (religious) terrorism involves a strategy of communication[31] analogous to performative nation-building. Regardless of the circumstances acts of terrorism are only meaningful when they are perceived as such by as broad a section of the public as possible and then interpreted, i.e. read correspondingly. With these public acts of repugnant violence the terrorists force the people to take note of the religious and political message behind the acts. This is a case of an extreme form of enforced communication between hidden actors and the public that receives the ideological message in a manner which compels it to pay attention. Since the real goal of violence exists independently of the act of violence and only uses the latter as a means to an end, the symbolic dimension, the impression created by the act of violence is its real content. Regardless of the actual number of victims the 'performance', the 'theatre' of the outburst of violence aims at a communication which consists of the symbolic reversal of the given power relations. The sudden and unexpected eruption of violence against the social or political body of the opponent reveals the latter's defencelessness and weakness and allows those who are actually powerless and weak to appear as masters of the situation. This in turn dictates the laws of further action. In its character as a symbolic performative act religious terrorism can be analysed in the same way as religious rituals or religious nationalism as performative nation-building. As shown above, performative acts not only reproduce reality, they also change it. The real content of terrorist violence consists both in the symbolic communication with the public as well as in the transformation of reality which is manifested each time in the behaviour of those directly and indirectly affected. If the aim is an adequate understanding of terrorism according to its own logic, these two dimensions which are analogous to performative nation-building will also have to be analysed and interpreted.

THE REPUBLIC OF INDIA BETWEEN *PUNYABHOOMI* AND *DAR AL-ISLAM*

Interestingly, the number of people killed in India through acts of terror has gone down considerably in recent years. The relatively good statistics available for India normally distinguish between different categories of victims. If one, however, includes civil victims, security forces and the terrorists themselves, we see that the number of victims was highest in 2001 (almost 5,840). Since then this number has been decreasing continuously. In 2004 the number of victims was 2,642, while a year later the figure stood at 2,519. These figures also allow us to draw conclusions about the context and the possible ideological motivations for the acts of violence. Between 1994 and 2005 a total of 18,151 civilians were killed in India by terrorist attacks. 10,483 of these were from Jammu & Kashmir, roughly 7,000 victims were recorded in the north-eastern region of the country and the rest were in the Punjab and other regions.[32] However, these figures do not allow any inferences about the organizations carrying out these attacks and their respective ideological background. Left-wing terrorism is altogether explicitly excluded from the data. However, the high ratio of the Kashmir-conflict indicates a strong quotient of religious-fundamentalist violence which mainly affects the civilian population, but also the security forces especially since the war between India and Pakistan in 1999 in which Islamist-terrorist groups also participated. Terrorism in the north-eastern region of the country can also be attributed to the secessionist movements there which are not all religiously motivated. In Punjab, however, terrorism motivated by religion plays a dominant role.

Against the backdrop of these statistical trends politicians and others assume that there has been a rise in religious terrorism which, in its varying forms, has succeeded in becoming the focus of national attention. Religious terrorism is thus also able to determine the political agenda.[33] This accumulation of attention also had a considerable influence on relations between the countries, especially with Pakistan, but also with Bangladesh, since the regional networking between terrorist organizations had, by then, increased significantly.

Terror and terrorism in India today consist of two differing trends, or two long-term developments which arose independently but which, in the meantime, are interrelated in specific ways. The first trend is the growing social anchoring of an extremist Hindu fundamentalism which has brought together politics, violence and public mobilization. After the genocide-like excesses against Muslims in 2002 in Gujarat in which many people died and countless others lost their livelihood, Chief Minister Narendra Modi actually tried to use the emergency situation to project himself to voters.

Modi's first opportunity came during the annual Jagannath Rath Yatra when a statue of the deity Jagannath is transported about 3 km through the narrow lanes of the old city in Ahmedabad. Already in the previous years this traditional popular event had offered extremist Hindu organizations an ideal setting for the enrolment of new members. In 2002 the Yatra began in June under the strictest security measures even as the civil commotion continued. These measures led to an exodus of several thousands of Muslims from the city for fear of renewed excesses and violent attacks. Modi did not see any reason to call off the Yatra, instead he led the procession himself in order to assert the 'right of the Hindus' to practise their religion freely. Only two months earlier Modi had asked the Muslims in Gujarat not to take out any processions during Muharram, since they would otherwise be responsible for any renewed violence.[34] The Yatra proceeded peacefully, but Modi used the atmosphere of fear to project himself as a defender of the Hindu cause. On 19 July, after the end of the legislature period, Modi dissolved the state assembly and asked the Election Commission in Delhi to announce new elections at the earliest. A fierce political debate broke out in the parliament in Delhi about the legality of elections under the present circumstances in Gujarat. After the Election Commission had examined the situation it declared that elections could take place in December 2002 at the earliest. Modi replied with renewed religious-nationalist actionism. At the end of September and the beginning of October Modi organized the 'Gujarat Gaurav Yatra', the journey of Gujarati pride, across the state. During this journey he had the opportunity to tell the people about his election manifesto which consisted mainly of old stereotypes and hostility against the Muslims. Thus, Modi alluded to the cliché about the numerical advantage that Muslims would soon have over Hindus which would help them to dominate India through a higher fertility rate:

> What should we do? Run relief camps for them? Do we want to open baby-producing centres? But for certain people that means 'hum paanch, hamare pachis' (we five and our 25). . . . We must teach a lesson to those who multiply like this.[35]

Before the actual election day on 12 December the VHP wanted to organize a Vijay Yatra.[36] As active support for Modi in the election campaign the VHP planned to start the journey on 17 November in Godhra and end it on 6 December at the Akshardham temple in Gandhinagar which had been attacked by Islamic fundamentalists in September. The date for the end of the journey would also mark the 'celebrations' for the tenth anniversary of the destruction of the Babri mosque.[37] The Election Commission, however, did not give permission for this undertaking and threatened to further postpone the elections. Since this was not in the chief minister's interests he prevented this plan and paved the way for the elections.

The second trend in India is the rise in the political significance of Islamist terror which has close organizational connections with Pakistan. The goal of these Islamic fundamentalist groups is the restoration of Islamic rule in South Asia and, thus, the transformation of India into an Islamic sphere of influence. The provocation through terror attacks aimed at military escalation in South Asia is a long-term process which, in India, initially appeared in the region of Kashmir. The conflict, which has existed since Independence, underwent a qualitative change since the end of the 1980s. Between 1988 and 1990 newly-established jihadist groups in India intervened in the conflict for the first time and fought for the independence of this Himalayan region. When the Indian government indulged in large-scale manipulation during local elections in 1987 the Jammu & Kashmir Liberation Front was established, followed by the Hizbul Mujaheddin in 1989 which had greater organizational capabilities. Between 1991 and 1995 the pro-Pakistan groups in the Indian part of Kashmir gained considerable ground and increasingly marginalized the moderate forces in the Valley. From 1996, or 1997, the number of foreign, Islamic-fundamentalist mercenaries in the Valley greatly increased.[38] This process, which is still going on, began at the time of the political rise of the Taliban in Afghanistan, leading to references about the 'Talibanization' of the Kashmir-conflict in the relevant literature.[39] According to conservative estimates the number of foreign mercenaries has increased from 15 (1990) to 60-70 per cent today.[40] The growing significance of the Pakistan intelligence service (Inter-Service Intelligence, ISI) in this regional conflict also took place during this time.[41] The regional terror in Kashmir entered the national stage for the first time in October 2001 when four suicide-bombers of the Jaish-e-Mohammed, a radical-Islamist group established in 1999, exploded a car bomb in front of the assembly building in Srinagar killing 32 people and causing immense damage. For the first time an establishment of the Indian state was the direct goal of a terrorist attack. Islamist terror thus succeeded in becoming a national concern in India. On 13 December of the same year the Jaish-e-Mohammed went a step further in their attack on the state when five of its members attacked the Indian parliament in New Delhi with grenades, machine guns and explosives. The parliament was in session at that time. With 11 people dead, the number of victims was relatively low, but the political resonance was enormous. When the responsibility for the act became clear the Indian government–led at that time by the Hindu-nationalist BJP which traditionally has strained relations with Pakistan–ordered the mobilization of Indian troops on the border with Pakistan. The then home minister, L.K. Advani, accused the Pakistan government of inaction and of indirect collusion through the involvement of the Pakistan intelligence service.[42] There was no follow-up to this aggressive posturing, but for several months the threat of war remained acute. The terrorist attacks on local trains in Mumbai on 11 July 2006 were carried out by the Lashkar-e-Taiba, a group operating out of Pakistan, and were a sign that Islamist groups in India had improved their organizational capacities.[43] When several attacks are carried out simultaneously–which is very complicated from an organizational and logistical perspective–it leads to greater chaos than individual attacks and bears testimony to the increased capabilities of the terrorists.

Both these trends–the rise of Hindu-fundamentalism in India, on the one hand, and the increased political significance of Islamist terror, on the other–not only exist alongside each other, but they also interact. The first tendencies of this logic of terror and counter-terror were already evident in 1993 when a series of 13 bomb-attacks occurred in Mumbai as a result of the violence against Muslims in the aftermath of the Babri episode in Ayodhya. The people who had carried out these attacks were located in the milieu of the Islamist mafia. More than 250 people died in these retaliatory attacks and over 700 were injured. In a direct reaction to the pogrom-like excesses of violence against Muslims in Gujarat in 2002 two members of the Lashkar-e-Taiba carried out an attack on the Akshardham temple in Gandhinagar, the capital of Gujarat. On 5 July 2005 five men tried to storm the barricades around the ruins of the mosque in Ayodhya. They threw hand-grenades and engaged the security forces in an exchange of fire in which all five perpetrators died. The Lashkar-e-Taiba was deemed to have been responsible for this attack also. It is said to have trained the five attackers who came into India through Nepal. In a countermove Hindu-fundamentalist groups in India called for stronger measures against Pakistan and, to this end, applied pressure on the government.[44] This act of terror clearly demonstrates the political logic of terror and counter-terror. In Indian domestic politics Ayodhya is a highly sensitive and symbolically laden place which now stands for the increasing strength of radical Hinduism and hostilities against Muslims. The only aim of the attack was to force a violent confrontation between Hindu fundamentalists and Islamist extremists which would, in turn, escalate the conflict between India and Pakistan with the goal of establishing a new Islamic rule in South Asia in the aftermath of this–possibly also nuclear–conflict.[45] At present, therefore, domestic politics in India is determined by this fatal logic of terror and counter-terror which severely limits the possibilities for action. The change of government in 2004, when the Hindu-nationalist BJP was voted out, reduced tensions in the short-term, since pressure on the religious minorities was reduced. This is one of the first conditions to break out of the vicious circle of terror and counter-terror. The confrontation between the Indian state and Islamist terrorism, however, continues, as does the conflict in Kashmir.

THE OLIGOPOLY OF VIOLENCE IN PAKISTAN

Pakistan differs from India not only in the nature of its statehood which has traditionally been closely linked with Islam and, since Zia-ul-Haq's dictatorship, also with Islamic fundamentalism. On account of India's rising economic and military strength Pakistan's strategic importance for the USA had been steadily decreasing. The catastrophe of 11 September 2001 made it the focus of Washington's interests again. Pakistan became the decisive front-line state in the war against terror as defined by the USA. As a result, sanctions that had been in place since the nuclear tests in 1998 were lifted and Pakistan was once again at the top of the list of countries receiving American financial aid.[46] USA's traditional ally in the days of the Cold War thus regained a privileged status in Washington's political calculations, although this only served to cover up, or even exacerbate, changes in Pakistan but did not resolve any problems.

After the previously discussed changes of the state in Pakistan in the 1980s which brought about a greater involvement of radical-Islamic organizations in national and local politics and, especially, in the education sector, the 1990s were chiefly a decade of increasing poverty and worsening internal security. The significant decline in economic growth, a further deterioration of the infrastructure in the country and the precarious financial condition of the state as a whole led to a rise in poverty. The number of people living below the poverty-line rose in the period from 1987/8 till 1999/2000 from 17 to 32 per cent.[47] This was accompanied by a steady worsening of internal security which further undermined the state's monopoly on violence.

At the same time the social relevance of radical-Islamic forces increased, especially through their involvement in the education sector. In many religious-extremist milieus work in education is a priority since it ensures the continuation or the spread of one's world-view and also helps in training reliable recruits. Since the government neglected to register the religious schools (*madrasas*) in the country and to place them under state control, there are no exact figures about the number of such schools. According to the Home Ministry in Islamabad there are about 13,500 religious schools in Pakistan. Other estimates name a figure of at least 20,000.[48] Those schools among these roughly 20,000 that are not registered have about 1.5 million pupils and their syllabi are not subjected to any form of control.[49] The largest network of such schools is run by the Jamiat Ulema-e-Islami which, on a local level in Baluchistan, was a coalition partner of the military dictator Pervez Musharraf. For reasons of political strategy, therefore, the dictatorial government found it difficult to show greater initiative in this area. This, however, makes Pakistan one of the most important training-grounds for followers of a radical-Islamic ideology whose activities are, by no means, limited to the territory of Pakistan. Within the country Islamist groups like the Jaish-e-Mohammed, the Lashkar-e-Taiba or the Harkat-ul-Mujaheddin—all established in the last 25 years—mainly carry out terrorist attacks on the Shiite minority and thus contribute to a further deterioration of the security situation.[50]

Along with the previously mentioned increase in *jihadi* activities in Kashmir—even on the Pakistan side—the new dimensions of terrorism in Pakistan are mainly the regional and trans-national networks that have grown in recent years. The events in Afghanistan, which brought the Taliban to power and thus also strengthened the presence of the al-Qaida, are directly linked with changes in Pakistan. The difficult domestic situation in Pakistan enabled a close and intensive cooperation between radical-Islamic organizations in the country and the then new political rulers in Afghanistan. The Pakistani military was also involved in this. Its military personnel helped to train the Islamist cadres, covered up the financial transactions of the concerned organizations and provided logistical support. Although the motives for this cooperation have not been fully established, these are most likely to be a combination of strategic interest in consolidating the political power of the Taliban and ideological allegiance.[51] Some of the Islamist groups in Pakistan also have trans-national connections. The Pakistani or Kashmiri diasporas in North America, western Europe or in the Gulf states help to maintain training camps outside the region and recruit new cadre.[52]

An additional political factor in connection with terrorism is the Pakistan intelligence service, the ISI. The Indian government has repeatedly accused the ISI of complicity in terror attacks and of supporting terrorist networks that are working against India. The assumptions range from financial support and propaganda to training of terrorists.[53] Whatever be the case, the fact remains that in

Pakistan institutions of the state, like the military and the intelligence service, are closely linked with radical Islamic organizations which, for their part, increase their social relevance through their growing involvement in the education sector. The break-down of the state, which has affected an increasing number of areas of social life in recent years, has become the decisive condition for the emergence of an oligopoly of violence in Pakistan in which the state itself is only one of many players.

TERRORISM IN AND FROM BANGLADESH

Like Pakistan, Bangladesh also has immense economic problems and a political system that is only partly functional. Since its Independence in 1971 Bangladesh has progressed in numerous areas of social development, such as life-expectancy or primary education. Despite this, state expenditure on health and education, for example, remains very low and the population falls back on alternative offers including those from radical Islamist groups. The unproven figure of 64,000 schools—a number that has sharply risen in recent years—bears witness to these deficits.[54] This is accompanied by an extremely inefficient political system. In two successive years (2000 and 2001) Transparency International declared Bangladesh to be the most corrupt country in the world.[55] The nepotism of the two-party system that has been established since the restoration of democracy in 1991 is severely criticized by the people of Bangladesh. In contrast to this, the Jamaat-e-Islami, an Islamic fundamentalist party, presents itself as a party free of corruption. It also functions far more efficiently than the two ruling parties and has therefore been able to record a slow but steady political ascendancy.[56]

Since its Independence Bangladesh, like India, was confronted with different forms of terrorism, of which Islamic terrorism was and is only one kind. Along with the earlier mentioned political party, the Jamaat-e-Islami, there are mainly two fundamentalist organizations that form the focus of critical assessments of Islamism in Bangladesh: the Jagrat Muslim Janata Bangladesh (Awakened Muslim Masses of Bangladesh) which was established in 2003 with the goal of an Islamic revolution, and the Jamaat-al-Mujaheddin Bangladesh (Party of God's Warriors of Bangladesh) which has been carrying out a violent struggle against democracy since 1998 with the aim of establishing Islamic law.[57] Bomb attacks by these two groups in recent years have been directed mainly against the ruling parties, claiming the life of a former finance minister in January 2005.[58] In August of the same year more than 500 bombs exploded in Bangladesh which were directed against institutions of the state, against journalists and lawyers. Responsibility for these attacks has been laid at the door of the Jamaat-al-Mujaheddin.[59] On the whole, however, there is a lack of research on Islamism in Bangladesh which makes it difficult to arrive at any definite conclusions about the real extent of the problem in the country. India has repeatedly accused Bangladesh of supporting the secessionist movements in north-east India, or of not taking adequate steps against such groups operating from their national territory. According to Indian sources, the Pakistan intelligence service, the ISI, is also supporting the activities of these groups.[60] According to police reports the ISI is also linked to Pakistani and international Islamist networks in Bangladesh which are said, for example, to have planned the attacks in Morocco in 2004.[61] The attack on the American Information and Cultural Centre in Kolkata in January 2002 is also said to have been initiated in Bangladesh.[62] However, there is no clear proof of this.

Estimates of the extent to which Bangladesh has been infiltrated by radical Islamic organizations differ. However, developments appear to have taken place which indicate that the process of radicalization through religious-fundamentalist groups is bound to increase in the years to come. Given the combination of a politically irrelevant parliament and a corrupt administration Bangladesh does not have the necessary democratic and legal means to defend itself against this internal collapse of the state.

CONCLUSION

Against the backdrop of the long history of terrorism as a political strategy in South Asia the region today is again important for what has become transnational terrorism. Pakistan's position, in particular, and the developments in its territory have a significance which goes far beyond the subcontinent. In South Asia itself terrorism motivated by religion is directly linked with relations between the countries concerned on the one hand, viz. India, Pakistan and Bangladesh, and, on the other, with internal political developments in these countries. As speech-acts, these acts of terrorism are not only able to convey a message each time, but they also succeed in changing reality and, therefore, also the political conditions. South Asia thus finds itself in a dilemma which, to a great extent, these countries have either allowed to happen or have even actively created.

If these states do not undertake any counter-measures, which consist, first and foremost, in fulfilling the duties of the state effectively, the relevance of terrorism will only increase. Given South Asia's ethnic and religious composition such a development would be disastrous, even from an international point-of-view, since two nuclear powers in the region are engaged in a lasting Cold War which has already been affected by terrorist attacks and could continue to do so in the future.

NOTES

1. Heehs, 1998, p. 6.
2. Cf. for this Mehra/Sharma, 2006, pp. 45f.
3. Hazarika, 2006; cf. also Mehra/Sharma, 2006, p. 50.
4. Hussain, 2004.
5. Cf. for this Schied, 2004, pp. 235f.
6. International Crisis Group, 2006.
7. For the concept of 'Transnational Terrorism', cf. Schneckener, 2006, p. 49.
8. Cf. Wickramsinghe, 2006, esp. p. 382.
9. For the difference between genocide and terrorism for example, cf. Ali, 2004.
10. Andersen/Sloan, 1995, p. 348; Waldmann, 2003, p. 88; Waldmann, 2005.
11. Franck, 2007.

12. Waldmann, 2005, p. 15.
13. Cf. Derrida/Habermas, 2003, p. 57.
14. Thackrah, 2004, p. 264.
15. Austin, 1962; for the use of the speech-act theory and Bourdieu's application of the same to the context of religious violence, cf. Juergensmeyer, 2004, p. 175 and Six, 2006, pp. 193f.
16. Mitra, 1991, p. 764.
17. Kothari, 1964.
18. Chatterjee, 1998, pp. 353f.
19. Mitra, 1991, p. 760.
20. For the decline in the authority of state institutions, cf. Kaviraj, 1984. On the rise of Hindu nationalism in this context see Mitra, 1990, pp. 86f.
21. Ganguly, 2007, p. 76.
22. Cf. Jinnah's speech to the Constituent Assembly on 11 August 1947, reproduced in the original in Hay, 1991, pp. 385-7, here p. 387.
23. Nasr, 2002, p. 88.
24. Ganguly, 2007, p. 80.
25. Rao, 2004, pp. 194f.
26. Khan, 2006, pp. 181f.
27. International Crisis Group, 2006, p. 5.
28. Ahmed, 2003, pp. 360f.
29. Cf. for this Juergensmeyer, 2001, Chap. 1.
30. Riesebrodt, 2004, pp. 23f.
31. Cf. Anderson/Sloan 1995, p. 348; Waldmann, 2003, p. 88.
32. The figures have been taken from the South Asia terrorism portal and can be seen in http://www.satp.org/satporgtp/countries/india/database/fatalities.htm. Last seen 3 June 2007. The data explicitly excludes left-wing terrorism.
33. Cf. for this, for example, Witschel, 2003, p. 21.
34. Bunsha, 2002, p. 6.
35. Bunsha, 2002a.
36. Hindi, literally the victory journey.
37. Bunsha, 2002b.
38. Khan, 2006, p. 168.
39. Cf. for example, Rashid, 1999 and Evans, 2001.
40. Khan, 2006, p. 169.
41. Knudsen, 2002, p. 39.

42. Advani, 2001.
43. Swami, 2006.
44. Cf. for this Ramakrishnan, 2005.
45. Cf. for this, for example, the pamphlet 'Why are we waging Jihad?' by the Lashkar-e-Taiba, which can be seen in: http://www.satp.org/satporgtp/countries/india/states/jandk/terrorist_outfits/lashkar_e_ toiba.htm. Last seen 3 June 2007.
46. Cf. for this Cheema, 2003, pp. 48f.
47. Hussain, 2003, p. 132.
48. International Crisis Group, 2007, p. 5.
49. International Crisis Group, 2004.
50. Schneckener, 2006, pp. 92f.
51. Sreedhar, 2004, pp. 64f; cf. also Schneckener, 2006, pp. 83f.
52. Schneckener, 2006, p. 94.
53. Rao, 2004, pp. 186 and 194.
54. Lintner, 2002.
55. Rahman, 2003, p. 169.
56. Rahman, 2003, p. 172; Bangladesh assessment, 2006, to be found in http://www.satp.org/satporgtp/countries/bangladesh/index.htm. Last seen 3 June 2007.
57. International Crisis Group, 2006, p. 16.
58. Khaṇ, 2006, p. 180.
59. Chattopadhyay/Habib, 2006.
60. Rahman, 2003, p. 176.
61. Chattopadhyay/Habib, 2006.
62. International Crisis Group, 2006, p. 17.

CHAPTER 8

Spectacular Politics, Power and Constructed Consensus: Some Conclusions

Having discussed historical examples from colonial and post-colonial India we can now once again summarize and elucidate the insights gained in order to return to the theoretical questions formulated at the beginning. Going beyond India's historical and cultural specificities the attempt will be to show patterns that are relevant also for the general debate on nationalism, politics and religion. Such an attempt initially appears to be difficult since the specificities of South Asia's historical experiences, especially the consequences of colonial subjugation which reach into the present, are too distinct to fit into a general formulation. Nevertheless, the following thoughts demonstrate interesting parallels to other post-colonial societies in the context of increasing economic liberalization. The sociological debates around this focus on themes such as fundamentalism, globalization or the general return of religion as the decisive framework of meaning not only in post-colonial societies, but also in the West.[1] After the theoretical failure of theories of modernization we now see that contrary to expectations religious nationalism and even fundamentalism determine social realities in these complex, post-colonial societies like India with a renewed emphasis and presence.

This is why an attempt is being made here to conclude by trying to gain some insights from the historical examples for further theoretical discussions on this broad theme. In what follows Pierre Bourdieu's concept of the 'field' will be used in order to propose an alternative understanding of politics that allows for an adequate discussion and analysis of the role of religion. This approach is interesting insofar as it was developed by Bourdieu with reference to the historical and social transformation of Algerian (i.e. of an African) society. If one conceives of politics or nationalism as a field, quasi as a discursive terrain on which contesting versions of national self-understanding, contesting ideas of the meaning of religion or contesting concepts of anti-colonial and post-colonial politics are fought out in order to achieve the social 'power to formulate', it allows for a more adequate discussion of the different cyclical booms of politicized religion. It also obviates the necessity of getting involved in the logic of secularization which, in the long-term, proceeds from the disappearance of religion. Religion as a discourse always remains in reserve as an alternative, especially in politics, even though it may not play a dominant role in different periods and epochs. This non-secular, alternative understanding of politics comes to the fore, especially in crisis situations, when the 'ontological certainties'[2] of a society appear to be threatened. Religion always offers this imagined security, even after secular phases of national politics.

STRATEGIES FOR THE MEDIATION OF POLITICAL CONTENT: DISCOURSE AND PERFORMANCE

The concept of performative nation-building that has been sketched out essentially attempts to answer a very simple question, namely how a concrete political and participatory programme can be developed out of a theoretical and initially very abstract idea of a nation—a programme that can enthuse people, gain their commitment and thus become a historically important factor. This question arises from the fact that the concept of nation, in contrast to other more limited forms of collective identity like the family or regional units such as the village or city, goes far beyond the range of personal experience and is, therefore, difficult to perceive and experience in the same measure. In order to translate the idea of a nation into concrete political programmes which will be perceived as such and deemed relevant by the citizens of this 'imagined community' (Benedict Anderson), strategies of translation, representation and communication become important. These transform the theoretical discourse on nation into a concrete political programme that allows for both collective imagination and individual participation. In the preceding chapters I, therefore, undertook a threefold analytical classification of nationalism as a political discourse to which I would like to draw attention again. I had proposed a distinction between the content of political rhetoric, the strategies of the discourse and, finally, the actual means of realization with which, for example, nationalist politicians try to establish and popularize their version of nation. The first aspect, the contents of political rhetoric, reflects the ideological understanding of the central protagonists and reproduces the content of nationalist ideologies. The strategies of discourse, the second aspect of the nationalist discourse, can be taken to mean 'a more or less specific plan of action which helps to achieve a political, psychological or other goal'.[3] This stage of planning thus differs from the precise strategies through which the plans are finally transformed into action. Whereas this last distinction is comprehensible on a theoretical level, the historical examples in the case of India have shown that, on a practical plane, these plans made by the concerned historical players are not always available and that the interim stage therefore merges with the actual means of realization, the strategies of performative nation-building. Two aspects then remain to be analysed. Firstly, the discursive strategies prepare the theoretical and conceptual ground of nationalism as a political programme. As if working on a drawing board, they outline the collective self-understanding of the nation and determine the direction political action should take to achieve nation-building. Secondly, performance functions as an actionist method to mediate and realize nationalism. It quasi creates the nation as an experiential and, more importantly, as a participatory reality. These two elements, to be precise, constitute a historical chronology, since the second element is the concrete manifestation and execution of the first. Often, however, when translated into practise, the content-component of nation-building either enters into a stage of reformulation or performative nation-building is only an unsatisfactory attempt at practical transformation of the contents. These flexible configurations of the relations between content and form, between discourse and performance have to be kept in mind. Nevertheless, this bipartite division of religious nation-building remains valid and can also serve as a guide for the following conclusions derived from the examples of the history of modern India.

Let us first look at the contents in the discursive strategy of Indian nationalism. In the examples described earlier the process was initiated by Gandhi's attempts at the beginning of the 1920s to expand the movement for Independence, hitherto restricted to small individual groups, into a mass movement. Within the framework of his broad symbolic repertoire Gandhi mainly used the religious and political question of the Khilafat movement in order to establish his version of an inclusive nationalism and in order to bring the Muslims, who were being increasingly marginalized within the Congress, into the movement under the Congress banner. Even before Gandhi there were numerous attempts, such as the Cow Protection movement at the end of the nineteenth century or the Swadeshi movement at the beginning of the twentieth century, to establish a collective religious-nationalist or even an explicitly anti-colonial identity through performative strategies. These attempts, however, were limited to certain regions and for various, even organizational, reasons they had a limited political significance. Gandhi was, therefore, the first to successfully attempt the use of performative strategies as a means of political communication on an all-India level. His person, onto which ideas of religious and political freedom were projected, as described earlier, was just as important in this process as were his political ideas of a nation defined by religious integration for all Indians, especially also for Indian women.

In contrast to this, Hindu nationalism subscribes to an exclusivist concept of nation. Hindu nationalist actors are not limited to the explicitly political field. Outside the main political arena the cadres of the RSS or even of the VHP, the World Hindu Association, try to work on forming the new community of Hindus and building a nation according to their ideas. The arguments used to legitimise this are not the same in all cases and are, furthermore, one-sided and selective when referring to the history of the country. The players generally single out isolated elements with strong ideological overtones in an understanding of a Hindu nationalist past, present and future and use this to intervene in what is for them a crisis-ridden reality. Taken together, the attempts by a politicized Hinduism to change reality and to justify these ideologically result in an argumentative pattern which represents the overarching framework of interpretation. At the same time, this pattern reproduces the understanding of the representatives of this school of thought in their times. Since these players see themselves as executors of a historical mission, the historical development and the background for the rise of a social, national reality is decisive. The significance of Hindu nationalist utopias and visions becomes visible only when individual life is placed in the context of a larger flow of time with its idealized beginning, its historical mistakes and erroneous developments linked with the idea of a return to glorious origins. The point of departure and the culmination of social commitment is the 'golden age' which marks the ideal condition in every regard as a social utopia. The basic understanding of problems, especially with regard to the dismal present, is derived from this and all attempts at reform and national renaissance under the banner of religion are directed towards this. When this original condition is described it resembles a social uterus where there was originally trust between all humans, on the one hand, and between man and the cosmos, on the other, where neither transgressions nor wicked intentions disturbed this harmonious accord. Such a portrayal clearly borrows from Hindu religious mythology and transforms this material into an actual historical utopia. History and mythology thus merge in this first stage and create the alluring illusion of a co-existence between men and gods.

It was mainly the Shuddhi movement in the 1920s which made the process of inner decay the theme of religious-political activity and talked about some essential elements of this 'decline'. As a result of the censuses that were carried out every ten years by the British from 1911 onwards it was possible for the first time to visualize the ratio between the religious communities.[4] A numerical competition arose between these communities, and this had an enormous 'pedagogic and disciplinary function'[5] within the Indian population. The awareness of numerical changes in the ratio of Hindus to the religious minorities, whose numbers were increasing mainly due to conversions, created a new framework of reference for politics in South Asia. Besides conversion, the religious nationalists among Hindus discovered other religious and cultural aspects that could apparently explain the decline in the ratio of Hindus to the total population. The ban on widow-remarriage, child marriage, shortcomings in the systematic, especially physical, upbringing of children, etc., were all held responsible for the organic decline of Hindus.[6] Historically, Buddhism and Jainism, as religions that emerged from within Hinduism, were seen as examples for the decline in the valour of Hindu society.[7] Criticism of these religions as well as the rejection of Gandhi's methods constitute the core elements of the Hindu right-wing after 1920 and the writings of Veer Savarkar are especially full of attacks on the ideals and the political concepts of an uncompromising non-violence.[8] It was felt that only when non-violence appeared in the form of Jainism and Buddhism, which are considered by Hindu nationalism to be Hindu forms of belief,[9] did Hindu society become vulnerable to attacks from the outside, i.e. to threats from other non-Indian religions. The early arrival of Christianity was considered one of the first in a series of such events. The St. Thomas Christians in south India established this insidious process of foreign religious and cultural 'infiltration' by settling down in India and by drawing Hindus away from the Hindu nation through conversion. The 'invasion of Islam', especially the establishment of Mughal rule, are interpreted as the first stage of foreign rule which laid the ground for the centuries-long subjugation of Hindus to the will of religious minorities. The dogmatic and organizational unity of the monotheistic religions of the Near East are always portrayed in this context as an advantage in the interreligious struggle for survival,[10] but they are also criticized and counteracted with a stereotypical orientalist notion of 'Hindu tolerance'. The outcome of all these historical images is a kind of religious social Darwinism which sees the different religious communities in a demographic fight for survival out of which only the dogmatically and organizationally strongest would emerge victorious.

Finally, the inner decay and the external threat constitute the framework for a diagnosis of the condition of Hinduism which, in this view, legitimizes the nationalist offensive. This 'victimization' projects a self-image in the role of a victim in almost all spheres of social reality necessitating an equally comprehensive resistance. It is only this self-perception of Hindus which offers a point of departure for an all-encompassing critique and a reform in the spirit of Hindu nationalism. Not only the BJP, but also the VHP and the RSS, always use the expression 'holistic approach'[11] when giving statements on topical issues in order to portray their alternative to what they see as hopeless times. This means that there is a comprehensively different concept for the Hindu nation encompassing all spheres of life ranging from the national economy and defence policies to the social system as well as family and sexuality. From this Hindu nationalism also derives a fundamental de-legitimating of the post-colonial state which is interpreted as a project of 'pandering to the minorities' and which should, therefore, be rejected in the interest of the emancipation of the Hindu majority.

Organization (*sangathan*) and the renewed strengthening of Hindus as a national collective are considered to be the correct strategy to confront the crisis of the times. Essentially this ranges from the organization of Hindu society in local cadres to an armaments race and posing as a superpower. Almost all imaginable means of militarization are used which also directly provoke hostilities against the minorities. The process of a social re-armament is aimed at removing all inner and external wrongs and is combined, on occasion, with notions of cleansing and social as well as religious purity in order to pave the way for a collective advancement.

The long-term goal is the return to the 'golden age' which will not simply be re-established, but will be realized anew in the principles of its inner functioning with modern technological and scientific means. The point of departure and the culminating point of Hindu nationalist discourses is thus constituted by a socio-political utopia that shows the Hindus as one of the superior civilizations of the world and, therefore, accords them a correspondingly privileged position in the world, i.e. the status of a superpower.

With regard to the second dimension of performative nation-building, the stage of actual realization and its strategies, a few fundamental features also need to be summed up which characterize the very different methods used in the course of the twentieth century. Performative politics clearly has the potential to transcend cleavages within a society and create a political space beyond existing fragmentations. As illustrated before, the Khilafat movement was Gandhi's performative reaction to several developments undermining the effort to construct a united and effective political opposition to the British colonial regime. Within the Indian National Congress, the alienation of Muslim members and Muslim leaders had started already before the First World War and was, at the beginning of the Khilafat movement, a long-term trend within this political organization. For Gandhi it became crucial to develop a political strategy that would enable the INC to close its ranks again and integrate Muslims again more convincingly than before at the decision-making level as well as at the ground level of the organization. Additionally, the British had recently supported this process of political alienation of Indian Muslims. In 1909, the reforms initiated by the liberal Secretary of State for India, John Morley, and the conservative Indian Viceroy, Lord Minto, introduced separate electorates for Muslims which 'gave birth to a sense of Muslims being a religio-political entity in the colonial image—of being unified, cohesive and segregated from Hindus. They were homogenized like castes and tribes and suitably accommodated within political schemes and bureaucratic designs.'[12] This structural feature introduced into Indian politics was a severe challenge to the INC's claim to represent the whole of India, including Muslims and other religious groups. Furthermore, these reforms had a far-reaching effect insofar as they reinforced the idea of religious communities as the basis for political entities:

> Separate electorates created the space for reinforcing religious identities, a process which was, both in conception and articulation, profoundly divisive. In effect, the Morley-Minto Reforms ingeniously challenged those assumptions which guided many nationalists to cultivate a pan-Indian identity, and through a judicious mixture of concessions and guarantees undermined the broadly secular foundations of Indian nationalism.[13]

I cannot discuss here as to how far Mushirul Hasan's interpretation of the 'secular foundations of Indian nationalism' is justified or not—it seems to me, as discussed above, that these 'foundations' were far less 'secular' than assumed. However, what is interesting about the Khilafat movement is that this form of performative nation-building challenged the growing divisions between Hindus and Muslims in the Independence movement but did little or nothing about the use of religious markers for the definition of political entities. On the contrary, it reinforced the notion of distinct Muslim issues such as the Khilafat and demanded the Hindus' solidarity in the name of a unified Indian movement. The result was more an affirmation of the perception that Hindus and Muslims constitute two distinct political entities. The unifying effect of the performance, however, concerned the existing social cleavages on the one hand, i.e. different belongings to caste and class, and regional divisions on the other, as the Khilafat movement achieved a really 'national' mobilization with different degrees of participation in various parts of India.

Similar effects of performative politics in the sense of bridging gaps can be seen in more recent examples. In the discussion on the social background of the rise of the BJP it became clear that the party succeeded in forming a social block of partly very different castes and classes and in maintaining this as a unified political constituency, at least in the short-term. Through their religious-nationalist campaigns the BJP attempted, among other things, to establish a variously defined consensus among as large a section of Hindu society as possible in order to close the ranks behind the immediate party members. In his remarks on liberal society John Rawls has used the term 'overlapping consensus' to describe how a political consensus is established beyond cultural differences.[14] In its efforts to establish an overlapping consensus Hindu nationalism puts a two-dimensional strategy into operation. On the one hand, Hindutva as a religious-cultural nationalism forces religious minorities into submission and deliberately excludes them from a definition of national self-understanding, since it proceeds from an essential Hindu core of the Indian nation which it justifies historically. In this context Hindu nationalism actually undermines the formation of a consensus which would include all citizens regardless of their cultural and religious specificities. On the other hand, however, Hindu nationalism uses strategies of performative nation-building to undertake the formulation, the enactment and the political instrumentalization of an overlapping consensus among Hindus. Precisely because Hinduism represents an irreducible religious and cultural plurality, the players of the Hindu-right do not attempt to sketch an exact dogmatic or a political canon for all Hindus, limiting themselves instead to general characteristics of all Hindus beyond the concrete teachings. Cow worship, the waters of India's holy rivers, the goddess 'Mother India' or Rama's birthplace are not specific religious contents but general symbols of the non-Islamic or non-Christian which can be drawn upon for the formulation and political realization of a nation of Hindus. When Rawls says that 'religion and philosophical concepts' tend to 'be general and comprehensive' and that is the reason why they are not suitable for establishing a religious and philosophical overlapping consensus,[15] it shows that he has the Western concept of religion in mind which is strongly oriented towards a confessional definition. A concept of religion oriented towards the Indian reality, however, should be understood rather as a 'life praxis anchored in consensual action'[16] as 'common sense' derived from lived and orally handed-down traditions which constitute an unspoken and common, yet extremely heterogeneous framework of social action over which it has a great influence. An important part of this diversity of conventions and modes of communication also works beyond individual religions and constitutes important bridges between religions in the daily life of Indian society. Besides this, there are also separate practices which are specific to Islam or Hinduism and which can therefore be drawn upon for the formulation of a collective consciousness of all Hindus, Muslims or Christians. In the case of Hinduism, however, these are not dogmatic contents but common practices of daily life or religious activities in all regions which, on closer examination, distinguish Hindus from Muslims or Christians.

The political and ritual campaigns focus on these very limited aspects of the Hindu way of life and reformulate them in the context of political requirements. This means, firstly, that characteristics of religious life that were previously not so important have to be made meaningful. The transformation of the divine ruler, Rama, traditionally described as an androgynous, charitable person, into the aggressive masculine crusader against the Muslims in the framework of Hindu-nationalist propaganda clearly shows this process at work.[17] Secondly, the religious forms of expression themselves change in the process of socio-political appropriation and thereby get transformed into public spectacles for political means. Both aspects radicalize religious contents and place greater emphasis on the function of religion as a demarcation from people of other faiths. Religion as co-ordinated action in agreement with traditions and with other believers thus functions in the production of an overlapping consensus, as that unconscious but existent 'intuitive thought' which Rawls mentions as the point of departure for a consensus. In contrast to this, however, the outcome of religious consensus-building is not a liberal-democratic, open society but a nationalist accord of preferably all Hindus which is built on a fundamental dissent, namely against religious minorities.

RELIGIOUS NATIONALISM AS A POLITICAL FIELD

Indian studies on nationalism today offer a plethora of theoretical positions. Accordingly, the ways of approaching the topic are diverse and, in many cases, contradictory to one another. Numerous studies of nationalism, especially older ones, demarcate this phenomenon, which is in their view basically a secular, modern one, from all attempts at a religious and cultural definition of an Indian nation that are, for their part, strongly devalued.[18] This kind of interpretation is not only historiographic, it is itself historical. In the 1920s, in the decade when Hindu nationalism enjoyed a highly favourable climate, the Indian National Congress began to interpret religious forms of nationalism as an opposition to actual nationalism, or even to deny that it constituted a form of nationalism at all. The term used to describe it was 'communalism' which was actually a relic of colonial and orientalist influenced historiography.[19] After Independence this interpretation of religious nationalism continued and it determined the discourse on nationalism, especially among Marxist historians. Bipan Chandra, for example, used the word 'communalism' to describe the belief 'that a group of people has common social, political and economic interests because they belong to a particular religion'.[20] In Chandra's understanding, in 'communalism', as against nationalism, it is religion which defines social relationships and also determines the secular, i.e. worldly interests of a group. Viewed from this perspective communal ideology and interreligious violence are tied-up in a grave reciprocal action where violence serves to spread the ideology and ideology helps to justify violence.[21] The basis of all this, however, it is felt, is a 'false consciousness of the social reality' in India,[22] making it the task of genuine nationalism, i.e. the Congress party under Nehru, to enlighten the people about the real causes of misery and the competing political as well as economic interests. In this interpretive framework religion is simply understood as an instrument which is used by the elites to ensure their political and economic resources and power. On the other hand, however, religion *per se* does not have any real significance as a 'cement of communal ideology and politics'.[23] Even the standard book by A.R. Desai,[24] which was first published in 1948 and remained valid for a long time, contains important preliminary work with regard to this perspective. Desai's argument in this work establishes the close connection between the process of India's de-industrialization under British rule and the rise of nationalism. Hinduism as a 'conglomerate of religious cults'[25] and the religious reform movements of the nineteenth century served as a backdrop for the conflict that developed over the decades between the Indian elites and the long-term interests of the British.[26]

During the course of the events of the 1990s many historians tried to open up this Marxist approach and develop another evaluation of culture and religion in the framework of nationalism or of politics in general. However, they did not give up the dichotomy of (good) nationalism, on the one hand, and (evil) 'communalism' on the other. K.N. Panikkar attempted to approach the events involving a religious-cultural mobilization through a reassessment and a closer observation of the religious-cultural context at the local level.[27] Paul R. Brass interpreted nationalism as an elite phenomenon which, in its religious form, primarily serves to increase group-cohesion and guarantee protection of interests in the public sphere. According to him, the secret behind the successes of mobilization lay in the felicitous choice of religious symbols.[28]

Another important change in Indian studies on nationalism came about in the 1980s when, similar to culture studies in the West, a widespread engagement with Antonio Gramsci began, leading to a reassessment of religious and cultural aspects in history. Partha Chatterjee's first important work on nationalism in India works with Gramsci's formula of the 'passive revolution'. In three stages, consisting of the moment of departure, the moment of manoeuvre and the moment of arrival, Chatterjee discusses the development of the nationalist discourse as well as that of capitalist, socio-economic changes.[29] Without going into the details of his analysis Chatterjee's reference to a dual division of reality, especially in the early phase of nationalism, is of great theoretical importance for the assessment of culture and religion within the political discourse in colonial India. Especially in the 'moment of departure' which, to a great extent, was undertaken and initiated by religious nationalists, culture constituted a decisive terrain of the strategic contest for autonomy and national self-consciousness:

> Nationalist thought at its moment of departure formulates the following characteristic answer: it asserts that the superiority of the West lies in the materiality of its culture, exemplified by its science, technology and love of progress. But the East is superior in the spiritual aspect of culture. True modernity for the non-European nations would lie in combining the superior material qualities of Western cultures with the spiritual greatness of the East.[30]

Chatterjee reiterated and extended this approach in his second book on nationalism in India and used it to explain the constitution of difference itself in colonized societies.[31]

The framework for this theoretical approach is the interpretation of culture as a 'battleground', as the territory where the contest for social and political hegemony takes place as Gramsci has repeatedly suggested in his Prison Notebooks.[32] This function of culture helps in the formation of a 'historical block', a historical alliance of different social classes and camps who come together for a strategic cooperation to co-ordinate their interests and who not only communicate but also implement their claim to power with the help of culture and religion. In other words, the elites use culture and religion as manipulative means in their own interests.[33] Other authors also tried to use Gramsci's concrete remarks about the rise of fascism in Italy of the 1920s theoretically and came up with corresponding analogies about the events in Ayodhya.[34] This approach focuses almost entirely on the changes in the economic field and the social transformation of 'classes' without going into the role of culture and religion explicitly.[35] This theoretical approach is also controversial because of the problem of historical analogies with fascist Italy and the doubtful application of this very specific concept to the equally specific circumstances in India during the 1990s.

Indian social scientists who are reassessing modernity in the light of post-modern theoretical constructions in the West go a step further in the autonomy they grant to culture and religion in the context of political developments and post-colonial statehood. In doing this they also arrive at a re-evaluation of these aspects of Indian reality. These Indian scholars try to develop a quasi-'Indian' concept of autonomy in demarcation to Western dominance; a concept that is more oriented towards pre-modern ways of life in India and which one can, therefore, neither call modern nor post-modern.[36] For T.N. Madan, Ashis Nandy and others the essence of India, even as a nation, is to be found in pre-modern conventions, cultural practices and in the non-politicized everyday understanding of religion. This essence, according to them, should be mobilized in the fight against fundamentalism and religious intolerance.[37] Strictly speaking, these scholars have enormous problems with the concept of nation itself, since its link with modernity cannot be ignored without abandoning the concept as such. By looking at structural violence, especially against groups in a post-colonial society that are marginalized because of their culture and religion, they attempt to rupture the modern model of national statehood which, according to them, is responsible for the widespread and systematic denial of the subaltern.[38] This 'post-nationalism'[39] criticizes the wrong developments and the violence associated with the enforcement of national self-consciousness through a fundamental critique of this form of political discourse. At the same time it also offers alternative approaches to the question of political organization. The most important change that is required, according to them, is the reassessment of culture and religion in matters of statehood. Only when these defining characteristics are taken into account can one find a non-violent and realistic organizational form, i.e. a form that corresponds to the diversity of these societies.

Against the backdrop of these theoretical developments I will, while concluding, attempt to sketch out another approach for understanding politics and religion which also takes these present developments into account. I propose that religious nationalism be understood both as a discursive as well as a performative field in which there is a struggle for the power to define as also for political power. The concept of the field has been borrowed from Bourdieu, but it has to be re-interpreted here. Bourdieu develops the concept of the field on the basis of fundamental questions about the inner functioning of societies:

> With the exception of the least differentiated societies . . . all societies appear as social spaces, that is, as structures of differences that can only be understood by constructing the generative principle which objectively grounds those differences. This principle is none other than the structure of the distribution of the forms of power or the kinds of capital[40] which are effective in the social universe under consideration—and which vary according to the specific place and moment at hand.[41]

Society is thus an accumulation of different structures which function according to their own specific rules and confer or legitimize strength and power within that universe in accordance with these rules. Economy, politics, religion, art, etc., are all structures which pervade society and establish their own, relatively autonomous, spheres of life. Bourdieu calls these spheres fields.

Within these fields the respective players not only heed and observe the rules of the field, but these rules are also further developed with the passage of time and the struggles that take place to gain hegemony. Bourdieu's definition of the religious field makes it clear what is at stake here:

> To be more precise, religion contributes to the (masked) establishing of the principles that structure the manner in which the world is perceived and thought about, especially the social world, to the extent that it enforces a system of practices and ideas whose objective structure, based on a principle of political division, appears as the natural-supernatural structure of the cosmos.[42]

Fields are, therefore, not only the structuring elements of society as a social space, but they also determine two kinds of aspects through their praxis: firstly, the world of ideas, by defining and establishing the categories of judgement and thought in general and, secondly, the actions by laying down the clearly demarcated sphere of possibilities of action, thus limiting the choice of realistic options. The political field, for example, is thus the place where 'the competing players present in it [create] political products'[43] which not only include programmes, analyses, commentaries and concepts, but mainly also the problems themselves and their solutions. An aspect of the competition within these fields and, especially, in politics is to appropriate the power to formulate problems and solutions and to thus enforce one's own version against that of the rivals. This 'power to formulate' (Sloterdijk) is also linked with the ability to determine political praxis and to project oneself as the only legitimate representative of passive players, i.e. the voters and citizens.

Under the conditions of modern statehood the political field transforms itself into a field of nationalism that functions according to its own specific rules and within which different players fight for the power to define and establish their own versions. Modern statehood constitutes the required conditions to which the differing versions of the nation as a political and imagined collective try to react. Statehood demands, among other things, that the collective be made culturally uniform in order to establish an ideological equivalent of the central administrative state and in order to guarantee the necessary cohesion of the population as citizens of the state. Statehood thus also demands that cultural criteria of inclusion and exclusion are formulated so that the limits of administration are ideologically marked and also cognitively established. Finally, statehood requires the formulation of applicable categories that can enable a collective, i.e. overall national definition of shared problems and their solutions in the future, in order to gain a jargon, a political grammar, corresponding to the political conditions of the modern administrative state and to thus establish the state itself as a cognitive category.

These fundamental requirements, however, lead in modern times to a very heterogeneous field of nationalism within which there is a struggle for the power to formulate and for the performative construction of nation. Differing versions of nation fulfil the listed requirements of the modern state in very different ways. Religious nationalism, such as Hindu nationalism, thus enters the field of struggle as one version among many. On the basis of common guidelines, the shared rules of the discourse within the field of nationalism, it is wrong not to characterize religious forms of nationalism for what they are and, instead, to dismiss them with the word 'communalism' as quasi-qualitatively lesser forms of an otherwise respectable (since anti-colonial) form of discourse. In its functional logic religious nationalism fulfils the same requirements as the secular version does, the difference being that in its replies to the reality of the modern state its concept of the national collective with its external borders and its cultural self-understanding is completely different. All forms of colonial and post-colonial nationalism share a catalogue of questions and relevant political requirements which arise out of the nature of statehood itself and can be answered in many different ways. This also gives rise to the great flexibility of the versions and players in this field, to the ever-present simultaneity of many forms of nationalism which find varying responses from the people. Which version has an upper hand at a particular time depends on the social background of its representatives and corresponding developments among the population. The concrete form of nationalism in its cultural specificity has to prove itself as an attractive ideology for ensuring power and resources. Therefore, the profits to be gained from social and symbolic capital as well as the threat of its loss constitute the essential motivations for a reformulation of nationalist ideology. Historical changes in the economic and political fields of a society are, therefore, the powerful caesura that gives rise to alternative nationalist ideologies since they communicate social changes in corresponding cultural terms. Through this cultural concretization the struggle for hegemony in society as a social space is continued in a relatively autonomous manner.

The public sphere plays an important role in the political field and in the confrontation between different nationalist discourses. As indicated in the previous chapters, the public sphere is subjected to fundamental changes especially in the course of the modernization of a society. These changes also affect the access to the public sphere for different social groups and players. The transition from the anti-colonialism of a relatively small group, consisting primarily of Western-educated lawyers, to the mass movement of the 1920s and the 1930s, or the opening-up of the modern Indian TV-sector in the 1990s represent important changes in the definition of the public sphere and access to it. The contests for power and hegemony that are carried out in the political field are also reflected in the constitution of the public sphere, which is itself a product of relations of power:

> The point here is that the public sphere is a space *necessarily* (and not just contingently) articulated by power. And everyone who enters it must address power's disposition of people and things, the dependence of some on the goodwill of others.[44]

Talal Asad also elucidates this structure of the public sphere which requires more than the physical ability to speak. It is equally necessary to be actually heard:

> If one's speech has no effect whatever it can hardly be said to be in the public sphere, no matter how loudly one shouts. *To make others listen* even if they would prefer not to hear, to speak to some consequence so that something in the political world is affected, to come to a conclusion, to have the authority to make practical decisions on the basis of that conclusion—these are all presupposed in the idea of free public debate as a liberal virtue. But these performatives are not open equally to everyone because the domain of free speech is always shaped by preestablished limits.[45]

Performative nation-building is the repertoire for playing out these power-struggles which involve not only definitions and political hegemony but also the formation of the public sphere and its control. Even the example of terrorism (legitimized by religion) discussed in the previous chapter is a performative strategy of fear with the aim to make others listen.

With this understanding of nationalism as a field of discourse and action it is possible to view the boom of Hindu nationalism in the 1990s not only as a paradigm-shift and as the supplanting of the 'secular' nationalism of the Congress party, but also as the cyclical zenith of an individual version among many others that has latently existed since colonial rule and which in the concrete historical circumstances found its 'translators' and users among the BJP and its leaders.

A final point while talking about nationalism in modern India needs to be made with reference to Rabindranath Tagore, the Indian Nobel Prize winner from Bengal. Tagore once likened India to the ocean thus accurately characterizing the essence of this country in its size, its vastness and its sheer unlimited capacity for maintaining its equanimity. Against the backdrop of this perspective the writer tried to clarify his position on the phenomenon of nationalism to a Western audience and to explain why he considered this school of thought to be inappropriate for his country.[46] In his comments on nationalism Tagore criticizes the basic unsuitability of the idea of an Indian nation because of the high and, in end effect, inhuman, degree of abstraction from reality that it entails:

> This abstract being, the Nation, is ruling India. We have seen in our country some brand of tinned food advertised as entirely made and packed without being touched by hand. This description applies to the governing of India, which is as little touched by the human hand as possible. . . . But we, who are governed, are not mere abstraction. We, on our side, are individuals with living sensibilities.[47]

This 'octopus of abstractions' that is being spread successfully in all spheres of society would allow not only the colonial government, but every government set up in the name of nation, however it is defined, to practise inhumanity and would systematically alienate it from the people of the country, their diversity and differences. For Tagore, therefore, nationalism bears the root of evil within itself and it is the basic structures of nationalism which would lead to suffering and violence in India:

What is the Nation? It is the aspect of a whole people as an organized power. This organization incessantly keeps up the insistence of the population on becoming strong and efficient. But this strenuous effort after strength and efficiency drains man's energy from his higher nature where he is self-sacrificing and creative. . . . Nationalism is a great menace. It is the particular thing, which for years has been at the bottom of India's troubles. And inasmuch as we have been ruled and dominated by a nation that is strictly political in its attitude, we have tried to develop within ourselves, despite our inheritance from the past, a belief in our eventual political destiny.[48]

With this understanding of the problem Tagore opened up, before Gandhi, new horizons for a fundamental critique of nationalism. He saw the compulsion for homogenization and the intrinsic urge for power as necessary correlations of the political instrument of nationalism, even if the short-term political successes of mobilization for anti-colonial commitment were convincing. The history of modern India in the twentieth century proves that his fears were not unfounded. The concept of a nation, regardless of the concrete formulation of every individual version, necessarily reduces the vast plurality of the religious and cultural landscape of the country with its intrinsic tendency towards violence. For Tagore, the only adequate way out of these constraints consisted in an extensive federalism within the country as well as an 'intensive internationalism' under the principle of neutrality with regard to foreign affairs.[49] Both principles were meant to be applied in a strictly non-violent manner. Following Tagore, the question remains as to what extent not only has religious nationalism currently become a massive problem for India, but also whether one needs to think about another, fundamentally different concept of statehood which not only does not reduce the differences between individuals but, on the contrary, declares these differences to be the actual content.

NOTES

1. Cf., among others, Giddens, 2001, Eisenstadt, 1998, Marty/ Appelby, 1996, Meyer, 1989 and 1989a, Riesebrodt, 1998 and 2000, etc.
2. Giddens, 1999, p. 164.
3. Wodak et al., 1998, p. 73.
4. Jones, 1981; Datta, 1993.
5. Appadurai, 1998, p. 120.
6. Cf. for example, Shraddhanand, 1926 and Parmanand, 1936.
7. Savarkar, 1989.
8. Cf. for example, Savarkar, 1984, pp. 98f; 1989, pp. 17-25; Savarkar in Grover 1992a, pp. 172f, etc.
9. Cf. the speech by Malaviya in *The Leader* (22 August 1923); Savarkar, 1989.
10. Saraswati, 1915.
11. Cf. BJP, 1998, Thengadi, 1992, Seshadri, 1991, Malkani, 1980.
12. Hasan, 2001a, p. 35.
13. Ibid.
14. See for example, Rawls, 1994, 1994a, 1994b.
15. Rawls, 1994a, p. 343.
16. Rothermund, 2003, p. 183.
17 See for this Kapur, 1993.
18. See for example, Chandra, 1994, pp. 62ff; also Chandra, 1989.
19. For details about this cf. Pandey, 1999, Introduction.
20. Chandra, 1987, p. 1; cf. also Chandra, 1992, p. 45.
21. Chandra, 1991, p. 132; see also Chandra, 1994, p. 7.
22. Chandra, 1987, p. 24.
23. Ibid., pp. 159f.
24. Desai, 1976.
25. Ibid., p. 5.
26. Ibid., pp. 282ff.
27. See for this, among others, Panikkar, 1991, 1993, 1993a, 2001, etc.
28. Cf. Brass, 1974, 1979, 1991 as well as Robinson, 1977 for critical comments on Brass' statements.
29. Chatterjee, 1986.
30. Ibid., p. 51. See for this also Chatterjee, 1997a, p. 32.
31. Chatterjee, 1993, pp. 5f.

32. Cf. the good selection from the Prison Notebooks on the topic of culture and politics in Gramsci, 1991, the introduction to it by Sabine Kebir who outlines Gramsci's concept of culture very clearly. Cf. also Gramsci, 1986, especially pp. 219ff, pp. 268-73.
33. A consistent application of Gramsci's ideas in this sense is offered by Barlas, 1995, especially chapter 2.
34. See for example, Ahmad, 1993 and 1993a.
35. On the use of the concept of fascism for the concrete Indian context see also Sarkar, 1993, Patnaik, 1993 as also the systematic critique of these by Vanaik, 1994. Brass/Vanaik, 2002, pp. 13f. provide a history of the uses of the concept of fascism in India.
36. Joseph, 1998, p. 155.
37. See for example Madan, 1997 and 1998, Nandy, 1988, Bharucha, 1993, Sugata Bose, 1998, etc.
38. For the subaltern perspective see the comments by Chakrabarty, 1995 and 1995a.
39. This term was originally used by Edward Said and is taken from Gandhi, 1999, p. 124.
40. Besides economic capital Bourdieu identifies other forms of capital such as social, symbolic or cultural capital. See for this Bourdieu, 1997a, Chap. 3.
41. Bourdieu, 1998, p. 32.
42. Bourdieu, 2000, p. 49.
43. Bourdieu, 2001, p. 13.
44. Asad, 2003, p. 184.
45. Ibid.
46. Tagore delivered these speeches in 1916 in the USA and they were first published a year later in the original English version.
47. Tagore, 1996, pp. 422f.
48. Ibid., p. 458.
49. Cf. for this the analyses by Nandy, 1998, pp. 4-8.

Abbreviations

AIADMK	All-India Anna Dravida Munnetra Kazhagam
AICC	All-India Congress Committee
BJP	Bharatiya Janata Party
CWMG	*Collected Works of Mahatma Gandhi*, NMML (Year/Volume/Page)
HD	Government of India, Home Department, NAI (Year/File Number, Month/Page)
HDP	Government of India, Home Department Political, NAI (Year/File Number, Month/Page)
HDPD	Government of India, Home Department Political Deposit, NAI (Year/File Number, Month/Page)
HDPP	Government of India, Home Department Political Proceedings, NAI (Year/File Number, Month/Page)
HM	Hizbul Mujaheddin
INC	Indian National Congress
ISI	Inter-Service-Intelligence (Pakistan)
JKLF	Jammu & Kashmir Liberation Front
JP	M.R. Jayakar Papers, NAI (File Number/Page)
LeT	Lashkar-e-Taiba
MP	Moonje Papers, NAI (Roll Number/Date)
NAI	National Archives of India, New Delhi
NMML	Nehru Memorial Museum & Library, New Delhi.
NPUPAO	Notes on the Press, United Provinces of Agra and Oudh, NAI (Year/Number/Page)
PPA	Punjab Press Abstract, NAI (Year/Number/Page)
RIPCPB	Report on Indian Papers published in the Central Provinces and Berar, NAI (Year/Number/Page)
RSS	Rashtriya Swayamsevak Sangh
SJM	Swadeshi Jagaran Manch
TIM	Tanzim Islahul Muslimeen
TOI	*Times of India*
UP	Uttar Pradesh
VHP	Vishwa Hindu Parishad

Bibliography

Advani, L.K., 'A Tale of Two Temples', in *Indian Express*, 30 July 1989.

——, Statement in Parliament by Home Minister L.K. Advani on Terrorist Attack on Parliament House on 13 December 2001 (BJP Publication No. E/18/2001), New Delhi, 2001.

Ahmad, Aijaz, 'Fascism and National Culture: Reading Gramsci in the Days of Hindutva', *Social Scientist*, 21/3-4, 1993, pp. 32-68.

——, 'Culture, Community, Nation: On the Ruins of Ayodhya', *Social Scientist*, 21/7-8, 1993, pp. 17-48.

Ahmad, Imtiaz, 'Introduction', in Imtiaz Ahmad (ed.), *Ritual and Religion among Muslims in India*, New Delhi, 1984, pp. 1-20.

——, 'Contemporary Terrorism and the State, Non-State, and the Interstate: Newer Drinks, Newer Bottles', in Sridhar K. Khatri and Gert W. Kueck (eds.), *Terrorism in South Asia: Impact on Development and Democratic Process*, New Delhi, 2003, pp. 353-87.

Alam, Javed, *India: Living with Modernity*, New Delhi, 1999.

Ali, Amir, 'Terrorism and Genocide: Making Sense of the Senselessness', *Economic and Political Weekly*, 7 February 2004.

Aloysius, G., 'Caste in and above History', in S.L. Sharma and T.K. Oommen (eds.), *Nation and National Identity in South Asia*, New Delhi, 2000, pp. 151-73.

——, *Nationalism without a Nation in India*, 4th edn., New Delhi, 2002.

Ananthu, T.S., *Going Beyond the Intellect: A Gandhian Approach to Scientific Education*, New Delhi, 1981.

Anderson, Benedict, *Die Erfindung der Nation. Zur Karriere eines erfolgreichen Konzepts*, Erweiterte Ausgabe, Berlin, 1998.

Anderson, Sean and Stephen Sloan, *Historical Dictionary of Terrorism* (Historical Dictionaries of Religions, Philosophies and Movements, no. 4), London, 1995.

Appadorai, A., *Documents on Political Thought in Modern India*, vol. I, Bombay, 1973.

——, *Documents on Political Thought in Modern India*, vol. II, Bombay, 1976.

——, *Indian Political Thinking in the Twentieth Century: An Introductory Survey*, 2nd edn., New Delhi, 1987.

Appadurai, Arjun, 'Number in the Colonial Imagination', in Arjun Appadurai (ed.), *Modernity at Large: Cultural Dimensions of Globalization*, Minneapolis, London, 1998, pp. 114-35.

Arendt, Hannah, *Über die Revolution*, 4th edn., Munich, Zurich, 2000.

Armstrong, John A., 'Religious Nationalism and Collective Violence', *Nations and Nationalism*, 3/4, 1997, pp. 597-606.

Asad, Talal, *Formations of the Secular: Christianity, Islam, Modernity*, Stanford, 2003.

Ashraf, Ali, 'Khilafat Movement: A Factor in Muslim Separatism', in Mushirul Hasan (ed.), *Communal and Pan-Islamic Trends in Colonial India*, New Delhi, 1985, pp. 82-100.

Assmann, Jan, *Das kulturelle Gedächtnis. Schrift, Erinnerung und politische Identität in frühen Hochkulturen*, 2nd edn., Munich, 1999.

Audehm, Kathrin, 'Die Macht der Sprache. Performative Magie bei Pierre Bourdieu', in Christoph Wulf/Michael Göhlich/Jörg Zirfas (eds.), *Grundlagen des Performativen. Eine Einführung in die Zusammenhänge von Sprache, Macht und Handeln*, Weinheim, Munich, 2001, pp. 101-28.

Austin, J.L., *How to Do Things with Words*, Oxford, 1962.

Azad, Maulana Abul Kalam, *India Wins Freedom*, The Complete Version (original 1959), Hyderabad, 1989.

Banerjee, Sikata, 'Civic and Cultural Nationalism in India', in Brass/Vanaik (eds.), 2002a, pp. 50-82.

Barlas, Asma, *Democracy, Nationalism and Communalism: The Colonial Legacy in South Asia*, Boulder, Colorado, Oxford, Lahore, 1995.

Basu, Tapan, Pradip Datta, Sumit Sarkar, Tanika Sarkar and Sambuddha Sen, *Khaki Shorts and Saffron Flags: A Critique of the Hindu Right*, New Delhi, 1993.

Basu, Subho and Surajit C. Mukhopadhayay, 'The Crisis of the Centralized Nation State: Regionalization and Electoral Politics in India in 1990s', in Subho Basu and Suranjan Das (eds.), *Electoral Politics in South Asia*, Calcutta, 2000, pp. 201-34.

Bayly, C.A., 'Patriotism and Nationalism', in Bayly, 1998a, pp. 98-132.

——, *Origins of Nationality in South Asia: Patriotism and Ethical Government in the Making of Modern India*, Delhi, 1998a.

Ben-Amos, Avner, 'Der letzte Gang des großen Mannes. Die Staatsbegräbnisse in Frankreichs Dritter Republik', in Etienne François, Hannes Siegrist and Jakob Vogel (eds.), *Nation und Emotion: Deutschland und Frankreich im Vergleich, 19 und 20, Jahrhundert*, Göttingen, 1995, pp. 232-51.

Berding, Helmut (ed.), *Nationales Bewußtsein und kollektive Identität. Studien zur Entwicklung des kollektiven Bewußtseins in der Neuzeit 2*, Frankfurt/Main, 1994.

Bhabha, Homi (ed.), *Nation and Narration*, London, New York, 1990.

Bharucha, Rustom, *The Question of Faith*, New Delhi, 1993.

Bharatiya Janata Party (BJP), *Resolutions Adopted at the National Executive Meeting*, 9 to 11 June 1989, Palampur, New Delhi, 1989.

——, *Election Manifesto, Lok Sabha Elections*, New Delhi, 1989a.

——, *Towards Ram Rajya. Mid-Term Poll to Lok Sabha, May 1991: Our Commitments*, New Delhi, 1991.

——, *Election Manifesto, Lok Sabha Elections*, New Delhi, 1998.

Bidwai, Praful, and Achin Vanaik, *South Asia on a Short Fuse: Nuclear Politics and the Future of Global Disarmament*, New Delhi, 2001.

Bin-Laden, Osama, 'To Our Muslim brothers in Pakistan', 24.9.2001. http://www.pbs.org/newshour/bb/military/terroristattack7binladen-letter_9-24.html (last seen: 13.12.2005)

——, 'Letter to America', 24.11.2002. http://observer. guardian.co.uk/print/0,3858,4552895-110490,00.html (last seen: 13.12.2005)

Bittner, Rüdiger, 'Die Hoffnung auf politischen Konsens', in Philosophische Gesellschaft Bad Homburg and Wilfried Hinsch (eds.), *Zur Idee des politischen Liberalismus. John Rawls in der Diskussion*, Frankfurt/Main, 1997, pp. 39-51.

Bose, Sugata, 'Nation, Reason and Religion: India's Independence in International Perspective', *Economic and Political Weekly*, 1 August 1998, pp. 2090-7.

Bourdieu, Pierre, *Entwurf einer Theorie der Praxis auf der ethnologischen Grundlage der kabylischen Gesellschaft*, Frankfurt/Main, 1976.

Bourdieu, Pierre, *Zur Soziologie der symbolischen Formen*, 6. Aufl., Frankfurt/Main, 1997.

——, *Die verborgenen Mechanismen der Macht. Schriften zu Politik und Kultur* 1, Hamburg, 1997.

——, *Practical Reason: On the Theory of Action*, Stanford, California, 1998. (German *Praktische Vernunft*, Frankfurt/Main, 1998.)

——, *Das religiöse Feld. Texte zur Ökonomie des Heilsgeschehens*, Konstanz, 2000.

——, *Pascalian Meditations*, Stanford, California, 2000. (German *Meditationen. Zur Kritik scholastischer Vernunft*, Frankfurt/Main 2001.)

——, *Das politische Feld. Zur Kritik der politischen Vernunft*, Konstanz, 2001.

Bourdieu, Pierre and Sozialer Sinn, *Kritik der theoretischen Vernuft,* 3. Aufl., Frankfurt/Main, 1999.

Brass, Paul, *Language, Religion and Politics in North India*, Cambridge, 1974.

——, 'Elite Groups, Symbol Manipulation and Ethnic Identity Among the Muslims of South Asia', in David Taylor and Malcolm Yapp (eds.), *Political Identity in South Asia*, London, Dublin, 1979, pp. 35-77.

——, *Ethnicity and Nationalism: Theory and Comparison*, New Delhi, Newbury Park, London, 1991.

Brass, Paul R. and Achin Vanaik, 'Introduction', in Brass and Vanaik 2002a, pp. 1-17.

Brass, Paul R. and Achin Vanaik (eds.), *Competing Nationalisms in South Asia: Essays for Asghar Ali Engineer*, Hyderabad, 2002a.

Brenan, Timothy, 'The National Longing for Form', in Bhabha, 1990, pp. 44-70.

Brown, Judith M., 'Gandhi's Leadership', in B.N. Pandey (ed.), *Leadership in South Asia*, New Delhi, 1977, pp. 563-89.

Buck, David D., 'Dimensions of Ethnic and Cultural Nationalism in Asia: A Symposium', *The Journal for Asian Studies*, vol. 53, no. 1, 1994, pp. 3-9.

Bunsha, Dionne, 'Chariots of Fear', *Frontline*, 2 August 2002, pp. 4-8.

——, 'The Modi Road Show', *Frontline*, 19 October 2002.

——, 'Yatra Drama', *Frontline*, 6 December 2002.

——, 'Still a Burning Question', *Frontline* 3 (2005).

Butler, Judith, *Frames of War: When Is Life Grievable?*, London, New York, 2009.

Chakrabarty, Dipesh, 'Radical Histories and Question of Enlightenment Rationalism: Some Recent Critiques of Subaltern Studies', *Economic and Political Weekly*, 8 April 1995, pp. 751-9.

——, 'Modernity and Ethnicity in India: A History of the Present', *Economic and Political Weekly*, 30 December 1995, pp. 3373-80.

Chakravarti, Uma, 'Saffroning the Past: Of Myths, Histories and Right-Wing Agendas', *Economic and Political Weekly*, 31 January 1998, pp. 225-32.

Chamupati, Pandit, *Ten Principles of Arya Samaj*, Jullundur, n.d.

Chandra, Bipin, *Communalism in Modern India*, 2nd edn., New Delhi, 1987.

——, *India's Struggle for Independence 1857-1947*, New Delhi, 1989.

——, 'Communalism and the State: Some Issues in India', in K.N. Panikkar (ed.), *Communalism in India: History, Politics and Culture*, New Delhi, 1991, pp. 132-41.

——, *The Epic Struggle*, New Delhi, 1992.

——, *Ideology and Politics in Modern India*, New Delhi, 1994.

Chatterjee, Partha, *Nationalist Thought and the Colonial World: A Derivative Discourse?*, Delhi, 1986.

——, *The Nation and Its Fragments: Colonial and Postcolonial Histories*, Delhi, 1993.

——, 'History and the Nationalization of Hinduism', in Vasudha Dalmia and Heinrich von Stietencron (eds.), *Representing Hinduism: The Construction of Religious Traditions and National Identity*, New Delhi, Thousand Oaks, London, pp. 103-28.

——, *A Possible India: Essays in Political Criticism*, Delhi, 1997.

——, 'Beyond the Nation or Within?', *Economic and Political Weekly*, vol. 32, nos. 1-2, pp. 30-4.

——, 'Secularism and Tolerance', in Rajeev Bhargava (ed.), *Secularism and its Critics*, Delhi, 1998, pp. 345-79.

Chattopadhyay, Suhrid Sankar and Haroon Habib, 'Challenges in the East', *Frontline*, 1 (2006), pp. 11-13.

Cheema, Pervaiz Iqbal, 'Post-11 September Developments: A Pakistani Perspective', in Dipankar Banerjee and Gert W. Kueck (eds.), *South Asia and the War on Terrorism. Analysing the Implications of 11 September*, New Delhi, 2003, pp. 39-50.

Chibber, Pradeep K. and Subhash Misra, 'Hindus and the Babri Masjid: The Sectional Basis of Communal Attitudes', *Asian Survey*, vol. 33, no. 7, 1993, pp. 665-72.

Chiriyankandath, James, 'An Analysis of Lok-Sabha Elections 1952-91', in Mitra/Chiriyankandath, 1992, pp. 269-71.

Corbridge, Stuart, 'The Militarization of All Hindudom? The Bharatiya Janata Party, the Bomb, and the Political Spaces of Hindu Nationalism', *Economy and Society*, vol. 28, no. 2, 1999, pp. 222-55.

Crouch, Colin, *Post-democracy*, Cambridge (UK), Malden (USA), 2004.

Da Matta, Roberto, 'Constraint and License: A Preliminary Study of Two Brazilian National Rituals', in S.F. Moore and B.G. Myerhoff (eds)., *Secular Ritual*, Assen, Amsterdam, 1977, pp. 244-64.

Dalmia-Lüderitz, Vasudha, 'Television and Tradition: Some Observations on the Serialization of the Ramayana', in Monika Thiel-Horstmann (ed)., *Ramayana and Ramayanas, Khoj: A Series of Modern South Asian Studies*, vol. 3, Wiesbaden, 1991, pp. 207-28.

Dalton, Dennis, 'Gandhi's Style of Leadership', in B.N. Pandey (ed.), *Leadership in South Asia*, New Delhi, 1977, pp. 590-631.

——, 'Gandhi's Originality', in J. Parel Anthony (ed.), *Gandhi, Freedom, and Self-Rule*, New Delhi, 2002, pp. 63-85.

Datta, Pradip K., 'VHP's Ram in Ayodhya: Reincarnation Through Ideology and Organisation', *Economic and Political Weekly*, 2 November 1991, pp. 2517-26.

——,'"Dying Hindus": Production of Hindu Communal Common

Sense in Early 20th Century Bengal', *Economic and Political Weekly*, 19 June 1993, pp. 1305-19.

Davis, Richard H., 'The Iconography of Rama's Chariot', in David Ludden (ed.), *Contesting the Nation: Religion, Community, and the Politics of Democracy in India*, Philadelphia, 1996, pp. 27-54.

Deol, Harnik, *Religion and Nationalism in India: The Case of Punjab*, London, New York, 2000.

Derrida, Jacques and Jürgen Habermas, *Le "concept" du 11 septembre. Dialogue à New York (octobre-décembre 2001) avec Giovanna Borradori*, Paris, 2004.

Desai, A.R., *Social Background of Indian Nationalism*, 5th edn., Bombay, 1976.

Desai, Radhika, 'Culturalism and Contemporary Right: Indian Bourgeoisie and Political Hindutva', *Economic and Political Weekly*, 20 March 1999, pp. 695-712.

——, 'Forward March of Hindutva Halted?', *New Left Review*, 30 (November/December), 2004, pp. 49-67.

Deshpande, Satish, 'Communalising the Nation-Space: Notes on Spatial Strategies of Hindutva', *Economic and Political Weekly*, vol. 30, no. 50, 1995, pp. 3220-7.

Deutsch, Karl W., *Nationalism and Social Communication: An Inquiry into the Foundations of Nationality*, 2nd edn. (orig. 1953), Cambridge, 1966.

Dubashi, Jay, *The Road To Ayodhya*, New Delhi, 1992.

Durkheim, Emile, *Die elementaren Formen des religiösen Lebens*, Frankfurt/Main, 1981.

Edelmann, Murray, *Politik als Ritual. Die symbolische Funktion staatlicher Institutionen und politischen Handelns*, Frankfurt/Main, New York, 1990.

Eisenstadt, Shmuel Noah, *Die Antinomien der Moderne. Die jakobinischen Grundzüge der Moderne und des Fundamentalismus*, Frankfurt/Main, 1998.

Farmer, Victoria L., 'Mass Media: Images, Mobilization, and Communalism', in Ludden, 1996, pp. 98-115.

Evans, Alexander, 'Talibanising Kashmir?', *The World Today*, 14-16 December 2009.

Farmer, Victoria L., 'Depicting the Nation: Media Politics in Independent India', in Francine Frankel, Zoya Hasan, Rajeev Bhargava and Balveer Arora (eds.)., *Transforming India: Social and Political Dynamics of Democracy*, New Delhi 2000, pp. 254-87.

Flynn, Barbara Wilmat, 'The Communalization of Politics: National Political Activity in India 1926-1930', unpublished dissertation, Duke University, 1974 (Microfilm, Nehru Memorial Museum & Library).

François, Etienne, Hannes Siegrist and Jakob Vogel, 'Die Nation. Vorstellungen, Inszenierungen, Emotionen', in François/Siegrist/ Vogel, 1995a, pp. 13-35.

François, Etienne, Hannes Siegrist and Jakob Vogel (eds), *Nation und Emotion. Deutschland und Frankreich im Vergleich. 19. und 20. Jahrhundert*, Göttingen, 1995a.

Franck, Georg, *Ökonomie der Aufmerksamkeit. Ein Entwurf*, Munich, 2007.

Frankel, Francine R., 'Middle Classes and Castes in India's Politics: Prospects for Political Accommodation', in Atul Kohli (ed.), *India's Democracy: An Analysis of Changing State-Society Relations*, Princeton, New Jersey, 1988, pp. 225-61.

Freitag, Sandria B., *Collective Action and Community: Public Areas and the Emergence of Communalism in North India*, Delhi, 1990.

Freitag, Sandria B., 'Visions of the Nation: Theorizing the Nexus Between Creation, Consumption, and Participation in the Public Sphere', in Rachel Dwyer and Christopher Pinney (eds.), *Pleasure and the Nation: The History, Politics and Consumption of Public Culture in India*, New Delhi, 2001, pp. 35-75.

Frykenberg, Robert Eric, 'The Emergence of Modern Hinduism as a Concept and as an Institution: A Reappraisal With Special Reference to South India', in Günther Sontheimer and Hermann Kulke (eds.), *Hinduism Reconsidered*, New Delhi, pp. 29-49.

Fuchs, Martin, *Der Kampf um Differenz. Repräsentation, Subjektivität und soziale Bewegungen. Das Beispiel Indien*, Frankfurt/Main, 1999.

Gandhi, Mohandas Karamchand, *To the Hindus and Muslims*, ed. Anand T. Hingorani, Karachi, 1942.

——, *Collected Works of Mahatma Gandhi*, New Delhi, 1958-84.

——, *An Autobiography or The Story of My Experiments With Truth*, London, 1982.

——, *The Way to Communal Harmony*, 3rd edn., Ahmedabad, 1994.

Gandhi, Leela, *Postcolonial Theory: A Critical Introduction*, Delhi, 1999.

Ganguly, Sumit, 'The Roots of Religious Violence in India, Pakistan and Bangladesh', in Linell E. Cady and Sheldon W. Simon (eds.), *Religion and Conflict in South and Southeast Asia: Disrupting Violence*, London, New York, 2007, pp. 70-84.

Geertz, Clifford, 'After the Revolution: The Fate of Nationalism in the New States', in Geertz, 1973a, pp. 234-54.

——, *The Interpretation of Cultures: Selected Essays by Clifford Geertz*, New York, 1973a.

——, *Welt in Stücken. Kultur und Politik am Ende des 20. Jahrhunderts*, Vienna, 1996.

Gellner, Ernest, *Thought and Change*, London, 1965.

——, *Nations and Nationalism*, Oxford, 1983.

——, *Encounters with Nationalism*, Oxford (UK), Cambridge (USA), 1994.

——, *Nationalismus. Kultur und Macht*, Berlin, 1999.

Ghai, R.K., *Shuddhi Movement in India (A Study of Its Socio-political Dimensions)*, New Delhi, 1990.

Ghosh, Amitav, *Countdown*, Delhi, 1999.

Gode, P.K. and C.G. Karve (eds.), *V.S. Apte's The Practical Sanskrit-English Dictionary*, vol. III, Poona, 1959.

Giddens, Anthony, *Konsequenzen der Moderne*, Frankfurt/Main, 1999.

——, *Entfesselte Welt. Wie die Globalisierung unser Leben verändert*, Frankfurt/Main, 2001.

Gold, Daniel, 'Organized Hinduisms: From Vedic Truth to Hindu Nation', in Martin E. Marty/Scott R. Appleby (eds.), *Fundamentalisms Observed* (*The Fundamentalism Project*, vol. 1), Chicago, London, 1991, pp. 531-93.

Golwalkar, M.S., *Spotlights: Guruji Answers*, Bangalore, 1974.

Goody, Jack, 'Religion and Ritual: The Definitional Problem', *The British Journal of Sociology*, vol. 12, no. 2, pp. 142-64.

——, 'Against, Ritual: Loosely Structured Thoughts on a Loosely Defined Topic', in S.F. Moore and B.G. Myerhoff (eds.), *Secular Ritual*, Assen, Amsterdam, 1977, pp. 25-35.

Gopal, Krishna, 'The Development of the Indian National Congress as a Mass Organization, 1918-1923', *Journal of Asian Studies*, vol. 25, no. 3, pp. 413-30.

Gopal, Sarvepalli, 'Introduction', in S. Gopal (ed.), *Anatomy of a Confrontation: The Babri-Masjid-Ramjanmabhoomi Issue*, New Delhi, 1991, pp. 11-21.

Gordon, Richard, 'The Hindu Mahasabha and the Indian National Congress, 1915 to 1926', *Modern Asian Studies*, vol. 9, no. 2, pp. 145-203.

Government of India, Ministry of Information and Broadcasting, *Mass Media in India 1994-95*, New Delhi, 1995.

Graham, James Reid, 'The Arya Samaj as a Reformation in Hinduism with Special Reference to Caste', Unpublished dissertation, Yale University (Microfilm, Nehru Memorial Museum & Library), New Delhi, 1943.

Gramsci, Antonio, *Zu Politik, Geschichte und Kultur. Ausgewählte Schriften*, Frankfurt/Main, 1986.

——, *Marxismus und Kultur. Ideologie, Alltag, Literatur*, 3rd edn., Hamburg, 1991.

Grosby, Steven, 'Nationality and Religion', in Montserrat Guibernau and John Hutchinson (eds.), *Understanding Nationalism*, Cambridge, 2001, pp. 97-119.

Grover, Verinder, *Political Thinkers of Modern India*, vol. 13: *Bipin Chandra Pal*, New Delhi, 1992.

——, *Political Thinkers of Modern India*, vol. 14: *V.D. Savarkar*, New Delhi, 1992.

Gupta, N.L. (ed.), *Nehru on Communalism*, New Delhi, 1965.

Gupta, Dipankar, *Interrogating Caste: Understanding Hierarchy and Difference in Indian Society*, New Delhi, 2000.

Hall, Stuart, 'Der Westen und der Rest: Diskurs und Macht', in Hall, 1994, pp. 137-79.

——, 'Die Frage der kulturellen Identität', in Hall, 1994, pp. 180-222.

——, *Rassismus und kulturelle Identität. Ausgewählte Schriften 2*, Hamburg, 1994.

Hall, John A., *The State of the Nation: Ernest Gellner and the Theory of Nationalism*, Cambridge, 1998.

Hansen, Thomas Blom, 'Politics as Permanent Performance: The Production of Political Authority in the Locality', in John Zavos, Andrew Wyatt and Vernon Hewitt (eds.), *The Politics of Cultural Mobilization in India*, New Delhi, 2004, pp. 19-36.

——, 'RSS and the Popularisation of Hindutva', *Economic & Political Weekly*, vol. 16, no. 10, 1993, pp. 2270-2.

——, 'BJP and the Politics of Hindutva in Maharashtra', in Blom Hansen and Jaffrelot (eds.), 1998, pp. 121-62.

——, *The Saffron Wave: Democracy and Hindu Nationalism in Modern India*, Princeton, New Jersey, 1999.

Hansen, Thomas Blom and Christophe Jaffrelot (eds.), *The BJP and the Compulsions of Politics in India*, Delhi, 1998.

Hasan, Mushirul, 'Introduction: The Khilafat Movement: A Reappraisal', in M. Hasan (ed.), *Communal and Pan-Islamic Trends in Colonial India*, New Delhi, 1985, pp. 1-16.

——, 'The Muslim Mass Contact Campaign: Analysis of a Strategy of Political Mobilization', in Richard Sisson and Stanley Wolpert (eds.), *Congress and Indian Nationalism: The Pre-Independence Phase*, Delhi, 1988, pp. 198-222.

——, *Nationalism and Communal Politics in India, 1885-1930*, New Delhi, 1991.

——, *Legacy of a Divided Nation: India's Muslims since Independence*, New Delhi, 2001.

Hasan, Zoya, *Quest for Power: Oppositional Movements and Post-Congress Politics in Uttar Pradesh*, New Delhi, 1998.

——, 'Transfer of Power? Politics of Mass Mobilisation in UP', *Economic and Political Weekly*, 24 November 2001, pp. 4401-9.

Hay, Stephen (ed.), *Sources of Indian Tradition*, vol. Two: *Modern India and Pakistan*, 2nd edn., New Delhi, 1992.

Hazarika, Sanjoy, 'Terrorism and Subalternity–III: India and the Subnationalist Movements in Mizoram and Nagaland', in Imtiaz Ahmed (ed.), *Understanding Terrorism in South Asia: Beyond Statistic Discourses*, New Delhi, 2006, pp. 345-70.

Heehs, Peter, *Nationalism, Terrorism, Communalism: Essays in Modern Indian History*, Delhi, 1998.

Hegel, Georg Wilhelm Friedrich, *Werke [in 20 Bänden]. Bd. 7: Grundlagen der Philosophie des Rechts oder Naturrecht und Staatswissenschaft im Grundrisse*, 2nd edn., Frankfurt/Main 1989.

Hitchcock, R.H., *Peasant Revolt in Malabar: A History of the Malabar Rebellion, 1921*, New Delhi, 1983 (orig. 1925).

Hobsbawm, Eric, *Nations and Nationalism since 1780: Programme, Myth, Reality*, 2nd edn., Cambridge, 1992.

Hussain, Akmal, 'Terrorism, Development and Democracy: The Case of Pakistan', in Sridhar K. Khatri and Gert W. Kueck (eds.), *Terrorism in South Asia: Impact on Development and Democratic Process*, New Delhi, 2003, pp. 123-34.

Hussain, Wasbir, 'Insurgency in India's Cross-border Links and Strategic Alliances', http://www.satp.org/satporgtp/publication/faultlines/volume17/Wasbir.pdf. (Last seen: 28 May 2007.)

Ilaiah, Kancha, *Why I am not a Hindu: A Sudra Critique of Hindutva Philosophy, Culture and Political Economy*, Kolkata, 1996.

International Crisis Group, 2004, *Unfulfilled Promises: Pakistan's Failure to Tackle Extremism* (Asia Report No. 73), http://www.crisisgroup.org/library/documents /asia/south_asia/073_unfulfil_promises_pakistan_ extr.pdf. (Last seen: 7 June 2007.)

International Crisis Group 2006, Bangladesh Today (Asia Report No. 121), http://www.crisisgroup.org/library/documents/asia/south_asia/121_bangladesh_ today.pdf (Last seen: 28 May 2007.)

International Crisis Group 2007, Pakistan: Karachi's Madrasas and Violent Extremism (Asia Report No. 130 – 29 March 2007), http://www.crisisgroup.org/library/documents/asia/south_asia/130_pakistan_ karachi_s_madrasas_and _violent_extremism.pdf. (Last seen: 7 June 2007.)

International Initiative for Justice 2003, Threatened Existence: A Feminist Analysis of the Genocide in Gujarat, http://www.onlinevolunteers.org/gujarat/reports/iijg/2003/. (Last seen: 4 June 2007.)

Jaffrelot, Christophe, 'Hindu Nationalism: Strategic Syncretism in Ideology Building', *Economic and Political Weekly*, 20-7 March 1993, pp. 517-24.

——, *The Hindu Nationalist Movement and Indian Politics, 1925 to the 1990: Strategies and Identity Building, Implantation and Mobilisation (with special reference to Central India)*, London, 1996.

——, 'Militant Hindus and the Conversion Issue (1885-1990): From Suddhi to Dharm Parivartan. Politicization and Diffusion of an "Invention of Tradition" ', in Jackie Assayag (ed.), *The Resources of History: Tradition, Narration and Nation in South Asia*, Paris, Pondichéry, 1999, pp. 127-49.

——, 'Hindu Nationalism and Democracy', in Francine Frankel et al. (eds.), *Transforming India: Social and Political Dynamics of Democracy*, New Delhi, 2000, pp. 353-78.

—— (ed.), *Pakistan: Nationalism Without a Nation?*, New Delhi, 2002.

——, *India's Silent Revolution: The Rise of the Low Castes in North Indian Politics*, Delhi, 2003.

Jambunathan, M.R. (ed.), *Swami Shraddhanand*, Mumbai, 1961.

Jones, Kenneth W., *Arya Dharm: Hindu Consciousness in 19th-Century Punjab*, New Delhi, 1976.

——, 'Religious Identity and the Indian Census', N. Gerald Barrier (ed.), *The Census in British India: New Perspectives*, New Delhi, 1981, pp. 73-101.

Jordens, J.T.F., 'Reconversion to Hinduism: The Shuddhi of the Arya Samaj', in G.A. Oddie (ed.), *Religion in South Asia: Religious Conversion and Revival Movements in South Asia in Medieval and Modern Times*, 2nd edn., New Delhi, 1991, pp. 215-30.

Joseph, Sarah, *Interrogating Culture: Critical Perspectives on Contemporary Social Theory*, New Delhi, Thousand Oaks, London, 1998.

Juergensmeyer, Mark, Terror im Namen Gottes. Ein Blick hinter die Kulissen des gewalttätigen Fundamentalismus, Freiburg, Basel, Vienna, 2003.

Kallscheuer Otto/Claus Leggewie, 'Deutsche Kulturnation versus französische Staatsnation? Eine ideengeschichtliche Stichprobe', in Berding, 1994, pp. 112-62.

Kane, Pandurang Vaman, *History of Dharmaśāstra (Ancient and Medieval Religious and Civil Law in India*), vol. I, part I, 2nd edn., Poona, 1968.

Kantha, Pramod K., 'The BJP and Indian Democracy: Elections, Bombs, and Beyond', in Ramashray Roy and Paul Wallace (eds.), *Indian Politics and the 1998 Election: Regionalism, Hindutva and State Politics*, New Delhi, Thousand Oaks, London, 1999, pp. 340-64.

Kapferer, Bruce, *Legends of People, Myths of State: Violence, Intolerance and Political Culture in Sri Lanka and Australia*, Washington, London, 1998.

Kapur, Anuradha, 'Deity to Crusader: The Changing Iconography of Ram', in Gyanendra Pandey (ed.), *Hindus and Others: The Question of Identity in India Today*, New Delhi, pp. 74-109.

Kaschuba, Wolfgang, 'Die Nation als Körper. Zur symbolischen Konstruktion 'nationaler' Alltagswelt', in François, Siegrist and Vogel (ed.), 1995, pp. 291-9.

Katju, Manjari, *Vishva Hindu Parishad and Indian Politics*, Hyderabad, 2003.

Kaur, Raminder, *Performative Politics and the Cultures of Hinduism: Public Uses of Religion in Western India*, Delhi, 2003.

Kaviraj, Sudipta, 'On the Crisis of Political Institutions in India', *Contributions to Indian Sociology* (new series) vol. 18, no. 2 (1984), pp. 223-43.

Kedourie, Elie, *Nationalism*, 4th edn., Oxford (UK), Cambridge (USA), 1993.

Kellas, James G., *The Politics of Nationalism and Ethnicity*, 2nd edn., Houndmills, Basingstoke, London, 1998.

Kertzer, David I., *Ritual, Politics, and Power*, New Haven, London, 1988.

Khan, Shahedul Anam, 'The State and the Limits of Counter-Terrorism-II: The Experience of India and Bangladesh', in Imtiaz Ahmed (ed.), *Understanding Terrorism in South Asia: Beyond Statistic Discourses*, New Delhi, 2006, pp. 153-201.

Klimkeit, Joachim, *Der politische Hinduismus: Indische Denker zwischen religiöser Reform und politischem Erwachen*, Wiesbaden, 1981.

Kohli, Atul, *State-directed Development: Political Power and Industrialization in the Global Periphery*, Cambridge, 2004.

Kothari, Rajni, 'The Congress, "System" in India', *Asian Survey*, vol. 4, no. 12, pp. 1161-73.

——, 'Introduction', in R. Kothari (ed.), *Caste in Indian Politics*, New Delhi, 1970, pp. 3-25.

Knudsen, Are, *Political Islam in South Asia*, Bergen, 2002.

Krüger, Horst, 'Hinduism and National Liberation Movement in India', in Günther Sontheimer and Hermann Kulke (eds.), *Hinduism Reconsidered*, New Delhi, 1989, pp. 81-92.

Kulkarni, Vaijayanti, 'BJP Says It On Video, With a Difference', *The Independent*, 11 April 1991.

Kumar, Keval J., 'Cable and Satellite Television in India: The Role of Advertising', in David French and Michael Richards (eds.), *Television in Contemporary Asia*, New Delhi, Thousand Oaks, London, 2000, pp. 111-29.

Kumar, Sunil, *Communalism and Secularism in Indian Politics: Study of the BJP*, Jaipur, New Delhi, 2001.

Kumar, Amrita and Prashun Bhaumik (eds.), *Lest We Forget, Gujarat 2002*, New Delhi, 2002.

Kushner, Harvey W., *Encyclopaedia of Terrorism*, Thousand Oaks, London, New Delhi, 2003.

Leggewie, Claus, 'Ethnizität, Nationalismus und multikulturelle Gesellschaft', in Berding, 1994, pp. 46-65.

Lévy, Bernard-Henri, *Gefährliche Reinheit*, Vienna, 1995.

Lieten, Georges Kristoffel, 'Kaste, Klasse und Kommunalismus', in Christian Weiß et al. (eds.), *Religion-Macht-Gewalt. Religiöser, Fundamentalismus' und Hindu-Moslem-Konflikte in Südasien*, Frankfurt/Main, 1996, pp. 126-51.

Lintner, Bertil, 'A Cocoon of Terror', *Far Eastern Economic Review*, 4 April 2002.

Lochtefeld, James G., 'New Wine, Old Skins: The Sangh Parivar and the Transformation of Hinduism', *Religion*, 26, pp. 101-17.

Ludden, David (ed.), *Contesting the Nation: Religion, Community, and the Politics of Democracy in India*, Philadelphia, 1996.

Lukács, Georg, *History and Class Consciousness: Studies in Marxist*

Dialectics (tr. by Rodney Livingstone), Cambridge, Massachusetts, 1972.

Maaß, Citha D., 'Indiens ehrgeiziges Nuklearkonzept', in Werner Draguhn (ed.), *Indien 2000*, Politik, Wirtschaft, Gesellschaft, Hamburg, 2000, pp. 243-73.

Madan, T.N., 'Religious Ideology and Social Structure: The Muslims and Hindus of Kashmir', Imtiaz Ahmad (ed.), *Ritual and Religion Among Muslims in India*, New Delhi, 1984, pp. 21-64.

——, *Modern Myths, Locked Minds: Secularism and Fundamentalism in India*, Delhi, 1997.

——, 'Secularism in its Place', in Rajeev Bhargava (ed.), *Secularism and its Critics*, Delhi, 1998, pp. 297-315.

——, *Non-Renunciation: Themes and Interpretation of Hindu Culture*, 3rd edn., New Delhi, 2001.

Malik, Ashok, 'The Mind of Young Voters', *India Today*, 27 September 1999.

Malinar, Angelika, 'The Bhagavatgita and the Mahabharata TV Serial: Domestic Drama and Dharmic Solutions', in Vasudha Dalmia and Heinrich von Stietencron (eds.), *Representing Hinduism: The Construction of Religious Traditions and National Identity*, New Delhi, Thousand Oaks, London, 1995, pp. 442-67.

Malkani, K.R., *The RSS Story*, New Delhi, 1980.

Mankekar, Purnima, *Screening Culture, Viewing Politics: Television, Womanhood and Nation in Modern India*, New Delhi, 2000.

Manor, James, 'Parties and Party System', in Atul Kohli (ed.), *India's Democracy: An Analysis of Changing State-Society Relations*, Princeton, New Jersey, 1988, pp. 62-98.

Manuel, Peter, 'Music, the Media, and Communal Relations in North India: Past and Present', in Ludden, 1996, pp. 119-39.

Marty, M.E. and A.S. Appleby (eds.), *Herausforderung Fundamentalismus. Radikale Christen, Moslems und Juden im Kampf gegen die Moderne*, Frankfurt/Main, 1996.

McGuire, John, Peter Reeves and Howard Brasted (eds.), *Politics of Violence: From Ayodhya to Behrampada* (Studies on Contemporary South Asia, no. 1), New Delhi, Thousand Oaks, London, 1996.

McLane, John R. (ed.), *The Political Awakening in India*, Englewood Cliffs, New Jersey, 1970.

Mehra, Ajay K. and O.P. Sharma, *Terrorism and the Rule of Law: An Indian Perspective* (KAF Publication Series no. 6), New Delhi, 2006.

Metcalf, Barbara Daly, 'Imagining Community: Polemical Debates in Colonial India', in Kenneth W. Jones (ed.), *Religious Controversy in British India: Dialogues in South Asian Languages*, Albany, 1992, pp. 229-40.

Thomas, Meyer, *Fundamentalismus. Aufstand gegen die Moderne*, Hamburg, 1989.

——, 'Fundamentalismus. Die andere Dialektik der Aufklärung', in T. Meyer (ed.), *Fundamentalismus in der modernen Welt. Die Internationale der Unvernunft*, Frankfurt/Main, 1989, pp. 13-22.

——, *Die Transformation des Politischen*, Frankfurt/Main, 1994.

Minault, Gail, *The Khilafat Movement: Religious Symbolism and Political Mobilization in India*, Delhi, 1982.

Mishra, Vinay Chandra (ed.), *Ram Janmabhoomi Babri Masjid: Historical Documents, Legal Opinions and Judgements*, Delhi, 1991.

Misra, B.B., *The Indian Middle Class: Their Growth in Modern Times*, London, 1961.

——, *The Unification and Division of India*, Delhi, 1990.

Mitra, Subrata Kumar, 'Between Transaction and Transcendence: The State and The Institutionalisation of Power in India', in Subrata Kumar Mitra (ed.), *The Post-Colonial State in Asia: Dialectics of Politics and Culture*, New York, 1990, pp. 73-99.

——, 'Desecularising the State: Religion and Politics in India after Independence', in *Comparative Studies in Society and History*, vol. 33 (1991), pp. 755-77.

Mitra, Subrata K. and James Chiriyankandath (eds.), *Electoral Politics in India: A Changing Landscape*, New Delhi, 1992.

Mitra, Subrata K. and V.B. Singh, *Democracy and Social Change in India: A Cross-sectional Analysis of the National Electorate*, New Delhi, Thousand Oaks, London, 1999.

Monier-Williams, Monier, *A Sanskrit-English Dictionary* (rpt. 1999), Delhi, 1899.

Moore, R.J. (ed.), *Tradition and Politics in South Asia*, New Delhi, 1979.

Moore, Sally F. and Barbara G. Myerhoff, 'Introduction: Secular Ritual: Forms and Meanings', in Moore and Myerhoff (eds.), *Secular Ritual*, Assen, Amsterdam, 1977, pp. 3-24.

Mortimer, Edward and Robert Fine (eds.), *People, Nation and State: The Meaning of Ethnicity and Nationalism*, London, New York, 1999.

Müller-Dohm, Stefan and Klaus Neumann-Braun, 'Kulturinszenierungen–Einleitende Betrachtungen über die Medien kultureller Sinnvermittlung', in Müller-Dohm and Braun (eds.), *Kulturinszenierungen*, Frankfurt/Main, 1995, pp. 9-23.

Muralidharan, Sukumar, 'Mandal, Mandir aur Masjid: Hindu Communalism and the Crisis of the State', in K.N. Panikkar (ed.), *Communalism in India: History, Politics and Culture*, New Delhi, 1991, pp. 196-218.

Nair, Diwan Bahadur C. Gopalan, *The Moplah Rebellion, 1921*, Calicut, 1923.

Nanda, B.R., *Gokhale, Gandhi and the Nehrus: Studies in Indian Nationalism*, London, 1974.

——, *Jawaharlal Nehru: Rebel and Statesman*, Delhi, 1998.

Nandy, Ashis, 'The Politics of Secularism and the Recovery of Religious Tolerance', *Alternatives*, vol. 13, no. 2, 1988, pp. 177-94.

——, 'The Politics of Ayodhya', in Rajeshwar Ghose (ed.), *In Quest of a Secular Symbol: Ayodhya and After* (South Asian Issues Monograph no. 2), Perth, 1996, pp. 72-81.

——, *The Illegitimacy of Nationalism: Rabindranath Tagore and the Politics of Self*, 3rd edn., Delhi, 1998.

——, 'The Political Culture of the Indian State', in Zoya Hasan (ed.), *Politics and the State in India* (Readings in the Indian Government and Politics 3), New Delhi, Thousand Oaks, London, 2000, pp. 64-88.

——, 'Obituary of a Culture', *Seminar*, no. 513, May 2002, pp. 15-18.

Nasr, S.V.R., 'Islam, the State and the Rise of Sectarian Militancy in Pakistan', in Christophe Jaffrelot (ed.), *Pakistan: Nationalism without a Nation?*, New Delhi, 2002, pp. 85-114.

Nayar, Baldev Raj, 'India in 2004: Regime Change in a Divided Democracy', *Asian Survey*, vol. 45, no. 1, 2004, pp. 71-82.

Nehru, Jawaharlal, *Selected Works of Jawaharlal Nehru (SWJN)*, vol. 5, New Delhi, 1973.

——, *Selected Works of Jawaharlal Nehru* (General Editor: S. Gopal), 2nd series, vol. 3, New Delhi, 1985.

——, *An Autobiography*, 9th edn., New Delhi, 1995 (orig. 1936).

——, *The Discovery of India*, 18th edn., New Delhi, 1998 (orig. 1946).

Noorani, A.G., 'Legal Aspects of the Issue', in Sarvepalli Gopal (ed.), *Anatomy of a Confrontation: The Babri-Masjid-Ramjanmabhoomi Issue*, New Delhi, 1991, pp. 58-98.

O'Leary, Brendan, 'Ernest Gellner's Diagnoses of Nationalism: A Critical Overview, or, What is Living and What is Dead in Ernest Gellner's Philosophy of Nationalism?', in John A. Hall (ed.), *The State of the Nation: Ernest Gellner in the Theory of Nationalism*, Cambridge 1998, pp. 40-88.

Padmanabhan, Mukund and Shiraz Sidhva, 'Chalo Ayodhya: On the Road With Advani's Rath Yatra', *Sunday*, 21-7 October 1990, pp. 60f.

Page, David, *Prelude to Partition: The Indian Muslims and the Imperial System of Control 1920-1932*, 2nd edn., Delhi, 1999.

Page, David and William Crawley, *Satellites over South Asia: Broadcasting Culture and the Public Interest*, New Delhi, Thousand Oaks, London, 2001.

Pandey, B.N., *Nehru*, New Delhi, 1976.

Pandey, Gyanendra, 'Congress and the Nation, 1917-1947', in Richard Sisson and Stanley Wolpert (eds.), *Congress and Indian Nationalism: The Pre-Independence Phase*, Delhi, 1988, pp. 121-33.

——, 'Which of Us Are Hindus?', in G. Pandey (ed.), *Hindus and Others: The Question of Identity in India Today*, New Delhi, 1993, pp. 238-72.

——, *The Construction of Communalism in Colonial North India*, 6th edn., New Delhi, 1999.

Panikkar, K.N., 'Introduction', K.N. Panikkar (ed.), *Communalism in India: History, Politics and Culture*, New Delhi, 1991, pp. 1-16.

——, 'Religious Symbols and Political Mobilization: The Agitation for a Mandir at Ayodhya', *Social Scientist*, vol. 21, nos. 7-8, 1993, pp. 63-78.

——, 'Culture and Communalism', *Social Scientist*, vol. 21, nos. 3-4, 1993, pp. 24-31.

——, *Against the Lord and State: Religion and Peasant Uprising in Malabar 1836-1921*, 2nd edn., New Delhi, 2001.

Parekh, Bhikhu, *Defining National Identity in a Multicultural Society*, in Mortimer and Fine, 1999, pp. 66-74.

Parmanand, Bhai, *Hindu Sangathan*, Lahore, 1936.

Patel, Sujata, 'The Urban Factor', *Seminar* 411 (November) 1993, pp. 27-30.

Pathak, Avijit, *Indian Modernity: Contradictions, Paradoxes and Possibilities*, New Delhi, 1998.

Patnaik, Prabhat, 'The Fascism of Our Times', *Social Scientist*, vol. 21, nos. 3-4, 1993, pp. 69-77.

Platvoet, Jan, 'Ritual in Plural and Pluralist Societies: Instruments for Analysis', in Platvoet and Toorn, 1995, pp. 25-51.

——, 'Ritual as Confrontation: The Ayodhya Conflict', in Platvoet and Toorn, 1995, pp. 187-226.

Platvoet, Jan and Karel van der Toorn, 'Pluralism and Identity: An Epilogue', in Platvoet and Toorn, 1995, pp. 349-60.

Platvoet, Jan and Karel van der Toorn (eds.), *Pluralism and Identity: Studies in Ritual Behaviour* (Studies in History of Religions, vol. LXVII), Leiden, New York, Cologne, 1995.

Pollock, Sheldon, 'Ramayana and Political Imagination in India', *Journal of Asian Studies*, vol. 52, no. 2, 1993, pp. 261-97.

Rahman, A.K.M. Atiqar, 'Economic Costs of Terrorism in South Asia: The Case of Bangladesh', in Sridhar K. Khatri and Gert W. Kueck (eds.), *Terrorism in South Asia: Impact on Development and Democratic Process*, New Delhi, 2003, pp. 69-80.

Rai, Lala Lajpat, *A History of the Arya Samaj: An Account of Its*

Origin, Doctrines and Activities with a Biographical Sketch of the Founder (ed. Sri Ram Sharma), New Delhi, 1992 (orig. 1914).

Rajagopal, Arvind, 'Ram Janmabhoomi: Consumer Identity and Image-Based Politics', *Economic and Political Weekly*, 2 July 1994, pp. 1659-68.

——, *Politics After Television: Hindu Nationalism and the Reshaping of the Public in India*, Cambridge, 2001.

Ram, N., *Riding the Nuclear Tiger*, New Delhi, 1999.

Ramakrishnan, Venkitesh, 'Back to Ayodhya', *Frontline*, no. 15, 2005, pp. 4-9.

Rao, J. Laxmi Marasimha, 'Jihad and Cross-Border Terrorism in South Asia', A. Subramanyam Raju (ed.), *Terrorism in South Asia: Views from India*, New Delhi, 2004, pp. 173-204.

Rashid, Ahmed, 'Talibanisation', *The Nation*, 18 November, 1999.

Rawls, John, 'Der Gedanke des übergreifenden Konsenses', in Rawls, 1994c, pp. 293-332.

——, 'Der Bereich des Politischen und der Gedanke eines übergreifenden Konsenses', in Rawls, 1994c, pp. 333-63.

——, *Eine Theorie der Gerechtigkeit*, 8th edn., 1994, Frankfurt/Main.

——, *Die, Idee des politischen Liberalismus. Aufsätze 1978-1989*, ed. Wilfried Hirsch, Frankfurt/Main, 1994c.

Renan, Ernest, 'What is a Nation?' in Homi Bhabha (ed.), *Nation and Narration*, London, New York, 1990 (orig. 1882), pp. 8-22.

Riesebrodt, Martin, 'Fundamentalismus, Säkularisierung und die Risiken der Moderne', in Heiner Bielefeldt and Wilhelm Heitmeyer (eds.), *Politisierte Religion. Ursachen und Erscheinungsformen des modernen Fundamentalismus*, Frankfurt/Main, 1998, pp. 67-90.

——, *Die Rückkehr der Religionen. Fundamentalismus und der 'Kampf der Kulturen'*, Munich, 2000.

——, 'Was ist "Religiöser Fundamentalismus?', in Clemens Six, Martin Riesebrodt and Siegfried Haas (eds.), *Religiöser Fundamentalismus. Vom Kolonialismus zur Globalisierung* (Querschnitte 16), Innsbruck-Vienna-Munich-Bozen, 2004, pp. 13-32.

Robinson, Francis, 'Nation Formation: The Brass Thesis and Muslim Separatism', *Journal of Commonwealth & Comparative Politics*, vol. 15, no. 3, November 1997, pp. 215-30.

Rogers, John D., 'Post-Orientalism and the Interpretation of Premodern and Modern Political Identities: The Case of Sri Lanka', *The Journal of Asian Studies*, vol. 53, no. 1, 1994, pp. 10-23.

Rothermund, Dietmar, *Die politische Willensbildung in Indien 1900-1960*, Wiesbaden, 1965.

——, *The Phases of Indian Nationalism and Other Essays*, Mumbai, 1970.

——, 'Traditionalism and National Solidarity in India', in Moore, 1979, pp. 191-7.

——, 'Conflict as a Challenge to Legitimacy: A Historical Perspective', in Subrata K. Mitra and Dietmar Rothermund (eds.), *Legitimacy and Conflict in South Asia*, New Delhi, 1997, pp. 7-16.

——, 'The Fall-out of a New Political Regime in India', *Asien*, no. 68, 1998, pp. 5-20.

——, 'Multireligiosität in Indien', in Hartmann Lehmann (ed.), *Multireligiosität im vereinten Europa: Historische und juristische Aspekte (Sonderdruck)*, Göttingen, 2003, pp. 183-200.

Rudolph, Lloyd I., 'The Media and Cultural Politics', Mitra and Chiriyankandath, 1992, pp. 81-98.

Rudolph, Lloyd I. and Susanne Hoeber Rudolph, *The Modernity of Tradition: Political Development in India*, Chicago, London, 1984.

——, *In Pursuit of Lakshmi: The Political Economy of the Indian State*, Hyderabad, 1987.

Sankar, R. Vijaya, 'Rituals of Confrontation, *Frontline*, 26 October–8 November, 1991, pp. 14f.

Saraswati, Dayanand, *Light of Truth* (English Translation of the *Satyarth Prakash*, by Dr. Chiranjiva Bharadwaja), 2nd edn., Lahore, 1915.

Sarkar, Sumit, '*The Swadeshi Movement in Bengal' 1903-08*, New Delhi, 1973.

——, *Modern India: 1885-1947*, Delhi, 1983.

——, 'The Fascism of the Sangh Parivar', *Economic and Political Weekly*, 30 January 1993, pp. 163-7.

——, 'The BJP Bomb and Aspects of Nationalism', *Economic and Political Weekly*, 4-10 July 1998, pp. 1725-30.

——, 'Identity and Difference: Caste in the Formation of the Ideologies of Nationalism and Hindutva', in S. Sarkar (ed.), *Writing Social History*, 2nd edn., Delhi, 1998, pp. 359-90.

Savarkar, V.D., *Historic Statements*, ed. S.S. Savarkar and G.M. Joshi, Mumbai, 1967.

——, *Hindu Rashtra Darshan*, 2nd edn., Bombay, 1984.

——, *Hindutva: Who is a Hindu?*, 6th edn., Bombay, 1989.

Schied, Michael, 'Der religiöse Fundamentalismus in politischen Systemen: Pakistan im politischen Spannungsfeld von Religion, Ethnie und Ideologie', in Clemens Six, Martin Riesebrodt and Siegfried Haas (eds.), *Religiöser Fundamentalismus. Vom Kolonialismus zur Globalisierung* (Querschnitte 16), Innsbruck-Vienna-Munich-Bozen, 2004, pp. 227-45.

Schneckener, Ulrich, *Transnationaler Terrorismus. Charakter und Hintergründe des 'neuen' Terrorismus*, Frankfurt/Main, 2006.

Schnepel, Burkhard, 'Durga and the King: Ethnohistorical Aspects of Politico-Ritual Life in a South Orissan Jungle Kingdom', *Journal of the Royal Anthropological Institute*, vol. 1, no. 1, 1995, pp. 145-66.

Schwingel, Markus, *Pierre Bourdieu zur Einführung*, 3rd edn., Hamburg, 2000.

Searle, John R., *Speech Acts*, Cambridge, 1969.

Seshadri, H.V., 'The Shilanyas: What It Signifies', *Organiser*, 17 December 1989.

Seshadri, H.V., *Universal Spirit of Hindu Nationalism*, Madras, 1991.

Seunarine, J.F., *Reconversion to Hinduism Through Suddhi*, Madras, 1977.

Shafqat, Saeed, 'From Official Islam to Islamism: The Rise of Dawat-ul-Irshad and Lashkar-e-Taiba', in Jaffrelot, 2002, pp. 131-47.

Sharma, Sri Ram, *Mahatma Hansraj: Maker of Modern Punjab*, Lahore, 1941.

Shraddhanand, Sanyasi, *Hindu Sangathan: Saviour of a Dying Race*, Delhi, 1926.

Shri Ram Janamabhoomi Nyasa, *Some Frequently Asked Questions on Shri Rama Janmabhoomi of Ayodhya, Uttar Pradesh, India*, New Delhi, 2001.

Singh, Rajendra, *Ayodhya Episode: A Turning Point*, New Delhi, 1993.

Singh, V.B., *Elections in India. Volume 2: Data Handbook on Lok Sabha Elections 1986-1991*, New Delhi, Thousand Oaks, London, 1994.

Singh, V.B., 'Elections and Social Change in India: Results of National Election Study, 1996'. A Report Submitted to the Indian Council of Social Science Research, 1997, New Delhi (unpublished).

Sirinelli, Jean-François, 'Politische Kultur und nationale Emotion', in François, Siegrist and Vogel 1995, pp. 393-5.

Six, Clemens, *Hindi-Hindu-Hindustan: Politik und Religion im modernen Indien*, Vienna, 2006.

Six, Clemens, Martin Riesebrodt and Siegfried Haas (eds.), *Religiöser Fundamentalismus. Vom Kolonialismus zur Globalisierung*, Innsbruck, Vienna, Munich, Bozen, 2004.

Sloterdijk, Peter, *Luftbeben. An den Quellen des Terrors*, Frankfurt/ Main, 2002.

Smith, Anthony D., 'The Nation: Real or Imagined?', in Mortimer and Fine, 1999, pp. 36-42.

Spencer, Jonathan, 'Collective Violence and Everyday Practice in Sri Lanka', *Modern Asian Studies*, no. 3, 1990, pp. 603-23.

Sreedhar, T., 'New Trends in Terrorism and Violence: Pakistan-Taliban-Al Qaeda', in A. Subramanyam Raju (ed.), *Terrorism in South Asia: Views from India*, New Delhi, 2004, pp. 57-73.

Stietencron, Heinrich von, *Der Hinduismus*, Munich, 2001.

Subrahmaniam, Vidya and Smita Gupta, 'Changing the Face of Hinduism', *The Independent*, 18 November 1989.

Swami, Praveen, 'Maximum Terror and its Mechanisms', *Frontline*, vol. 14, 2006, pp. 4-9.

Tagore, Rabindranath, *The English Writings of Rabindranath Tagore*, vol. 2: *Plays, Stories, Essays*, ed. Sisir Kumar Das, New Delhi, 1996.

Thackrah, John Richard, *Dictionary of Terrorism*, 2nd edn., London, New York, 2004.

Tambiah, Stanley, 'A Performative Approach to Ritual', in Tambiah, 1985, pp. 123-66.

——, 'Form and Meaning of Magical Acts', in Tambiah, 1985, pp. 60-86.

——, *Culture, Thought and Social Action: An Anthropological Perspective*, Cambridge (USA), London, 1985.

——, 'Friends, 'Neighbours, Enemies, Strangers and Victim in Civilian Ethnic Riots', *Social Science and Medicine*, vol. 45, no. 8, 1997, pp. 1177-88.

Taylor, Charles, 'Nationalism and Modernity', in Hall, 1998, pp. 191-218.

Thapar, Romila, *The Past and Prejudice*, New Delhi, 1975.

——, 'Imagined Religious Communities? Ancient History and the Modern Search for Identity', *Modern Asian Studies*, vol. 23, no. 2, 1989, pp. 209-31.

——, 'The Ramayana Syndrome', *Seminar*, no. 353, 1989, pp. 71-5.

——, 'Epic and History: Tradition, Dissent and Politics in India', *Past and Present*, 125, 1989, pp. 3-26.

Thengadi, Dattopand, *National Pursuit*, Bangalore, 1992.

Thursby, G.R., *Hindu-Muslim Relations in British India: A Study of Controversy, Conflict, and Communal Movements in Northern India 1923-1928* (Studies in the History of Religions, vol. XXXV), Leiden, 1975.

Tibi, Bassam, *Nationalismus in der Dritten Welt am arabischen Beispiel*, Frankfurt/Main, 1971.

Tønnesson, Stein and Hans Antlöv, 'Asia in Theories of Nationalism and National Identity', in Tønneson and Antlöv (eds.), *Asian Forms of the Nation*, Richmond, Surrey, 1996, pp. 1-39.

Trevithick, Alan, 'Some Structual and Sequential Aspects of the British Imperial Assemblages at Delhi: 1877-1911', *Modern Asian Studies*, vol. 3, 1990, pp. 561-78.

Turner, Bryan S., *Citizenship and Capitalism*, London, 1986.

Upadhyaya, Prakash Chandra, 'The Politics of Indian Secularism', *Modern Asian Studies*, vol. 26, no. 4, 1992, pp. 815-53.

Varadarajan, Siddharth, 'Public Sphere, Mass Media and Mass Mobilisation', in Wien Kunsthalle et al. (eds.), *Kapital und Karma. Aktuelle Positionen indischer Kunst (Ausstellungskatalog)*, Ostfildern-Ruit, 2002, pp. 69-80.

Van Dyke, Virginia, 'Religious Mobilization and Sadhus in Politics: The Idealized versus Realpolitik', in Brass and Vanaik, 2002a, pp. 142-70.

Vanaik, Achin, 'Situating Threat of Hindu Nationalism: Problems with Fascist Paradigm', *Economic and Political Weekly*, 9 July 1994, pp. 1729-48.

——, *India in a Changing World: Problems, Limits and Successes of Its Foreign Policy, Tracts for the Times 9*, Hyderabad, 1995.

Veer, Peter van der, 'God Must Be Liberated! A Hindu Liberation Movement in Ayodhya', *Modern Asian Studies*, vol. 21, no. 2, 1987, pp. 283-301.

——, *Religious Nationalism: Hindus and Muslims in India*, Berkeley, Los Angeles, 1994.

——, 'Riots and Rituals: The Construction of Violence and Public Space in Hindu Nationalism', in Paul R. Brass (ed.), *Riots and Pogroms*, London, 1996, pp. 154-76.

——, *Gods on Earth: Religious Experience and Identity in Ayodhya*, Delhi, 1997.

——, *Imperial Encounters: Religion and Modernity in India and Britain*, New Delhi, 2001.

Viswanathan, Gauri, *Outside the Fold: Conversion, Modernity, and Belief*, Delhi, 1998.

Vivekananda, Swami, *The Complete Works of Swami Vivekananda*, vol. 4, Almora, 1928.

Vogt, Evon Z. and Suzanne Abel, 'On Political Rituals in Contemporary Mexico', in S.F. Moore and B.G. Myerhoff (eds.), *Secular Ritual*, Assen, Amsterdam, 1977, pp. 173-88.

Waldmann, Peter, 'Das terroristische Kalkül und seine Erfolgsaussichten', Wolfgang Schluchter (ed.), *Fundamentalismus Terrorismus Krieg*, Weilerswist, 2003, pp. 87-109.

——, *Terrorismus. Provokation der Macht*, Hamburg, 2005 (1st edn. 1998).

Wallace, Paul, 'Introduction: India's 1998 Election–Hindutva, the Tail Wags the Elephant, and Pokhran', in Ramashray Roy and Paul Wallace (eds.), *Indian Politics and the 1998 Election: Regionalism, Hindutva and State Politics*, New Delhi, Thousand Oaks, London, 1999, pp. 15-35.

Wertheim, W.F., 'Nationalismus und Führungselemente in Asien', in Heinrich August Winkler (ed.), Nationalismus, 2nd edn., Königstein/Ts. 1985, pp. 189-201.

Wickramsinghe, Nira, 'Unthinking the Terrorism-Globalization Nexus', in Imtiaz Ahmed (ed.), *Understanding Terrorism in South Asia: Beyond Statistic Discourses*, New Delhi, 2006, pp. 371-410.

Witschel, Georg, 'Global Terrorism: Trends and Response', in Sridhar K. Khatri and Gert W. Kueck (eds.), *Terrorism in South Asia: Impact on Development and Democratic Process*, New Delhi, 2003, pp. 21-31.

Wodak, Ruth et al., *Zur diskursiven Konstruktion nationaler Identität.* Frankfurt/Main, 1988.

Wulf, Christoph, Michael Göhlich and Jörg Zirfas, 'Sprache, Macht und Handeln–Aspekte des Performativen', in Wulf, Göhlich, Zirfas (eds.), *Grundlagen des Performativen: Eine Einführung in die Zusammenhänge von Sprache, Macht und Handeln*, Weinheim, Munich, 2001, pp. 9-24.

Yadav, Yogendra, 'The Elusive Mandate of 2004', *Economic and Political Weekly*, 18 December 2004, pp. 5383-95.

Yadav, Yogendra, Oliver Heath and Anindya Saha, 'Issues and the Verdict', *Frontline*, 26 November 1999, pp. 45-8.

Yadav, Yogendra, Alistair McMillan and Kanchan Chandra, 'Post-Poll: Who Voted for Whom?', *India Today*, 16 March 1998, pp. 49-52.

Yadav, Yogendra, Sanjay Kumar and Oliver Heath, 'The BJP's New Social Bloc', *Frontline*, 19 November 1999, pp. 31-40.

Yadav, Yogendra and P.M. Patel, 'Advantage BJP', *Frontline*, 20 December 2002.

Yagnik, Achyut and Suchitra Sheth, 'Whither Gujarat? Violence and After', *Economic and Political Weekly*, 16 March 2002, pp. 1009-11.

Yang, Anand A., 'Sacred Symbol and Sacred Space in Rural India: Community Mobilisation in the "Anti-Cow Killing" of 1983', *Comparative Studies of Society and History*, vol. 22, no. 4, 1980, pp. 576-96.

Zavos, John, *The Emergence of Hindu Nationalism*, New Delhi, 2000.

——, 'Understanding Politics Through Performance in Colonial and Postcolonial India', in Timothy Fitzgerald (ed.), *Religion and the Secular, Historical and Colonial Formations*, London, *Oakville* 2007, pp. 135-52.

Zavos, John, Andrew Wyatt and Vernon Hewitt, 'De-constructing the Nation: Politics and Cultural Mobilization in India', in John Zavos, Andrew Wyatt and Vernon Hewitt (eds.), *The Politics of Cultural Mobilization in India*, New Delhi, 2004, pp. 1-15.

Index

(Page numbers in italic refer to footnotes)